VERBAL AND NON-VERBAL COMMUNICATION

Verbal and Non-verbal Communication

Aakash
PhD. in Mass Communication and Journalism
M. Phil. in Mass Communication and Journalism, M.M.C.
P.G. Diploma in Radio & Television Journalism

AMAN PUBLICATIONS
NEW DELHI

Published by
Rajiv Jain for Aman Publications
LG-4A, Ganpati Bhawan,
4675-B/21, Ansari Road,
Darya Ganj, Delhi - 110002
PH: 23255012, 23282127
E-mail: sshjbs@yahoo.com

First Published – 2010

ISBN-81-8204-060-4
ISBN-978-81-8204-060-1

SOLE DISTRIBUTOR
JINDAL BOOK SERVICES
LG-4A, Ganpati Bhawan,
4675-B/21, Ansari Road,
Darya Ganj, Delhi - 110002

Jacket Designed by :
S.M. Graphics

Printed by:
Balaji Offset, Delhi, India

Preface

The basis of communication is the interaction between people. Verbal communication is one way for people to communicate face-to-face. Some of the key components of verbal communication are sound, words, speaking, and language. At birth, most people have vocal cords, which produce sounds. As a child grows it learns how to form these sounds into words. Some words may be imitative of natural sounds, but others may come from expressions of emotion, such as laughter or crying. Words alone have no meaning. Only people can put meaning into words. As meaning is assigned to words, language develops, which leads to the development of speaking.

The actual origin of language is subject to considerable speculation. Some theorists believe it is an outgrowth of group activities such as working together or dancing. Others believe that language developed from basic sounds and gestures.

Nonverbal communication has received much attention in the areas of business presentation, sales and marketing, and the development of social skills. Little attention, however, has been given to its importance in general communication despite major differences in cultural use and interpretation of body language, expression, personal space and other nonverbal tools. It is estimated that less than ten percent of interpersonal communication involves words, the remainder being made up of voice tone, sounds and a variety of devices such as kinetics (movement), haptics (touch), oculesics (eye-contact), proxemics (space) and chronomics (time) as well as posture, sound symbols and silence, which either replace or accompany words. Different studies have identified a wide variety of types of nonverbal communication.

—Author

Contents

Contents

1

Verbal Communication

The basis of communication is the interaction between people. Verbal communication is one way for people to communicate face-to-face. Some of the key components of verbal communication are sound, words, speaking, and language. At birth, most people have vocal cords, which produce sounds. As a child grows it learns how to form these sounds into words. Some words may be imitative of natural sounds, but others may come from expressions of emotion, such as laughter or crying. Words alone have no meaning. Only people can put meaning into words. As meaning is assigned to words, language develops, which leads to the development of speaking.

The actual origin of language is subject to considerable speculation. Some theorists believe it is an outgrowth of group activities such as working together or dancing. Others believe that language developed from basic sounds and gestures.

Over 3,000 languages and major dialects are spoken in the world today. The development of languages reflects class, gender, profession, age group, and other social factors. The huge variety of languages usually creates difficulties between different languages, but even within a single language there can be many problems in understanding. Through speaking we try to eliminate this misunderstanding, but sometimes this is a very hard thing to do. Just as we assume that our messages are clearly received, so we assume that because something is important to us, it is important to others. As time has proven this is not at all true. Many problems can arise is speaking and the only way to solve these problems is through experience.

Speaking can be looked at in two major areas: interpersonal and public speaking. Since the majority of speaking is an interpersonal process, to communicate effectively we must not simply clean up our language, but learn to relate to people. In interpersonal speaking, etiquette is very important. To be an effective communicator one must speak in a manner that is not offending to the receiver. Etiquette also plays an important role in an area that has developed in most all business settings: hierarchical communication. In business today, hierarchical communication is of utmost importance to all members involved.

The other major area of speaking is public speaking. From the origin of time, it has been obvious that some people are just better public speakers than others. Because of this, today a good speaker can earn a living by speaking to people in a public setting. Some of the major areas of public speaking are speaking to persuade, speaking to inform, and speaking to inspire or motivate.

To learn more about verbal communication in the previously mentioned areas, just follow these links:

Interpersonal Speaking

Verbal communication is an essential part of business and when it is executed correctly, good things happen. Here are a few different ideas and styles to remember when speaking to anyone in a business setting.

Because speaking is such an indelible activity, we tend to do it without much thought. But, that casual approach can be a problem in business. Have you ever wished you could make a second, first impression because you said something that was out of character or embarrassing? That comment that you didn't think about before you said, has created an image in someone's mind that can not be replaced even when you meant something totally different. When it comes to oral communication, your goal should be to take advantage of its positive characteristics while minimizing the dangers.

Speaking can be used as a tool to accomplish your objectives. But, first you must break the habit of talkingspontaneously without planning what you're going to say or how you're going to say it. You must learn to manage the impression you create by consciously tailoring your remarks and delivery style to suit the situation. Here are some things which will make you an effective communicator:

- Remember to become aware of what you are saying.
- Apply the same process you use in written communication when you are communicating orally.
- Before you speak, think about your purpose, your main idea, and your audience.
- Organize your thoughts in a logical way.
- Decide on a style that, that suits the occasion and then edit your remarks mentally.
- As you speak, watch the other person to see whether your message is making the desired impression. If not, revise it and try again.

Remember that various situations call for different speaking styles, just as various writing assignments call for different writing styles. Here are four different styles that will suit every occasion:

1. Expressive Style is spontaneous, conversational, and uninhibited. Use this when you are expressing your feelings, joking, complaining, or socializing.

For example: "No way am I going to let that need force an incentive-pay plan on UPS workers."

2. Directive Style is an authoritative and judgemental style. We use this style to give orders, exert leadership, pass judgement, or state our opinions.

For example: "I want Mike Romig to explain the new pay plan to each manager."

3.Problem-Solving Style is rational, objective, unbiased, and bland. This is the style most commonly used in business dealings. We use it when we are solving problems and conveying routine information.

For example: "Stacy Lee might be able to present the plan more favourably."

4. Meta Style is used to discuss the communication process itself. Meta language enable us to talk about our interactions.

For example: "We seem to be having a hard time agreeing on the specifics of the incentive-pay plan."

Following these few helpful tips will increase your communication awareness which will ultimately increase your value as an employee. Nice communicating with you!

Hierarchical Communication

People communicate in businesses with each other most often by oral communication. This talking takes place between mangers, coworkers and subordinates alike. In organizations, communication skill is used to send messages 64% of the time. That is why it is important to understand all the concept of communication.

Have you ever noticed how people communicate differently to their bosses than they would communicate to their coworkers? This difference in communication is due to the chain of command. Managers or "bosses" are typically in an influential position over their employees. Managers have authority or the right to give orders and expect the orders to be obeyed. Many employees may feel that any bad attitude or disagreement with their superior may result in a bad relationship with the boss and therefore create a bad work environment or job description.

In most cases employees talk to their coworkers in a friendly manner. The overall standard is that workers will speak more freely and openly to their fellow workers than to their superiors. When workers talk to each other and relay information on to other workers it is called the "grapevine". The grapevine is the unofficial way that communication takes place in an organization. It is neither authorized nor supported by the organization. Information is spread by word or mouth and even through electronic means today. The grapevine can be used by an "open" company and it will have accurate information however, in an authoritative culture the rumour mill may not be accurate.

Communication from a manager to a subordinate is also different. One reason for this may be because of the arising concern by managers not to offend their workers or say the wrong thing. In today's society, lawsuits run rapid over conversations that some employees may take offensive from their bosses. Managers have a responsibility to know and follow guidelines of good business communication etiquette.

The last type of difference in communication is between the male and female sexes. It was found that when men talk, they do so to emphasize status and independence. Women are found to talk to create connections and intimacy. Women speak about a problem as a means of promoting closeness and to gain support and connection while men talk to solve a problem or give advice.

Etiquette

In today's competitive business environment, social skills and proper etiquette can mean the difference between finding and winning the job of your career and standing still in your career. The confidence of knowing you can hold your own in any social setting, from the white-knuckled nervousness of a first interview to a casual business lunch, can change the way people perceive and judge you. The key to proper business etiquette is: "Do unto others as they would want you to do unto them."

To be successful in the business world, a person must use proper verbal etiquette. One important aspect of verbal etiquette is a proper introduction. Every day we encounter people in a variety of business and social situations. The way we meet and greet them creates lasting impressions and paves the way for a productive encounter. Introductions project information. Besides the obvious elements of name, title, and affiliation, an introduction conveys a level of respect and reflects how the person making the introduction views the other person's status. Mastering the art of the introduction will help put you and the people you are introducing at ease. Learning the basics-and they are not very difficult-is the first step.

Basic points to remember when making introductions:

- The most important point about introductions is to always make them, even if you can't remember names. Failing to do so causes embarrassment and discomfort. If given a choice, most people would prefer you to make the introduction incorrectly, even if you forgot their name, rather than stand there unacknowledged and disregarded.
- A second important point in any introduction is the order of names. The name of the person being introduced is

mentioned last, and the person to whom the introduction is made is mentioned first. In a business setting, introductions are based on power and hierarchy. Simply, persons of lesser authority are introduced to persons of greater authority. Gender plays no role in business etiquette; nor does it affect the order of introductions.

Another important aspect of verbal etiquette is the way in which people address others in a business setting. Once introduced, improperly addressing superiors, colleagues, customers and clients, or subordinates at future meetings may create tension and will create a negative impression. Generally, it is appropriate to address subordinates and others with whom an informal relationship has been established by their first name. In formal relationships, or when the relationship status is unknown, it is necessary to refer to the individual using the appropriate gender-specific title. When gender-specific titles are necessary, use Mister (Mr.) to address men, Misses (Mrs.) to address married women, and Miss (Ms.) to address women who are single or whose marital status is unknown. Following are more specific rules for addressing others in business settings:

- Superiors: Always address superiors with the appropriate gender-specific title, unless he/she gives express permission to do otherwise.
- Colleagues: It is generally accepted procedure to address colleagues by first name. Exceptions arise when the relationship is formal or unfamiliar.
- Subordinates: If the superior has established an informal relationship with the subordinate, use of first names is appropriate. If the relationship is formal or unfamiliar, the appropriate gender-specific title is necessary.
- Clients and Customers: Most relationships with clients or customers are formal, dictating appropriate gender-specific titles. Occasionally, though, an amiable relationship has been established and would allow the use of first names.

A third aspect of business etiquette is proper telephone procedure. Since much of today's business is done over the phone, using correct telephone etiquette is more important than ever. Lasting impressions may be formed during and after telephone conversations, and business people, in order to be successful, must maintain a positive impression. This dictates that people use proper telephone etiquette. There are seven different aspects of telephone etiquette to consider.

1. General Telephone Etiquette

   Identify yourself, with your first and last name, when answering the phone.

   Return phones calls within 24 hours, and apologize if the call is late.

   Identify yourself when you place a call. Say your name, the company, business or department you represent. Then state the nature of your call. If you do not identify yourself, expect to be asked and do not take offense.

2. Interoffice Phone Etiquette

   Don't hover outside a coworker's office or cubicle waiting for him or her to finish up a phone call.

   Leave, and try again later.

   Don't listen in on coworkers' phone conversations. If you share office space with someone, this may be unavoidable, but try to keep busy while the person is talking – and never comment on what you've just overheard!

3. Voice Mail

   Outgoing messages should include your name and company name. If applicable, mention the job you handle to prevent having to route the message to someone else.

   Let the caller know how to reach a live person in an emergency.

   Keep your outgoing message current. If you're going to be out of the office, your message should say so. When you go away, state the date you'll be back and whether or not you'll be calling in for messages, or whom to contact in your absence.

4. Call-Waiting

   Unless you are expecting an urgent call and say so, it's impolite to continually put the person to whom you're speaking on hold while you take another call. Say, "I have another call, can you hold just a second?" Take the other call, explain you're on another line and will call back shortly. Then quickly return to your first caller.

5. Speakerphones

   Although a speakerphone is a great convenience when several people need to participate in a conference call, in a two-person conversation, it often annoys or offends the person whose voice is broadcast. Use it sparingly, and always tell the person on the other end that a speakerphone is being used. Try to avoid using it with a client.

6. Cellular phones

   Try to remove yourself from a public area to a quiet corner of the room so as not to bother others.

   If you must make or take a call, keep it short and as discrete as possible.

7. Placing someone on hold

   Make sure it's for a good reason, such as pulling the person's file or answering another line.

   Ask the person if he or she will hold, and wait for a response rather than assuming the answer is yes.

   Never keep a caller on hold for more than a minute. If you have to take longer than that, return to the person and tell them that you absolute have to take a few minutes longer, and ask if she wouldn't prefer that you call her back."

   When you return to the caller, thank them for holding.

Public Speaking

Seven Steps to Creating an Effective Speech

The first step in making a speech is choosing a topic. We will assume you already have a topic since your qualifications, the audience, or the occasion usually determines it. If you do not have a topic, your most effective speeches will come from a topic you are familiar with or that you want to learn more about.

The second step is to define the purpose of your speech. Are you speaking to persuade your audience, inform your audience, or a combination of the two? And, what are you persuading your audience to do, or what are you informing them about? The answers to these questions will define the purpose of your speech. The third step is to get to know your audience. Get to know the demographic features of your audience. You want to know how large the audience will be, what sort of setting or conditions you will be speaking in, how the audience feels about the topic, and how the audience feels about you as the speaker. Gauge how important these factors will be on the speaking situation and adjust your speech accordingly. Keep in mind the audience is the focus of your speech, and you re looking for a positive response from them.

The fourth step is to gather information for your speech. There are countless sources of information, but here are a few: interviews, the Internet, scholarly journals, government documents, newspapers, and magazines. This information can be used in your speech in a variety of ways. It may be used to supply examples for supporting your ideas, or as statistics to quantify your ideas.

The fifth step is to organize your speech. Start by identifying the main points you want to make, and then put them in an order that makes sense to your topic. You can order them chronologically if your topic covers a sequence of events; spatially if you are describing something from top to bottom, east to west, or according to some other avenue; or, problem-solution order if you are presenting a problem followed by a solution.

The sixth step is adding an introduction to your speech. The introduction is aimed at getting the attention of your audience. There are several ways to accomplish this, the most common are: relating the topic to the audience, shocking the audience with an intriguing or astonishing statement, questioning the audience, or telling a suspenseful or provocative story. The next phases of the introduction are to state the topic of your speech so the audience will know what you are going to talk about, and to preview the main points of your speech so the audience will know what to listen for.

The seventh step is adding a conclusion to your speech. First, signal to the audience that your speech is coming to a close by using phrases such as "In conclusion," In closing," and "Let me end by saying." Second, reinforce the main point of your speech.

2

Significance of Good Verbal Communication

Why is Good Verbal Communication so Important?

When it comes to business, verbal communication is very important for the reason being that you are dealing with a variety of people through out the day. In some cases you may deal with people who have different culture, ages and with different levels of experience.

Now take for example the way you converse with a family member or friend around your same age, you interact with them with a lot of confidence, there is without doubt that verbal communication is expressed with much ease, and perhaps you may speak differently from the way you speak with a person related to business. Imagine if you expressed yourself the same way with a customer who has different culture, is much older than you and have many years of experience in his field. Most likely yourthoughts will be difficult to express. Thus it is necessary to have proper skill when using verbal communication while dealing with different people.

How to Acquire Better Verbal Communication

First of all you need to be aware of the fact that you must be flexible with people depending on the circumstances. Let us say you are presenting a speech in front of an audience at work, and you express yourthoughts using business vocabulary. Now what if your audience where to be unfamiliar with the terms you are using, it is without question you will notice the audience lose focused attention to what you are saying, so then you must be flexible and change the way you are expressing yourthoughts by using words that are more comprehendible to the audience. It is suggested to build skills by attending a college course related to business communication. When you are attending the class you will then be forced to communicate more organized. Try to use the opportunity to overcome the fear of talking to a big crowd and a stranger while you are in class.

Besides attending a class that teaches business communication, you may also want to consider working in a job-field that involves working with strangers, such job can be a form of practice to gain confidence in yourself and help reduce shyness and intimidation.

Another form of practice can be talking to older relatives and friends, about a topic that involves expressing emotions and strongopinions or a discussion that may concern experiences. Such communication helps you to accumulate skills to express yourself in a more formal and proper manner. When practicing with your relatives or friends it is important for you to back up your opinions or statements with facts. In order to have references about your subject it is suggested to read and study about it. Like for example, if you where to discuss the issue that we are all facing today such as the world's economy for instance, then you may obtain the facts from the news paper, the news, Internet, and you can even get it from books.

Verbal Communication

How do you Define Verbal Communication?

It is the spoken, oral, and unwritten way of communicating. It makes use of words, vocabulary, numbers and symbols and is organized in sentences. This communication skill is not reserved for the selected few. It is an ability that each and every one should develop to improve relationships and interactions. Everyone's mind is forever having thoughts and they are primarily in pictures and words. Words spoken affect your life as well as others. They have the power to create emotions and move people to take action. When you communicate clearly, you activate your mind and that of others and you stimulate creativity.

You create your reality with your senses, the eyes, ears and feelings and words and symbols are used to create the meanings. This is why you are encouraged to read and watch informative materials, listen to motivational audio programs and attend classes or seminars that relate to your line of work or objectives. Positive and uplifting spokenwords motivate and inspire.

How to Improve Verbal Communication Skill.

Using positive words to challenge limiting beliefs.

Phrase your words clearly and positively. Your words and the explanations you give affect thoughts and determine emotions.

Questioning helps challenge beliefs. According to Michael Hall, a belief is a thought to which you have said "yes", and you have affirmed by saying, "I believe this". It takes questions worded specifically before you can fully agree.

Your customers, children or partners agreeing and saying "Yes" to your suggestions and opinions indicate that you were able to influence and change their beliefs and thoughts from your spoken or written persuasion.

Telling or narrating a story. One of the ways to let others understand your message is by telling a story, reading a quote or telling a joke. Verbal communication through stories carries power to induce the person to relate to what you are saying or suggesting. A joke usually helps people relax more and is opened to listen to you.

The way you deliver the story can affect the thinking, emotions and behaviour of the listeners. He is able to imagine the experience and will produce a response. A story narrated with eloquent can give hope to people who are in dire need for encouragement.

Asking the right questions.

Questioning yourself or others with precise words allow for correct answers. It will make a difference if you were to ask a "why" or a "how" question. The former gives you a lot of reasons, understandings and explanations while the later set your brain thinking for a solution, useful information and a strategy.

By asking questions and wording them specifically, you will invite a positive debate and interaction that will benefit all involved.

You become a better listener and entice others to do the same. Unnecessary arguments are reduced when you are able to express yourself with great command of your language skills, through verbal communication.

Think and prepare before you speak.

Whether you are going to speak in public, talk to your boss, spouse or children, you have to think before you utter those words. Verbal abuse happens when you express yourself without thinking and instead allow your emotions to take over.

You have to project your thoughts first in your mind or in writing before speaking them out. This will enable you to prepare yourself with any objections that may arise. Thinking, preparing and imagining the most desirable outcome in your mind allow you to practice your presentation and getting them right.

Reduce your usage of verbal pauses.

Have you ever listened to how you speak and render your conversations? If you haven't and are unaware, request for someone to do so. How many times did you stop your sentences and added an "ah", "um" or "well"? You can also record your verbal communication and listen back to your style of speaking.

Too many of these will irritate your listeners or is perceived as uneasiness or uncertainty in what you are saying. In order to reduce the unnecessary verbal cues, listen to yourself and become aware of it. Then when you realize it coming, condition yourself to just a silent pause.

Avoid careless language.

Use your phrases with care. Talk and write in ways that allow for accurate description of your experience, thoughts or ideas. Don't expect people to assume and guess what you are trying to say.

Speak with specificity by avoiding words like always, never, every, or all. When you say to your spouse that he is always late when in fact he was late only twice, you are attracting an argument.

Parents like to compare their children by making statements like, "You are worse than your sister". What happens then? That will create resentment and a rebellious attitude.

Non-Verbal Communication Modes

What is Nonverbal Communication?

Definition (CBC): "nonverbal communication involves those nonverbal stimuli in a communication setting that are generated by both the source [speaker] and his or her use of the environment and that have potential message value for the source or receiver [listener] (Samovar et al). Basically it is sending and receiving messages in a variety of ways without the use of verbal codes (words). It is both intentional and unintentional. Most speakers / listeners are not conscious of this. It includes — but is not limited to:

o touch
o glance
o eye contact (gaze)
o volume
o vocal nuance
o proximity
o gestures
o facial expression ? pause (silence)
o intonation
o dress
o posture
o smell
o word choice and syntax
o sounds (paralanguage).

Broadly speaking, there are two basic categories of Non-verbal language:

- nonverbal messages produced by the body;
- nonverbal messages produced by the broad setting (time, space, silence).

Why is Non-verbal Communication Important?

Basically, it is one of the key aspects of communication (and especially important in a high-context culture). It has multiple functions:

- o Used to repeat the verbal message (e.g. point in a direction while stating directions.
- o Often used to accent a verbal message. (e.g. verbal tone indicates the actual meaning of the specific words).
- o Often complement the verbal message but also may contradict. E.g.: a nod reinforces a positive message (among Americans); a "wink" may contradict a stated positive message.
- o Regulate interactions (Non-verbal cues covey when the other person should speak or not speak).
- o May substitute for the verbal message (especially if it is blocked by noise, interruption, etc.) — i.e. gestures (finger to lips to indicate need for quiet), facial expressions (i.e. a nod instead of a yes).

Note the implications of the proverb: "Actions speak louder than words." In essence, this underscores the importance of Non-verbal communication. Non-verbal communication is especially significant in intercultural situations. Probably Non-verbal differences account for typical difficulties in communicating.

Cultural Differences in Non-verbal Communication

1. General Appearance and Dress: All cultures are concerned for how they look and make judgements based on looks and dress. Americans, for instance, appear almost obsessed with dress and personal attractiveness. Consider differing cultural standards on what is attractive in dress and on what constitutes modesty. Note ways dress is used as a sign of status?
2. Body Movement: We send information on attitude toward person (facing or leaning towards another), emotional statue (tapping fingers, jiggling coins), and desire to control the environment (moving towards or away from a person).

   More than 700,000 possible motions we can make — so impossible to categorize them all! But just need to be aware the body movement and position is a key ingredient in sending messages.
3. Posture: Consider the following actions and note cultural differences:

- o Bowing (not done, criticized, or affected in US; shows rank in Japan)
- o Slouching (rude in most Northern European areas)
- o Hands in pocket (disrespectful in Turkey)
- o Sitting with legs crossed (offensive in Ghana, Turkey)
- o Showing soles of feet. (Offensive in Thailand, Saudi Arabia)
- o Even in US, there is a gender difference on acceptable posture?

4. Gestures: Impossible to catalogue them all. But need to recognize: 1) incredible possibility and variety and 2) that an acceptable in one's own culture may be offensive in another. In addition, amount of gesturing varies from culture to culture. Some cultures are animated; other restrained. Restrained cultures often feel animated cultures lack manners and overall restraint. Animated cultures often feel restrained cultures lack emotion or interest.

Even simple things like using hands to point and count differ.

Pointing : US with index finger; Germany with little finger; Japanese with entire hand (in fact most Asians consider pointing with index finger to be rude)

Counting: Thumb = 1 in Germany, 5 in Japan, middle finger for 1 in Indonesia.

5. Facial Expressions: While some say that facial expressions are identical, meaning attached to them differs. Majority opinion is that these do have similar meanings worldwide with respect to smiling, crying, or showing anger, sorrow, or disgust. However, the intensity varies from culture to culture. Note the following:
   - o Many Asian cultures suppress facial expression as much as possible.
   - o Many Mediterranean (Latino / Arabic) cultures exaggerate grief or sadness while most American men hide grief or sorrow.
   - o Some see "animated" expressions as a sign of a lack of control.

- o Too much smiling is viewed in as a sign of shallowness.
- o Women smile more than men.

6. Eye Contact and Gaze: In USA, eye contact indicates: degree of attention or interest, influences attitude change or persuasion, regulates interaction, communicates emotion, defines power and status, and has a central role in managing impressions of others.
   - o Western cultures — see direct eye to eye contact as positive (advise children to look a person in the eyes). But within USA, African-Americans use more eye contact when talking and less when listening with reverse true for Anglo Americans. This is a possible cause for some sense of unease between races in US. A prolonged gaze is often seen as a sign of sexual interest.
   - o Arabic cultures make prolonged eye-contact. — believe it shows interest and helps them understand truthfulness of the other person. (A person who doesn't reciprocate is seen as untrustworthy)
   - o Japan, Africa, Latin American, Caribbean — avoid eye contact to show respect.
7. Touch: Question: Why do we touch, where do we touch, and what meanings do we assign when someone else touches us?

Illustration: An African-American male goes into a convenience store recently taken over by new Korean immigrants. He gives a $20 bill for his purchase to Mrs Cho who is cashier and waits for his change. He is upset when his change is put down on the counter in front of him.

What is the problem? Traditional Korean (and many other Asian countries) don't touch strangers., especially between members of the opposite sex. But the African-American sees this as another example of discrimination (not touching him because he is black).

Basic answer: Touch is culturally determined! But each

culture has a clear concept of what parts of the body one may not touch. Basic message of touch is to affect or control — protect, support, disapprove (i.e. hug, kiss, hit, kick).

- o USA — handshake is common (even for strangers), hugs, kisses for those of opposite gender or of family (usually) on an increasingly more intimate basis. Note differences between African-Americans and Anglos in USA. Most African Americans touch on greeting but are annoyed if touched on the head (good boy, good girl overtones).
- o Islamic and Hindu: typically don't touch with the left hand. To do so is a social insult. Left hand is for toilet functions. Mannerly in India to break your bread only with your right hand (sometimes difficult for non-Indians)
- o Islamic cultures generally don't approve of any touching between genders (even hand shakes). But consider such touching (including hand holding, hugs) between same-sex to be appropriate.
- o Many Asians don't touch the head (Head houses the soul and a touch puts it in jeopardy).

  Basic patterns: Cultures (English, German, Scandinavian, Chinese, Japanese) with high emotional restraint concepts have little public touch; those which encourage emotion (Latino, Middle-East, Jewish) accept frequent touches.

Smell

- o USA — fear of offensive natural smells (billion dollar industry to mask objectionable odors with what is perceived to be pleasant) — again connected with "attractiveness" concept.
- o Many other cultures consider natural body odors as normal (Arabic).
- o Asian cultures (Filipino, Malay, Indonesian, Thai, Indian) stress frequent bathing — and often criticize USA of not bathing often enough!

Paralanguage

- o vocal characterizers (laugh, cry, yell, moan, whine, belch, yawn). These send different messages in different cultures (Japan — giggling indicates embarrassment; India – belch indicates satisfaction)
- o vocal qualifiers (volume, pitch, rhythm, tempo, and tone). Loudness indicates strength in Arabic cultures and softness indicates weakness; indicates confidence and authority to the Germans,; indicates impoliteness to the Thais; indicates loss of control to the Japanese. (Generally, one learns not to "shout" in Asia for nearly any reason!). Gender based as well: women tend to speak higher and more softly than men.
- o vocal segregates (un-huh, shh, uh, ooh, mmmh, humm, eh, mah, lah). Segregates indicate formality, acceptance, assent, uncertainty.

3

Non-verbal Communication: and Introduction

Nonverbal Communication

To learn more about nonverbal communication, just click on the following links:

Artifacts

Artifacts are often used to communicate information about oneself. Artifacts are objects, often clothes, jewelry, pictures, trinkets, which express one's interests, hobbies, status, or lifestyle. Often noted in democratic societies, where all are thought to be equal, artifacts are used to announce inequalities that for reasons of taste and conformity, cannot be expressed in words.

One of the most influential artifacts a person possesses is one's wardrobe. Much psychology and communication research supports that-at least in the observer's eyes-that clothes do make the man (or woman!).

Lefkowitz, Blake, and Mouton found in their own study that dress can even affect how willing others will be to follow you. This study found that significantly more individuals would follow a model's example in crossing against the "wait" signal when dressed in a business suit than when the same model crossed the street dressed in poor work clothes.

Manager Tip: Artifacts are key in establishing first impressions. If you are looking to improve your own professional style, make note of what artifacts gives strangers a professional look.

Haptics

Research has found that touching can create both positive and negative feelings. Your feelings are positive when the touch is perceived to be natural. A person gets the opposite feeling when the touch is perceived to be manipulative or insincere. Touch is experienced in many ways. Handshakes, pats, and kisses are just a few of the ways one can communicate by touching.

Manager Tip: A firm handshake says, "I care." A weak handshake says, "I care less."

Chronemics

Time, or chronemics, can be used very differently with respect to individuals and even cultures. Time perceptions include punctuality, willingness to wait, and interactions. Time use affects lifestyles, daily agendas, speed of speech and movements, how long people are willing to listen, etc. The way time is used can provide information about people as individuals. There are different perceptions about time usage and its value. Also, cultures differ in their usage of time. For example, in European and American societies, when men are interacting with women, they generally control the time use, talk more than women, and interrupt more than women. In the business world, Americans are expected to arrive to meetings on time and, usually, even early. On the other hand, they arrive late to parties and dances.

Manager Tip: When addressing the issues of time and punctuality, be specific as to what exactly is "on time." An employee may view arriving at 8:05-8:10 as acceptable, while the manager may see 8:10 as being late. By citing a specific time rather than using general phrases, communication can be improved and possible conflicts avoided.

Kinesics

Kinesics, or body language, is one of the most powerful ways that humans can communicate nonverbally. It is used to portray moods and emotions and to emphasize or contradict what is being said.

Body language is very important when in an interview. "To effectively communicate it's not always what you say, but what your body says, that makes the difference," according to Patricia Ball. There are various different types of body movement one can do to come across as being too strong or too weak. For example, when one first walks into the room and shakes hands with the interviewer you want to have good eye contact as well as a good firm hand shake. Not too strong, because you can come across as being a power player. Another important aspect to remember when you are on an interview and that is to mirror your interviewer, but not to the point that you over do it. For example, if the person that is giving you the interview crosses his/her arms than you can cross your arms. If he/she crosses their feet then you should cross your feet, but do it gradually.

The last two things to remember is when you first walk into the office do not cross anything unless the person that is doing the interviewing crosses his or hers first. Next when you are sitting down be relaxed as possible by opening your suit jacket. This shows the person that you are not tensed. The other aspect to remember is to lean forward in your chair, but not to close where you are in the individuals face. If you sit back in your chair you might be sending off signals, such as, aloofness or rejection. Finally, nonverbal communication can also be an effective sale when executives learn to read a client's body language.

Proxemics

One of the terms used in Non-verbal language is proxemics. Edward Hall defined proxemics in the 1950's and 1960's when he investigated man's use of personal space in contrast with fixed and semi-fixed feature space. Fixed feature is what it is fixed has in unmovable boundaries. Semi-fixed is fixed boundaries that can be moved like furniture. Proxemics can be divided in two other ways, physical and personal territory. Physical territory is like desks that are in front of the room of a classroom instead of center.

An example of the proxemic concept is that of stepping behind the desk of an associate at work and invading the personal zone. But what if it is the boss; do you have the authority? If it's a co-worker you probably do. A workplace where you sit is a primary tool in establishing certain communications and is his or her freedom to place that desk where and how it is a key element in personnel considerations. The cubicles don't offer the chance to allow the worker to rearrange the furniture to his or her preference, nor do they allow visitors. Extra room or the ability to move furniture in an office are both symbols of status.

Manager Tip: A manager can use proxemics to their advantage. The arrangement of an office space can show the attitude or personality of the manager. To establish a democratic and friendly style, speak with an employee side by side, such as at a table, rather than from behind a large, imposing desk.

Aspects of Nonverbal Communication

Nonverbal communication has received much attention in the areas of business presentation, sales and marketing, and the development of social skills. Little attention, however, has been given to its importance in general communication despite major differences in cultural use and interpretation of body language, expression, personal space and other nonverbal tools. It is estimated that less than ten percent of interpersonal communication involves words, the remainder being made up of voice tone, sounds and a variety of devices such as kinetics (movement), haptics (touch), oculesics (eye-contact), proxemics (space) and chronomics (time) as well as posture, sound symbols and silence, which either replace or accompany words. Different studies have identified a wide variety of types of nonverbal communication. The following is a relatively simple classification:

Kinesics : body motions (blushes, shrugs, eye movement, foot-tapping, drumming fingers)

Proxemics: spatial separation (in relation both the social and physical environment)

Haptics : touch

Oculesics : eye contact

Chronemics : use of time, waiting, pausing

Olfactics: smell

Vocalics : tone of voice, timbre, volume, speed

Sound Symbols: grunting, mmm, er, ah, uh-huh, mumbling,

Silence: absence of sound (muteness, stillness, secrecy)

Adornment: clothing, jewellery, hairstyle

Posture: position of the body (characteristic or assumed)

Locomotion: walking, running, staggering, limping

Expression: frowns, grimaces, smirks, smiles, pouting

It is often assumed that nonverbal communication is a transferable skill. However, there are two major problematic factors: firstly that, like speech, it has both form and function, and, secondly, that it is not always directly translatable. It is the first of these factors which makes nonverbal communication difficult to teach, and the second which leads to breakdowns and misunderstandings in intercultural communication.

Gestures, expressions and all other forms of nonverbal communication have functions, which, as with language, need to be taught along with their forms. In the same way as language items, some paralinguistic expressions have several functions, while nonverbal communication in general performs the three basic functions of managing identity, defining relationships, and conveying attitudes and feelings (but not ideas):

Form: Main Function (in some cultures)

Nod (Yes): Repeating

Shrug (I don't know): Substituting

Scratch head, quizzical look: Complementing

Tone of voice, pointing: Accenting

Hand raised: Regulating, turn taking

Head shake: Contradicting

Eye movements: Deceiving

Staring/Looking down or away: Dominating/Submitting

Raised fist: Aggression

Hand-shake: Socialising

Touching, kissing: Arousal

Over-adornment: Boasting

Misunderstandings occur because the functions of paralinguistic forms vary from culture to culture, although there are some universal nonverbals such as smiles, laughter and sour expressions. There are also differences according to gender and age. Nonverbal communication tends to be relatively ambiguous and open to interpretation while its influence often depends on the nature of the 'listener', particularly when it is unclear whether the messages conveyed are deliberate or unconscious.

Nonverbal indicators are most common in polychronic cultures, in which an individual often performs several tasks simultaneously. Nonverbal and verbal communication are normally inseparable, which, for example, is why it may seem so difficult to use the telephone in a foreign language.

It needs to be taught and practised situationally, in the right contexts, and with plenty of cultural input and awareness. Given its importance, there is a singular lack of material for the teacher which focuses on this aspect of communication, but here are a few techniques:

- Learners discuss the meaning of gestures and expressions (either demonstrated by the teacher, from pictures, or from existing published materials. This is particularly effective with multilingual classes.
- Learners watch a video clip without sound, then discuss and write the dialogue.
- Learners act out a dialogue using gesture and expression only:
  - A: Excuse me. Can you take a picture of me?
  - B: Yeah, sure.
  - A: Just press that button.
  - B: Er, which one?
  - A: The one on the top.
  - B: OK, right. Er.... can you move back a bit.
  - A: Is this OK?
  - B: Fine, now smile. That's it. Very nice.
  - A: Thanks.
  - B: Not at all. You've got a lovely smile. Er... fancy a drink?
  - A: OK, but I've got no money on me.
  - B: That's OK. I'll pay.

- Learners, in pairs, take turns in listening to each other for 30 seconds, using only nonverbal responses.

Nonverbal communication has implications for the teacher as well as the learner. It is often said that one can always recognise a language teacher by their use of gesture in normal conversation, while it is certainly true that a system of gestures has evolved which allows a teacher to perform aspects of classroom management quickly, quietly and efficiently. Gestures for 'work in pairs', 'open your books', 'listen' and 'write' are universal, while individual teachers have developed nonverbal repertoires involving the use of fingers to represent words, expressions to denote approval/disapproval and gestures to indicate time, tense and other linguistic features, and hence systems for instruction, correction and management which well-trained learners respond to immediately. The effective use of nonverbal cues assists in a wide range of classroom practices by adding an extra dimension to the language:

- reducing unnecessary teacher talking time
- increasing learner participation
- confidence building
- reducing fear of silence
- clear instructions
- efficient classroom management
- classroom atmosphere
- improving listening skills
- improving performance in pair and group activities
- self and peer correction
- avoiding misunderstandings
- improving intercultural competence.

Teachers, however, should always remember that the meanings of gestures and other nonverbal cues need to be taught in the same way as the meaning of essential classroom language, also that a number of nonverbal techniques already exist in their repertoire, such as the use of cuisenaire rods, colours and charts, adapted from the Silent Way. Make sure that the learners understand your codes, and teach them to use them themselves.

Non-verbal Communication And Patient Care

Non-verbal communication is a subtle form of communication that takes place in the initial three seconds after meeting someone for the first time and can continue through the entire interaction. Research indicates that Non-verbal communication accounts for approximately 70% of a communication episode. Non-verbal communication can impact the success of communication more acutely than the spoken word. Our culturally informed unconscious framework evaluates gestures, appearance, body language, the face, and how space is used. Yet, we arê rarely aware of how persons from other cultures perceive our Non-verbal communication or the subtle cues we have used to assess the person.

The following are case studies that provide examples of Non-verbal miscommunication that can sabotage a patient-provider encounter. Broad cultural generalizations are used for illustrative purposes. They should not be mistaken for stereotypes. A stereotype and a generalization may appear similar, but they function very differently. A stereotype is an ending point; no attempt is made to learn whether the individual in question fits the statement. A generalization is a beginning point; it indicates common trends, but further information is needed to ascertain whether the statement is appropriate to a particular individual. *Generalizations can serve as a guide to be accompanied by individualized in-person assessment. As a rule, ask the patient, rather than assume you know the patient's needs and wants.* If asked, patients will usually share their personal beliefs, practices and preferences related to prevention, diagnosis and treatment.

Eye Contact

Ellen was trying to teach her Navaho patient, Jim Nez, how to live with his newly diagnosed diabetes. She soon became extremely frustrated because she felt she was not getting through to him. He asked very few questions and never met her eyes. She reasoned from this that he was uninterested and therefore not listening to her.

It is rude to meet and hold eye contact with an elder or someone in a position of authority such as health professionals in most Latino, Asian, American Indian and many Arab countries.

It may be also considered a form of social aggression if a male insists on meeting and holding eye contact with a female.

Touch and Use of Space

A physician with a large medical group requested assistance encouraging young female patients to make and keep their first well woman appointment. The physician stated that this group had a high no-show rate and appointments did not go as smoothly as the physician would like.

Talk the patient through each exam so that the need for the physical contact is understood, prior to the initiation of the examination. Ease into the patients' personal space. If there are any concerns, ask before entering the three-foot zone. This will help ease the patient's level of discomfort and avoid any misinterpretation of physical contact. Additionally, physical contact between a male and female is strictly regulated in many cultures. An older female companion may be necessary during the visit. Gestures may have dramatically different meanings across cultures. It is best to think of gestures as a local dialect that is familiar only to insiders of the culture. Conservative use of hand or body gestures is recommended to avoid misunderstanding. In the case above, Elena took offense to Mr. Todd's innocent hand gesture. In the Philippines (and in Korea) the "come here" hand gesture is used to call animals.

Body Posture and Presentation

Many cultures prioritize respect for the family and demonstrate family respect in their manner of dress and presentation in public. Regardless of the economic resources that are available or the physical condition of the individual, going out in public involves creating an image that reflects positively on the family-the clothes are pressed, the hair is combed, and shoes are clean. A person's physical presentation is not an indicator of their economic situation.

Use of Voice

The use of voice is perhaps one of the most difficult forms of Non-verbal communication to change, as we rarely hear how we sound to others. If you speak too fast, you may be seen as not being interested in the patient. If you speak too loud, or too soft for the space involved, you may be perceived as domineering or lacking confidence. Expectations for the use of voice vary greatly between and within cultures, for male and female, and the young and old. *The best suggestion is to search for Non-verbal cues to determine*

Nonviolent Communication

Nonviolent Communication (NVC) is a process developed by Marshall Rosenberg and others, including Carl Rogers the famous American psychologist, pioneer of "client-centered therapy". It is a way to communicate with greater compassion and clarity. It focuses on two things: *honest self-expression* — exposing what matters to oneself in a way that's likely to inspire compassion in others, and *empathy* — listening with deep compassion. Two of the central tenets of nonviolent communication (also called "compassionate communication") is that everything a human being does (whether benign or hurtful) is an attempt to meet their human needs. NVC postulates that conflict between individuals or groups is a result of miscommunication about these needs, often because of coercive language or manipulative language (e.g., inducing fear, guilt, shame, praise, blame, duty, obligation, punishment, or reward).

One aim of NVC is to create a situation in which everyone's needs are met. The reasoning is that from a state of mutual understanding and compassion, new strategies will be generated that meet at least some needs of everyone.

In order to reach mutual understanding, NVC advocates expressing oneself in objective and neutral terms—talking about your (strictly objective) observations, feelings and needs—rather than in judgmental terms of good versus bad, right versus wrong, or fair versus unfair. Formal NVC self-expression follows four steps: making neutral *observations* (distinguished from interpretations/evaluations e.g. "I see that you are wearing a hat while standing in this building."), expressing *feelings* (emotions separate from reasons and interpretation e.g. "I am feeling puzzled"), expressing *needs* (deep motives e.g. "I have a need to learn about other people's motives for doing what they do") and making *requests* (clear, concrete, feasible and without an explicit or implicit demand e.g. "Please share with me, if you are willing, your reasons for wearing the hat in this building."). NVC advocates listening very carefully and patiently to the other party in a conflict. NVC advocates echoing that party's statements back to them, e.g. If someone said to you "You were very lucky indeed not to get shot when I saw you climbing over my garden wall last night." could be paraphrased as, "It sounds like you were nervous because your need for safety wasn't being met.")

The NVC model has three or four steps depending on the mode of use.

1. Observation
2. Feelings
3. Needs
4. Request (optional, depending on mode)

The two modes of use of the NVC model are

1. empathy, including both self-empathy, and empathy for another, and
2. honest self-expression, including "please" (request) and "thank you" (gratitude)

OFNR Model in More Detail

The four steps, when used in "self-expression" mode, work like this:

1. To observe without evaluation, judgment, or analysis,
2. To express feelings which these observations evoke,
3. To express needs connected with these feelings,
4. (optional) To make a specific request of another person to help meet an unmet need, and to enrich life of everyone involved. Essential in this is that the other person is to be left free to honour or decline the request.

In this recipe, offering an observation serves to give the listener a reference as to the subject. Offering a feeling (uncontaminated by interpretation and blame) tends to increase connection. Expressing needs, either met or unmet, provides connection and meaning. Finally, a request offers clarity as to what the speaker wants. Demands (for which there is only one acceptable response) do not meet the recipient's need for autonomy and tend to produce either submission or rebellion. Typically, neither of these responses is enjoyable for both parties. Both responses foster resentment and strain the relationship.

In contrast, it is felt that the consistent use of requests (for which no answer will trigger retaliation of any kind) leads to people experiencing the joy of giving. People will often say "yes" to a request out of the desire to contribute to one another, which NVC practitioners maintain is a stronger and more universal motivation than is commonly recognized. If a request yields a "no," the suggestion is to interpret that as information that a need exists that the requester was not aware of and may want to investigate. The need that originally motivated the request is more likely to be met through a strategy that respects all needs.

Empathy

Empathy, as practiced in NVC, is sometimes called "deep listening". It involves the listener connecting with the essential core of an individual's experience and offering a kindly energy of presence. The empathy process offered by NVC is often referred to as "giving empathy." It is more accurately a procedure that supports the development of true empathy. This process involves listening for, and sometimes guiding the other person towards describing:

1. Observations as to what happened,
2. Feelings evoked, sometimes guessing what feelings might be, if the other is (for example) in blame mode,
3. Needs both met and unmet, although the unmet needs are most likely to be provoking the feelings involved

The empathy process for another may be conducted out loud, as an interaction with that person, or silently, as an inner approach to awareness of that person's experience. Empathy brings about understanding of the needs of the one "receiving" empathy, and also relieves emotional charge.

Emotional charge is often uncomfortable and is a barrier to being able to hear others clearly and respond in a flexible fashion. Thus, empathy may be used to relieve distress and increase understanding and readiness for hearing.

Formal vs. Colloquial

When using NVC to communicate, one may use either formal or colloquial NVC. In formal NVC, one explicitly uses the steps of the processes for empathy and honest self-expression, and may overtly use words such as "feel" and "need." This may be well-received and effective, or may be experienced as odd and stilted. As an alternative, one may use colloquial or "street" NVC, in which the language is naturalized and may be considered NVC regardless of form so long as it springs from an awareness of needs and an intention to connect. Formal NVC is primarily used in teaching NVC and among NVC practitioners. Mastering formal NVC is recommended as a prerequisite to full effectiveness in speaking colloquial NVC.

Nonviolence

The name "nonviolent communication" refers to Mohandas Gandhi's philosophy of ahimsa or nonviolence. However, unlike Gandhi, Rosenberg endorses the use of protective force—the use of force to keep injury from occurring, so long as it is not punitive, i.e., force applied with the intention to punish or harm someone for a past deed. Rosenberg says the desire to punish and the use of punitive measures only exist in cultures that have moralistic good/evil worldviews. He points out that anthropologists have discovered cultures in many parts of the world in which the idea of someone being "bad" makes no sense. He says such cultures tend to be peaceful and do not rely on punitive force to correct maladaptive or harmful behaviours. One example of such a culture is the Semai people in Malaysia.

Programs

Rosenberg has used the concept of nonviolent communication in peace programs in conflict zones including Rwanda, Burundi, Nigeria, Malaysia, Indonesia, Sri Lanka, Colombia, the Middle East, Serbia, Croatia, and Ireland. The approach also has been used in projects of Restorative Justice; bringing prisoners, victims of crime, police and other interested parties together for healing and reconciliation. NVC is recognized by the government of Israel and several NVC training schools have been founded there. The theory has much in common with concepts used in mediation and conflict resolution and is used by some mediators in their work.

Behavioural Communication

Behavioural Communication is a psychological construct that addresses people's use of day-to-day behaviours as a form of communication. Specifically, it refers to people's tendency to express feelings, needs, and thoughts by means of indirect messages and behavioural impacts. Basically, any behaviour (or its absence when one is expected) may be judged as communicative if it has the intent to convey a message. For example, an expressive hairstyle, a show of a certain emotion (or emotional withdrawal), or simply doing (or not doing) the dishes all can be means by which people may convey messages to each other.

The construct of behavioural communication is conceived as a variable of Individual differences. This means that some people more than others tend to engage in behavioural communication in spite of the plausible alternatives of using verbal communication.

A measure of the construct, The Behavioural Communication Questionnaire (M. Ivanov, 2008), has been introduced at the Society for Personality Assessment conference in March, 2008. The conceptual framework of the construct has been presented at Western Psychological Association Conference in April, 2008.

Interpersonal Communication

Interpersonal communication is usually defined by communication scholars in numerous ways, usually describing participants who are dependent upon one another and have a shared history. Communication channels, the conceptualization of mediums that carry messages from sender to receiver, take two distinct forms: direct and indirect. Direct channels are obvious and easily recognized by the receiver. Both verbal and Non-verbal information is completely controlled by the sender. *Verbal* channels rely on words, as in written or spoken communication. *Non-verbal* channels encompass facial expressions, controlled body movements (police present hand gestures to control traffic), colour (red signals 'stop', green signals 'go'), and sound (warning sirens).

Indirect channels are usually recognized subconsciously by the receiver, and are not always under direct control of the sender. Body language, comprising most of the indirect channel, may inadvertently reveal one's true emotions, and thereby either unintentionally taint or bolster the believability of any intended verbal message. Subconscious reception and interpretation of these signals is often described with arbitrary terms like gut-feeling, hunch, or premonition.

Context refers to the conditions that precede or surround the communication. It consists of present or past events from which the meaning of the message is derived, though it may also, in the case of written communications, depend upon the statements preceding and following the quotation in question. Immediate surroundings may also colour the perceived meaning of words; normally safe discourse may easily become contextually ambiguous or offensive in a restroom or shower hall. These influences do not constitute the message by themselves, but rather these extraneous nuances subtly change the message's effective meaning. Ultimately, context includes the entire world, but usually refers to salient factors such as the following:

- Physical milieu: the season or weather, current physical location and environment
- Situational milieu: classroom, military conflict, supermarket checkout
- Cultural and linguistic backgrounds
- Developmental progress (maturity) or emotional state
- Complementary or contrasting roles: boss and employee; teacher and student; parent, child, and spouse; friend or enemy; partner or competitor

Improving Verbal Communications

Imaginative strategies are helping some internal audit departments to sharpen their verbal communications skills.

INTERNAL AUDITORS may possess all the financial and technical skills in the world; but if they can't develop a rapport with auditees and convince management to implement their ideas, they won't be very effective. Strong writing is an essential skill for internal auditors, of course; but oral communication skills are equally important. Christopher Hutchings, Assistant Vice President and Director of Corporate Auditing at the Coca-Cola Company, observes that "Being able to sell your ideas is as important as having ideas worth selling. You have to be a good communicator to be effective. You're attempting to provide a solution that may cost auditees money, time, and people. How you sell your ideas is critical."

In seven different internal audit shops around the U.S., several innovative approaches to improving oral communication have been developed. Although each approach is custom-tailored to the needs of the organization, these internal audit departments share a conviction that strong oral communications skills are crucial to their effectiveness.

Federal Express

Gene Bastedo, Director of Internal Auditing at Federal Express, maintains that "In the audit department, we are in the business of 'selling' our recommendations and ideas." In thinking about developing a course to help his internal audit staff enhance their selling capabilities, it occurred to Bastedo that he had a group of experts within his company: the sales staff. He reasoned, "Why go out and hire sales experts when we have people with the same skill sets in-house?" When Bastedo and his audit managers met with the Federal Express sales staff to discuss the proposed course, Bastedo explained that he wanted to stress open communication, service to clients, and quality management. It was agreed that one goal of the class would be to encourage the Federal Express sales staff to train auditors to think like salespeople.

In fact, auditors were trained to see things from the client's viewpoint, empathize with them, and prepare responses to their objections. "I understand how you feel, but here's what other people have found" might be one counter to an internal audit client's reservations. Areas such as nonverbal communication, listening, strategic communication systems, and overcoming obstacles to effective communication were stressed.

Audit manager Glenn Pearson met with the sales training department to review its curriculum and to determine which sections were best suited to internal auditors. In learning more about his counterparts' approaches, Pearson found many similarities between the way salespeople and internal auditors operate. "We're selling our audit recommendations and dealing with objections. We both apply similar techniques," Pearson observed.

The sales acronym APCOM — acceptance, purpose, consulting, overcoming objections, and motivating to act — provided a useful framework for auditors. Auditors were taught techniques to anticipate auditees' objections and strategies to overcome their resistance. Pearson did concede that, unlike auditors, sales professionals sell a product and base their arguments on its outstanding features. "Auditors aren't selling features. We're selling ideas and recommendations," Pearson pointed out, "and that can be more complex and ambiguous."

Feedback from auditors who took the class was very positive. Auditors realized that audit reports are often not enough to convince the auditee to implement recommendations. "You must see auditees as customers. Overcoming objections is a way to encourage them to implement our ideas. That's the bottom line," says Pearson. Stand Up and Present!

Levi Strauss

In a study that identified people's deepest fears, dying was ranked as the second most terrifying. First was delivering a speech before an audience. But David Garrett, currently director of Global Real Estate at Levi Strauss, spent 14 years as director of internal audit; he asserts that "Auditors have to present their findings not only to their peers but to local management. They have to be able to speak clearly and concisely."

That's why each auditor at Levi Strauss receives training in making presentations. Why are presentation skills so crucial to internal auditors? "Senior management has little time to spend reading audit reports," Garrett states. "They want their findings to be presented succinctly at a meeting and supported by a written document."

Members of Levi Strauss' internal audit staff are encouraged to become members of Toastmasters, a nonprofit organization dedicated to improving communication and public speaking skills. There are more than 8,000 Toastmasters' clubs worldwide, with 180,000 members.

Colin Kolankowski, a Levi Strauss internal auditor, said that he gained enormous confidence in his public speaking abilities through Toastmasters' weekly meetings and the opportunity to practice his presentation skills. After his first meeting, which covered basic techniques, Kolankowski delivered a five-minute speech on the Polish cavalry and the battle of Vienna in 1683, a favorite subject of his. He was trained to structure his speech in a logical way, stressing its beginning, middle, and end to see things from the viewpoint of his audience, and to focus on his effect on listeners. After delivering numerous speeches and receiving constructive feedback, his confidence level skyrocketed.

Kolankowski thinks that the improvement in his presentation skills has enhanced his capabilities as an internal auditor. At exit conferences, he is much better equipped to convey his recommendations in succinct language. Now he feels that his audience is friendly and wants to listen to him rather than judge him. About auditing, he admits that "Our subject can be dry and technical. To engage the listener is quite a skill." When an auditor feels confident about presentation skills, the anxiety that once was overwhelming at closing conferences dissipates.

Speaking is a Form of Acting

Coca-Cola USA

At the Coca-Cola Company, internal auditors are borrowing techniques from actors to improve their oral communication skills. "PowerTalk," a course introduced by the Bergerac Company, a Dallas-based consulting firm, teaches internal auditors to use acting techniques to enhance oral communication. "PowerTalk" stresses spontaneity as well as preparation. Don't write down every single word of your script; that usually leads to a stifled presentation, the class suggests. Donna Bingham, Human Resources Project Manager for Coca-Cola USA, says that the class stressed talking out the script, rather than writing everything down on paper. "The idea is that one's mind is like an internal computer," Bingham maintains. "Let your mind do the thinking.

And this way your audience will be enrapt rather than bored." Niki Flacks, chairman of Bergerac, contends that too many business presenters rely on overheads, slides, and visuals, forgetting their audience. "Communication," she writes in material distributed to students, "has become dehumanized, and audiences are drowning in overhead projections, pointers, and charts. If business communication is stilted, constricted, or monotonic, the listener's brain tunes out." "PowerTalk" encourages auditors to inject energy and vitality into their presentation skills.

When U.S. President Clinton delivered his 1993 State of the Union speech, he used a prepared speech, and then, apparently on the spur of the moment, injected his own ideas. A Newsweek writer noted that "It's becoming clear that for Bill Clinton a prepared text is an admission of failure. When he really knows his stuff, he feeds off his audience, customizing his message, sensing their needs and anxieties."

"PowerTalk" focuses on five key skills:

(1) Writing a thesis and a logical, concise, results-oriented outline.

(2) Mastering presenting skills, such as getting the audience involved.

(3) Rehearsing to review what you want to say.

(4) Concentrating on being listener-driven.

(5) Synthesizing all skills by creating a blue-print that can be applied to any speech.

During the "PowerTalk" course, students are videotaped several times so they can critique their own presentations. Instructors offer constructive feedback, as well. Participants are video-taped before learning the class's techniques, so that by class end, they can see themselves before, during, and after. "The class helps auditors to be themselves," states Bingham. "Auditors learn to enjoy making presentations, just as actors on stage learn to communicate their enthusiasm to their audience. Too many speech courses inhibit students by telling them to stand a certain way, to talk a certain way. Auditors who learn to plan their speeches and then add spontaneity will have the confidence to handle any presentation or audience."

Interviewing 101

Xerox Corporation

When Zsuzsanna Snow, Operations/Process Consultant with the Xerox Corporate Audit Department, asked the Xerox audit staff what kind of training they needed most, the majority requested a course in interviewing auditees. A quality improvement team developed an interviewing class and then presented it to a team of experienced auditors for their critiques and suggestions. The result: a class called Interview Training.

Facilitators who teach this one-day class stress group discussion rather than lecturing. Though the class has a syllabus, much of it centers around real-life situations confronting auditors. The class focuses on the key elements of the audit interview — preparation, learning about the area, asking good questions, planning the sequence of questions. Auditors are trained to handle surprising revelations and taught how to determine precisely the right person to interview.

Auditors are encouraged to build rapport with auditees and to be sensitive to their priorities and difficulties. In planning audits, the auditors work with auditees to determine objectives and to ask how they can assist auditees before initial interviews actually take place. "We want to move away from auditor and victim," Snow said succinctly.

The key to effective audit interviewing, Snow observes, is "showing respect for a fellow professional and demonstrating listening skills." Snow believes that, too frequently, auditors listen to facts and numbers and miss the nuances of communication. For example, suppose that an auditee is asked about an area's condition and replies, "I do get reports." If the auditee says nothing further, that could be a cue for the auditor to ask about the quality of the reports (or the lack thereof).

"By sharpening interviewing skills, auditors can build stronger partnerships with audit customers and learn more about the business environment so that they issue better recommendations," asserts Snow. "The goal of audit interviewing ultimately is issuing effective recommendations that auditees are enthusiastic about implementing."

Communication Excellence

Chase Manhattan Bank

Called "Communication Excellence" because it is based on strategies developed by observing master communicators at work, this class has proven effective in improving the communication skills of internal auditors at Chase Manhattan Bank. Carol Colone, manager of Professional Development for Chase General Auditing, teaches the course.

Colone says that the three-day class stresses "sensory acuity, outcome setting, rapport building, questioning, interpersonal effectiveness, meeting management, and presentation skills." Genie Z. Laborde, a California-based consultant, developed the class around the discipline of neurolinguistics and trained Carol Colone to teach it. Laborde defines neurolinguistics as "a set of skills that allows one to review the world in a new, more productive way." According to Laborde, author of Influencing with Integrity, these patterns "can be utilized by auditors to create win-win situations."

The communication model is founded on the idea that human beings "take in and present information to people through their five senses," says Colone. The class focuses on the three senses that play the greatest part in business situations—visual, auditory, and kinesthetic (or feeling).

Students are taught how to identify whether the person they are interacting with favors one of those senses and are then trained to employ different strategies to reach that person. Hence, if the person relies on his visual sense, the effective communicator may employ images to connect with them.

"One of the basic precepts of this class is that if what you are doing in a particular communication situation is not working, you should try something different," avers Colone. By stressing the senses, auditors learn to enhance their sensory acuity, or as Colone states it, "the ability to listen with their eyes as well as their ears." Why is this class perfect for internal auditors? Says Colone: "Internal auditors need to establish an effective communication link, very quickly, with people whom they may or may not be familiar. These skills enhance auditors' ability to build rapport with strangers and increase their ability to influence people."

Vicki Boatti, formerly a supervisor at Chase General Auditing who took the class, said it taught her to determine "whether you were getting true agreement as opposed to lip service." By making her more conscious of the communication process, she was able to focus on achieving what outcomes she wanted from a business interaction. Internal auditors employ tact and diplomacy to convince auditees that their recommendations will prove effective. Communication Excellence is helpful in this area because it stresses "the process of communication in addition to content. Most people aren't aware that, in certain instances, how they say something may be more important than what they're saying," notes Colone.

Auditors as Facilitators

General Electric

General Electric's Corporate Audit staff recognized that, after receiving feedback from auditees related to operational or process reviews, auditors were able to generate valuable ideas but they were not obtaining a high degree of acceptance from the businesses being audited. Since auditors visited a business area for only a temporary period, they were often not perceived as team members. To increase acceptance, consultant Ron Gager and Janice Poirier, program manager for Training and Development with General Electric Corporate Audit, developed a three-day class called Leadership Facilitation Skills.

The class trains auditors to become effective facilitators in groups. Each student has a chance to serve as the group's facilitator, designated facilitator, and team member. Students are videotaped in these roles and receive constructive feedback about how to improve their facilitating skills. According to Poirier, "The name of the game in GE is effecting change. You need to get buy-in from a group of people." The class aims to enhance each auditor's skill as "process consultants and to develop the facilitation skills necessary to serve as change agents with GE businesses." The syllabus of the class includes sections on understanding the difference between an expert and a consultant; group dynamics; knowing when and how to intervene in a group; strategies to problem-solve in a group; and learning/facilitation tools such as brainstorming.

This class meets an audit staff's needs because, as Anne Pellegrini, manager of Programs and Planning for the Corporate Audit staff at General Electric notes, much of an auditor's worth stems from his or her ability to influence many businesspeople. Anything that helps them become more effective team players helps them as auditors.

An effective auditor is frequently "not the one who comes up with the great idea" but who can encourage others to generate constructive recommendations," suggests Pellegrini. Since 40 percent of the auditing performed at General Electric involves operational reviews (the remaining 60 percent is financial and compliance review), auditors frequently work on teams in the business units. Pellegrini emphasizes that auditors still perform much of their financial work independently, but the skills mastered in this class help them become "better team members. That's not a skill that comes naturally for some auditors."

Dealing with Difficult People

Motorola Inc.

Auditees can be difficult. Even in an age focused on customer satisfaction, not all auditees want to hear the recommendations offered by internal auditors.

That's why the course "Dealing with Difficult People" has helped internal auditors at Motorola Inc. Bob Weber, senior manager for Corporate Financial Audit at Motorola, described the difficult situation that most auditors face.

They enter a business area where they do not work full-time, ask probing questions, and devise ways to improve the business. "Dealing with Difficult People," a course developed by the Dale Carnegie Institute, helps auditors to handle those difficult situations. Peter Soto, corporate audit manager at Motorola, says that the course helps auditors deliver what may be perceived as bad news. It stresses looking at matters from the auditee's viewpoint.

Weber notes that there are two ways to effect change. One is to impose your view, and the other involves asking questions so that the auditee arrives at his own conclusion — the same one that you intended. "Dealing with Difficult People" shows auditors how to achieve the second option.

Weber notes that when he attends closing sessions he can often pinpoint the auditors who have been through the "Dealing with Difficult People" class. "The difference between them and the others," he suggests, "is that they emphasize the positive — what can happen — while too many auditors accentuate the negative. When auditors emphasize what a new approach will do for auditees, not what they are doing wrong, those auditors are mastering the art of dealing with difficult people."

4

Making Sense of Non-verbal Communication

Nonverbal communications (NVC) is usually understood as the process of communication through sending and receiving wordless messages. i.e, language is not one source of communication, there are other means also. NVC can be communicated through gestures and touch (Haptic communication), by body language or posture, by facial expression and eye contact. NVC can be communicated through object communication such as clothing, hairstyles or even architecture, symbols and infographics. Speech contains nonverbal elements known as paralanguage, including voice quality, emotion and speaking style, as well as prosodic features such as rhythm, intonation and stress. Dance is also regarded as a nonverbal communication. Likewise, written texts have nonverbal elements such as handwriting style, spatial arrangement of words, or the use of emoticons. However, much of the study of nonverbal communication has focused on face-to-face interaction, where it can be classified into three principal areas: environmental conditions where communication takes place, the physical characteristics of the communicators, and behaviours of communicators during interaction.

Verbal vs. Oral Communication

Scholars in this field usually use a strict sense of the term "verbal", meaning "of or concerned with words," and do not use "verbal communication" as a synonym for oral or spoken communication. Thus, vocal sounds that are not considered to be words, such as a grunt, or singing a wordless note, are nonverbal.

Sign languages and writing are generally understood as forms of verbal communication, as both make use of words — although like speech, both may contain paralinguistic elements and often occur alongside nonverbal messages. Nonverbal communication can occur through any sensory channel — sight, sound, smell, touch or taste. NVC is important as: "When we speak (or listen), our attention is focused on words rather than body language. But our judgement includes both. An audience is simultaneously processing both verbal and nonverbal cues. Body movements are not usually positive or negative in and of themselves; rather, the situation and the message will determine the appraisal."

History

The first scientific study of nonverbal communication was Charles Darwin's book *The Expression of the Emotions in Man and Animals* (1872). He argued that all mammals show emotion reliably in their faces. Studies now range across a number of fields, including, linguistics, semiotics and social psychology.

Arbitrariness

While much nonverbal communication is based on arbitrary symbols, which differ from culture to culture, a large proportion is also to some extent iconic and may be universally understood. Paul Ekman's influential 1960s studies of facial expression determined that expressions of anger, disgust, fear, joy, sadness and surprise are universal.

Clothing and Bodily Characteristics

Elements such as physique, height, weight, hair, skin colour, gender, odors, and clothing send nonverbal messages during interaction. For example, a study, carried out in Vienna, Austria, of the clothing worn by women attending discotheques showed that in certain groups of women (especially women which were in town without their partners) motivation for sex, and levels of sexual hormones, were correlated with aspects of the clothing, especially the amount of skin displayed, and the presence of sheer clothing, e.g. at the arms. Thus, to some degree, clothing sent signals about interest in courtship. Research into height has generally found that taller people are perceived as being more impressive. A sample of managers in the UK and found that height was a key factor affecting who was promoted. Often people try to make themselves taller, for example, standing on a platform, when they want to make more of an impact with their speaking.

Physical Environment

Environmental factors such as furniture, architectural style, interior decorating, lighting conditions, colours, temperature, noise, and music affect the behaviour of communicators during interaction. The furniture itself can be seen as a nonverbal message

Proxemics

Proxemics is the study of how people use and perceive the physical space around them. The space between the sender and the receiver of a message influences the way the message is interpreted. The perception and use of space varies significantly across cultures and different settings within cultures. Space in nonverbal communication may be divided into four main categories: intimate, social, personal, and public space. The distance between communicators will also depend on sex, status, and social role.

Proxemics was first developed by Edward T. Hall during the 1950s and 60s. Hall's studies were inspired by earlier studies of how animals demonstrate territoriality. The term territoriality is still used in the study of proxemics to explain human behaviour regarding personal space. Tere are four such territories:

1. Primary territory: this refers to an area that is associated with someone who has exclusive use of it. For example, a house that others cannot enter without the owner's permission.
2. Secondary territory: unlike the previous type, there is no "right" to occupancy, but people may still feel some degree of ownership of a particular space. For example, someone may sit in the same seat on train every day and feel aggrieved if someone else sits there.
3. Public territory: this refers to an area that is available to all, but only for a set period, such as a parking space or a seat in a library. Although people have only a limited

claim over that space, they often exceed that claim. For example, it was found that people take longer to leave a parking space when someone is waiting to take that space.

4. Interaction territory: this is space created by others when they are interacting. For example, when a group is talking to each other on a footpath, others will walk around the group rather than disturb it.

Chronemics

Chronemics is the study of the use of time in nonverbal communication. The way we perceive time, structure our time and react to time is a powerful communication tool, and helps set the stage for communication. Time perceptions include punctuality and willingness to wait, the speed of speech and how long people are willing to listen. The timing and frequency of an action as well as the tempo and rhythm of communications within an interaction contributes to the interpretation of nonverbal messages. Gudykunst & Ting-Toomey (1988) identified 2 dominant time patterns:

- Monochronic time schedule (M-time): Time is seen as being very important and it is characterized by a linear pattern where the emphasis is on the use of time schedules and appointments. Time is viewed as something that can be controlled or wasted by individuals, and people tend to do one thing at a time. The M-pattern is typically found in North America and Northern Europe.
- Polychronic time schedule (P-time): Personal involvement is more important than schedules where the emphasis lies on personal relationships rather than keeping appointments on time. This is the usual pattern that is typically found in Latin America and the Middle East.

Movement and Body Position

Kinesics

Kinesics is the study of body movements, facial expressions, and gestures. It was developed by anthropologist Ray L. Birdwhistell in the 1950s. Kinesic behaviours include mutual gaze, smiling, facial warmth or pleasantness, childlike behaviours, direct body orientation, and the like. Birdwhistell proposed the term kineme to describe a minimal unit of visual expression, in analogy to a phoneme which is a minimal unit of sound.

Posture

Posture can be used to determine a participant's degree of attention or involvement, the difference in status between communicators, and the level of fondness a person has for the other communicator.

Studies investigating the impact of posture on interpersonal relationships suggest that mirror-image congruent postures, where one person's left side is parallel to the other's right side, leads to favorable perception of communicators and positive speech; a person who displays a forward lean or a decrease in a backwards lean also signify positive sentiment during communication. Posture is understood through such indicators as direction of lean, body orientation, arm position, and body openness.

Gesture

A gesture is a non-vocal bodily movement intended to express meaning. They may be articulated with the hands, arms or body, and also include movements of the head, face and eyes, such as winking, nodding, or rolling ones' eyes. The boundary between language and gesture, or verbal and nonverbal communication, can be hard to identify. It is suggested that gestures could be categorised into five types: emblems, illustrators, affect displays, regulators, and adaptors.

- *Emblems* are gestures with direct verbal translations, such as a goodbye wave;
- *illustrators* are gestures that depict what is said verbally, such as turning an imaginary steering wheel while talking about driving;
- an *affect display* is a gesture that conveys emotions, like a smile;
- *regulators* are gestures that control interaction;
- and finally, an *adaptor* is a gesture that facilitates the

release of bodily tension, such as quickly moving one's leg.

Gestures can also be categorised as either speech-independent or speech-related. Speech-independent gestures are dependent upon culturally accepted interpretation and have a direct verbal translation. A wave hello or a peace sign are examples of speech-independent gestures. Speech related gestures are used in parallel with verbal speech; this form of nonverbal communication is used to emphasize the message that is being communicated. Speech related gestures are intended to provide supplemental information to a verbal message such as pointing to an object of discussion. Gestures such as Mudra (Sanskrit) encode sophisticated information accessible to initiates that are privy to the subtlety of elements encoded in their tradition.

Haptics

Haptics is the study of touching as nonverbal communication. Touches that can be defined as communication include handshakes, holding hands, kissing (cheek, lips, hand), back slapping, high fives, a pat on the shoulder, and brushing an arm. Touching of oneself may include licking, picking, holding, and scratching. These behaviours are referred to as "adaptor" and may send messages that reveal the intentions or feelings of a communicator. The meaning conveyed from touch is highly dependent upon the context of the situation, the relationship between communicators, and the manner of touch. Humans communicate interpersonal closeness through a series of Non-verbal actions known as immediacy behaviours. Examples of immediacy behaviours are: smiling, touching,open body positions, and eye contact. Cultures that display these immediacy behaviours are known to be high contact cultures.

Eye Gaze

The study of the role of eyes in nonverbal communication is sometimes referred to as "oculesics". Eye contact can indicate interest, attention, and involvement. Gaze comprises the actions of looking while talking, looking while listening, amount of gaze, and frequency of glances, patterns of fixation, pupil dilation, and blink rate.

Touch

We communicate a great deal through touch. Think about the messages given by the following: a firm handshake, a timid tap on the shoulder, a warm bear hug, a reassuring pat on the back, a patronizing pat on the head, or a controlling grip on your arm can all be examples of nonverbal communication through touch.

Voice

We communicate with our voices, even when we are not using words. Nonverbal speech sounds such as tone, pitch, volume, inflection, rhythm, and rate are important communication elements. When we speak, other people "read" our voices in addition to listening to our words. These nonverbal speech sounds provide subtle but powerful clues into our true feelings and what we really mean. Think about how tone of voice, for example, can indicate sarcasm, anger, affection, or confidence.

Paralanguage

Paralanguage (sometimes called vocalics) is the study of nonverbal cues of the voice. Various acoustic properties of speech such as tone, pitch and accent, collectively known as prosody, can all give off nonverbal cues. Paralanguage may change the meaning of words. The linguist George L. Trager developed a classification system which consists of the voice set, voice qualities, and vocalization.

- The *voice set* is the context in which the speaker is speaking. This can include the situation, gender, mood, age and a person's culture.
- The *voice qualities* are volume, pitch, tempo, rhythm, articulation, resonance, nasality, and accent. They give each individual a unique "voice print".
- *Vocalization* consists of three subsections: characterizers, qualifiers and segregates. Characterizers are emotions expressed while speaking, such as laughing, crying, and yawning. A voice qualifier is the style of delivering a message-for example, yelling "Hey stop that!", as opposed to whispering "Hey stop that". Vocal segregates such as "uh-huh" notify the speaker that the listener is listening.

Functions of Nonverbal Communication

Argyle (1970) put forward the hypothesis that whereas spoken language is normally used for communicating information about events external to the speakers, Non-verbal codes are used to establish and maintain interpersonal relationships. It is considered more polite or nicer to communicate attitudes towards others non-verbally rather than verbally, for instance in order to avoid embarrassing situations.

Argyle (1988) concluded there are five primary functions of nonverbal bodily behaviour in human communication:

- Express emotions
- Express interpersonal attitudes
- To accompany speech in managing the cues of interaction between speakers and listeners
- Self-presentation of one's personality
- Rituals (greetings).

Concealing Deception

Nonverbal communication makes it easier to lie without being revealed. This is the conclusion of a study where people watched made-up interviews of persons accused of having stolen a wallet. The interviewees lied in about 50 % of the cases. People had access to either written transcripts of the interviews, or audio tape recordings, or video recordings. The more clues that were available to those watching, the larger was the trend that interviewees who actually lied were judged to be truthful. That is, people that are clever at lying can use voice tone and face expression to give the impression that they are truthful

The Relation between Verbal and Nonverbal Communication

An interesting question is: When two people are communicating face-to-face, how much of the meaning is communicated verbally, and how much is communicated non-verbally? This was investigated by Albert Mehrabian and reported in two papers,. The latter paper concluded: "It is suggested that the combined effect of simultaneous verbal, vocal, and facial attitude communications is a weighted sum of their independent effects-with coefficients of.07,.38, and .55, respectively." This "rule" that clues from spoken words, from the voice tone, and from the facial expression, contribute 7 %, 38 %, and 55 % respectively to the total meaning, is widely cited.

It is presented on all types of popular courses with statements like "scientists have found out that... ". In reality, however, it is extremely weakly founded.

First, it is based on the judgment of the meaning of single taperecorded words, i.e. a very artificial context. Second, the figures are obtained by combining results from two different studies which maybe cannot be combined. Third, it relates only to the communication of positive versus negative emotions. Fourth, it relates only to women, as men did not participate in the study.

Since then, other studies have analysed the relative contribution of verbal and nonverbal signals under more naturalistic situations. Argyle, using video tapes shown to the subjects, analysed the communication of submissive/dominant attitude and found that Non-verbal cues had 4.3 times the effect of verbal cues. The most important effect was that body posture communicated superior status in a very efficient way. On the other hand, a study by Hsee et al. had subjects judge a person on the dimension happy/sad and found that words spoken with minimal variation in intonation had an impact about 4 times larger than face expressions seen in a film without sound. Thus, the relative importance of spoken words and facial expressions may be very different in studies using different set-ups.

Interaction of Verbal and Nonverbal Communication

When communicating, nonverbal messages can interact with verbal messages in six ways: repeating, conflicting, complementing, substituting, regulating and accenting/moderating.

Repeating

"Repeating" consists of using gestures to strengthen a verbal message, such as pointing to the object of discussion.

Conflicting

Verbal and nonverbal messages within the same interaction can sometimes send opposing or conflicting messages. A person verbally expressing a statement of truth while simultaneously fidgeting or avoiding eye contact may convey a mixed message to the receiver in the interaction. Conflicting messages may occur for a variety of reasons often stemming from feelings of uncertainty, ambivalence, or frustration. When mixed messages occur, nonverbal communication becomes the primary tool people use to attain additional information to clarify the situation; great attention is placed on bodily movements and positioning when people perceive mixed messages during interactions.

Complementing

Accurate interpretation of messages is made easier when nonverbal and verbal communication complement each other. Nonverbal cues can be used to elaborate on verbal messages to reinforce the information sent when trying to achieve communicative goals; messages have been shown to be remembered better when nonverbal signals affirm the verbal exchange.

Substituting

Nonverbal behaviour is sometimes used as the sole channel for communication of a message. People learn to identify facial expressions, body movements, and body positioning as corresponding with specific feelings and intentions. Nonverbal signals can be used without verbal communication to convey messages; when nonverbal behaviour does not effectively communicate a message, verbal methods are used to enhance understanding.

Regulating

Nonverbal behaviour also regulates our conversations. For example, touching someone's arm can signal that you want to talk next or interrupt.

Accenting/Moderating

Nonverbal signals are used to alter the interpretation of verbal messages. Touch, voice pitch, and gestures are some of the tools people use to accent or amplify the message that is sent; nonverbal behaviour can also be used to moderate or tone down aspects of verbal messages as well. For example, a person who is verbally expressing anger may accent the verbal message by shaking a fist.

Dance and Nonverbal Communication

Dance is a form of nonverbal communication that requires the same underlying faculty in the brain for conceptualization, creativity and memory as does verbal language in speaking and writing. Means of self-expression, both forms have vocabulary (steps and gestures in dance), grammar (rules for putting the vocabulary together) and meaning. Dance, however, assembles (choreographs) these elements in a manner that more often resembles poetry, with its ambiguity and multiple, symbolic and elusive meanings.

Clinical Studies

From 1977 to 2004, the influence of disease and drugs on receptivity of nonverbal communication was studied by teams at three separate medical schools using a similar paradigm. Researchers at the University of Pittsburgh, Yale University and Ohio State University had subjects observe gamblers at a slot machine awaiting payoffs. The amount of this payoff was read by nonverbal transmission prior to reinforcement. This technique was developed by and the studies directed by psychologist, Dr. Robert E. Miller and psychiatrist, Dr. A. James Giannini. These groups reported diminished receptive ability in heroin addicts and phencyclidine abusers was contrasted with increased receptivity in cocaine addicts. Men with major depression manifested signicantly decreased ability to read nonverbal cues when compared with euthymic men.

Obese women and women with premenstrual syndrome were found to also possess diminished abilities to read these cues. In contradistinction, men with bipolar disorder possessed increased abilities.. A woman with total paralysis of the nerves of facial expression was found unable to transmit any nonverbal facial cues whatsoever.. Because of the changes in levels of accuracy on the levels of nonverbal receptivity, the members of the research team hypothesized a biochemical site in the brain which was operative for reception of nonverbal cues. Because certain drugs enhanced ability while others diminished it, the neurotransmitters dopamine and endorphin were considered to be likely etiological candidate. Based on the available data, however, the primary cause and primary effect could not be sorted out on the basis of the paradigm employed.

A byproduct of the work of the Pittsburgh/Yale/ Ohio State team was an investigation of the role of nonverbal facial cues in heterosexual nondate rape. Males who were serial rapists of adult women were studied for nonverbal receptive abilities. Their scores were the highest of any subgroup. Rape victims were next tested. It was reported that women who had been raped on at least two occasions by different perpetrators had a highly significant impairment in their abilities to read these cues in either male or female senders. These results were troubling, indicating a predator-prey model. The authors did note that whatever the nature of these preliminary findings the responsibility of the rapist was in no manner or level,diminished.

The final target of study for this group was the medical students they taught. Medical students at Ohio State University, Ohio University and Northest Ohio Medical College were invited to serve as subjects. Students indicating a preference for the specialties of family practice, psychiatry, pediatrics and obstetrics-gynecology achieved significantly higher levels of accuracy than those students who planned to train as surgeons, radiologists, or pathologists. Internal medicine and plastic surgery candidates scored at levels near the mean.

Difficulties

People vary in their ability to send and receive nonverbal communication. Thus, on average, to a moderate degree, women are better at nonverbal communication than are men.

Measurements of the ability to communicate nonverbally and the capacity to feel empathy have shown that the two abilities are independent of each other.

For people who have relatively large difficulties with nonverbal communication, this can pose significant challenges, especially in interpersonal relationships. There exist resources that are tailored specifically to these people, which attempt to assist those in understanding information which comes more easily to others. A specific group of persons that face these challenges are those with autism spectrum disorders, including Asperger syndrome.

Making Sense

Although there are misconceptions about the nature of nonverbal communication (Soucie, 1979), there being many popular, sometimes distorted beliefs, it is clear that humans share the meanings of their daily lives intersubjectively through verbal and nonverbal communication. Most daily conversations are conducted face-to-face, the body playing a supporting role in communication. In many circumstances, people use emblems or gestures that can stand alone. Most of the time, however, humans communicate with one another by combining spoken language with body "language".

Verbal and nonverbal communication are linked together synchronously, forming a complete presentation to the partipant or observer. This verbal and nonverbal interface must exist for humans to communicate fully. It is the body, however, that conveys most of the emotional semantics in communicative interactions. The potential of human communication is realized only when body messages and spoken messages work together synchronously and harmoniously. Dysfunction and confusion result when the spoken word is contradicted by body messages.

In face-to-face situations, the entire body is presented to the observer. In mediated situations, however, the body is masked. For example, when using e-mail, people substitute for emotions that are normally displayed in face-to-face situations by creating *emoticons* (Herring, 1996). Emotional and paralinguistic cues are artificially produced by e-mail users. It is only in face-to-face communication that the full communicative reportoire can be expressed. In face-to-face situations, people reveal emotions and rhetorical sensitivity as they construct joint, intersubjective nonverbal messages. They can create healthy relationships or they can create dysfunctional relationships.

Nonverbal skills and competencies, of course, are learned. Some pathologies exist, such as autism or schizophrenia, which appear to be neuro-chemically induced; other body related diseases, such as anexoria or body dysmorphic disease appear to be the result of distorted perceptions. Pathologies, such as these, are displayed in particular ways, as in a frozen smile, a reptilian stare, or a very thin body. Normally, however, individuals learn how to use and display their bodies just as they learned how to use spoken and written language, yet a number of scholars indicate that spoken language and nonverbal behaviour are processed in different ways in the brain (LeDoux, 1996).

People create a milieau and live within it; both the built and the natural environment are part of the context that influences human behaviour. Artifacts, such as buildings, clothes and communicative technologies are created by humans; these artifacts influence their behaviours in turn. The social environment includes dyadic, group and public situations, such as ceremonies and rituals in which humans engage themselves. The built environment includes houses and public structures. Cultural thoughtways influence how buildings are structured. For example, Frank Lloyd Wright, a prominent American architect, designed homes that fit into the environment; the Navajo designed the hogan, a round-shaped building that grew out of their values, beliefs and practices.

Aspects of Nonverbal Communication

The reader is aware that there are many ways to study nonverbal communication. For example, Affiliative Conflict Theory, The Expectancy-Norm Model, The Arousal-Labelling Model, The Arousal-Valence Model, The Discrepancy-Arousal Model and The Sequential-Functional Model are recent ways that researchers have investigated nonverbal communication with arousal being the central concern.. These recent models, just a few selected to illustrate the point, provide unique viewpoints and research models. These important models usually focus on narrow topics. The SI perspective, more aptly described as an approach, rather than a model or theory, is broad and it can include findings from other models without losing its integrity, although researchers from the SI background, tend to use qualitative, ethnographically research methods.. SI is compatible with a number of other approaches. Of course, the story of human communication is long and complex (Schramm, 1988) and researchers have approached the topic of human communication in multiple ways.

Interactionist Perspective

The Symbolic Interactionist perspective puts emphasis upon human action, or agentry, and upon intersubjectivity and interpretation. People try to make sense of the nonverbal behaviour of others and of themselves attaching meaning to the behaviours. Humans frame (Goffman, 1974) their worlds drawing upon their own personal experiences, their personal identity and life scripts. People respond to factual situations, to symbolic worlds found in literature, film, TV and books (Searle, 1995); they create meanings from what they observe others doing, in what they see themselves doing. They perceive, think, create lines of action, interact and then reflect upon the meaning of social events. The SI approach provides a way of looking at the naturally occuring world of human behaviour.

Framing Meaningful Acts

All human beings create action sequences. They go to school; they drive a car; they read books; they go to movies, sing, play sports and so on. These action sequences have symbolic value, recognized as forms of doing. Sequences of action are made up of singular acts; for example, people know how to drive cars, but they learned, mastering one simple act, then another. In this process, drivers create schemes; they know the procedural rules, the techniques and so on. Given sufficient practice, they drive almost nonconsciously.

Sequences of acts are usually planned in inner conversations with the self. When performed often, they become routine, requiring little pre-thinking. They are symbolic activities. Drivers invest meaning in what they are doing and derive meaning from doing it. They can tell others what it means to get a driver's license; they can share their joy in being able to take a trip. Whether the action is a simple handshake or a complex display of elaborate rituals, actions such as driving a car, human acts always carry a symbolic mantle, either from the actor's view or from the observer's view. In this sense, the study of nonverbal communication is communication about human actions. The meanings of human actions are shared intersubjectively, forming the basis of community (Blumer, 1969).

Symbolic interactionists suggest that the "actor" is always in the process of doing or thinking about doing; humans are influenced by others in interaction, in groups, institutions, society and culture. Society is not "out there"; rather humans engage interactively to produce society, engaging in self-talk, or conversations with themselves, to interpret behaviours. People take up multiple roles; indeed, they have many versions of themselves, not simply one, which are observed by themselves and others. People continually evaluate, negotiate, and produce "reality".

Nonverbal action is usually associated with verbal activity, although it can stand alone. It is dynamic and creative, but it may be patterned and somewhat predictable. Individuals may plan and create lines of action; on the other hand, they may act and react spontaneously. Although people are *agentive* on their own behalf, they are also interpreters of the actions of others. In short, they are performers and they are audience members. The human body is always present in social, interactive situations. In mediated situations, when people are on the telephone, for example, only the voice is heard; yet it sends nonverbal paralinguistic messages (Pittam, 1994). When e-mail is used, humans construct self images as they relate to others who cannot see them.

Obviously, the human body is a physical entity, but it is the symbolic meaning that humans attach to the body that is important. For example, when people wish to make their bodies beautiful or handsome, they work on the images that their culture or society presents to them. People share cultural meanings associated with beauty which vary from culture to culture. In the United States, the media portray the images of beauty in ways that are endlessly clear to the viewer, whether the observer accepts the images or not. In short, the participant in social interaction must decide what to do with the "stuff" of society, to try to make sense of it.

The Body and Identity

The sense of a body self, or *body identity* is inevitably connected to a sense of the social self. The body of course is ever present, always communicating, intended or not. Humans inevitably must construct or create meanings for their bodies, by taking account of the meanings that are imbedded in society and culture. People are able to make quite accurate statements about themselves, about their own bodies, although they may at times deceive themselves. Statements about the self and the body are designed to fit the circumstances (Leary, 1996). For example, people create fictitious selves on the internet, describing themselves in ways that they hope may appeal to others.

In this text, the author focuses on how people make sense of nonverbal communication. People perceive themselves and others symbolically, labelling their own bodies and the bodies of others. People hold conversations with themselves, about themselves, about others and about events. In short, there is a symbolic, cognitive activity involved in the presentation of self and in the interpretation of the nonverbal behaviours of others. In this text, this process is referred to as *sensemaking*, a word that is designed to suggest the often hidden symbolic activity that accompanies nonverbal communication.

Definition of Nonverbal Communication

There are scores of definitions and assumptions that researchers and scholars use to define nonverbal communication (1). One such definition says that nonverbal communication is comprised of all of the messages other than words that people use in interaction (Hecht & DeVito, 1990), a useful general approach, but it appears to fail to account for how people use words paralinguistically or how people create meaning in their interactions. To some extent, each definition reflects the training and tradition of the scholar involved. In everyday life, humans create meanings by drawing upon implicit assumptions rooted in their personal life experiences; in professional research, on the other hand, scholars make their assumptions explicit so that they are testable and useful.

There are several elements involved in human nonverbal

communication. Cultural, social and psychological factors enter into nonverbal communication in complex ways, as do gender, ethnicity, age and technology. The milieu, or social contexts, influence human nonverbal communication because these themes are deeply embedded in the contexts of everyday life. Each of these themes contain hidden codes. Space, time and the physical environment influence human nonverbal communication as well. These themes, or background factors, inevitably influence behaviour because people take account of the social contexts in which they act. Meaningful lines of action are best created when people are aware of the dynamics of the social context in which they find themselves. Nonverbal communication is deeply influenced by these dynamic elements.

Humans are *socialized* into their worlds but, in becoming socialized, they take part in their own creative unfolding, not being passive; the baby gradually learns to use her body in appropriate ways. As humans go through life to a gerontological or even a centenarian age, they learn to construct new ways of thinking and doing, to modify their own identities, to alter the ways that they use the body. Humans enact strategies of behaviour that will help them adapt and survive in a complex social world.

The Human Sensorium and Related Phenomena

Some texts about nonverbal communication include sections dealing with the sixth sense (Leathers, 1978). However, there has been considerable debate by researchers over whether humans can and do communicate by using the sxith sense. The field of study, called *parapsychology*, has inspired research from both sides, from the skeptics(Blackmore, 1990) to the believers (Tart,1989), the so-called goats and sheep. People who claim to have extrasensorial abilities are fairly numerous in popular American culture. In other cultures, similar powers may be invested in a shaman or a witch doctor (Castaneda, 1969). Although there is good reason to discuss the sixth sense, given its place in the popular mind and in the minds of some scholars, there is far less clarity about parapsychological research than there is about the five senses; which, when taken together are referred to as the human sensorium, the five basic senses which all primates have.

Ethologists, those who study animal behaviours, usually from an *evolutionary* perspective, point out the sensate differences that are found among various species. Dogs, for example, have a well developed sense of smell; owls have well developed hearing and visual abilities; and monkeys and chimpanzees have well developed tactile abilities. All creatures have a *neurological system*; they are sentient, capable of sensing things in their environment. Evolutionists and ethologists emphasize that this differential development of the senses is due to the need for each species to adapt to complex environmental circumstances in order to survive. Thus, animals who hunt at night need good vision, for example (Wilson, 1992).

Unlike most other primates, humans, who sit atop the primate evolutionary ladder, can knowingly improve the use of their senses. They can employ tools, develop their sensitivities, train the body, build muscles and so on, all of which seems to enable humans to take part in their own evolution. As an everyday example, the ordinary human may not be able to discern between the fine nuances and bouquets found in various wines, but the enologist, trained to do so, can detect and distinguish thousands of odors and tastes associated with wine. Indeed, chemists have created an elaborate vocabulary detailing very fine nuances of smells and tastes that is useful to specialists (Cain, 1990). Although some lower order animals seem to create tools and make plans (Eibl-Eibestadt, 1975), it is not clear how much cognitive ability primates share with humans, although recent evidence suggests that chimps and humans are not far apart genetically. Chimps have learned emblematic vocabularies (Sagan, 1977).

Smell and taste are referred to as chemical senses. That is, they are very closely associated with each other and in close proximity to the brain, serving rudimentary functions. They are referred to as *olfactory* and *gustatory* processes. As in the case of tactility, or touch, they come into play mostly when they are in immediate contact with foods or other items. The chemical senses change as humans age; they are affected by hormonal changes in women who are menstruating or giving birth. Smell and taste perform important basal functions, such as enhancing as food odors. A recent internationally based smell study, performed by National

Geographic revealed key differences between males and females on a smelling index and how culture influences perceptions of odors and taste. In short, there are cultural overlays resting on top of the physical function of smelling. Another line of inquiry suggests that humans have individualized olfactory signatures. Pheromones, active in lower order animals in the sexual act, may be active in humans, influencing the mating, courtship ritual. Scientific research needs to validate the possibility. Perfume makers would like to know the answer to the question! They have put a perfume on the market called Pheromone.

Oculesics, mentioned above, is a field of study that refers to the use of the eyes and eye movement, including to some extent, perceptual processes (Webbink, 1986). From early studies focusing on what happens when a cat sees a mouse—the iris opens automatically— (Hess, 1975) to recent research about the colour of they eyes, eye attraction and gaze behaviour, research about the eyes indicates that the eyes have directive features; that is, humans can influence others merely by the way they use their eyes. When a speaker suddenly looks to the side of the room, her observors may look there as well. Humans can encourage affiliation or they can discourage contact, merely by how they use their eyes. There are cultural, gender and ethnic differences among humans influencing how they use their eyes and in how that use is interpreted by observers. Staring is a common nonverbal activity found among lower order animals.

Aurality refers to the ability of humans to hear, an ability that varies highly among cultures. It also is age-related. The young enjoy loud music; the old enjoy softer music. Hearing can be improve with training. For example, a recent study showed that conductors could hear orchestral sounds that others in the orchestra could not detect. However, the human hearing mechanism does not permit them to hear as well as many lower order animals. In some lower order animals, the use of echolocation mechanisms help them as they hunt, mate or move about in the physical environment.

Tactility, or *haptics*, refers to one's ability to touch and feel, the skin being the largest sensitive organ in the human body. Touching has been associated with gentling and bonding in both humans and other primates (Montagu, 1971) and to attitudes about body accessibility (Jourard, 1966; Jones, 1994)) and self-confidence. The human skin is sufficiently sensitive that individuals can discern writing patterns performed on their backs, out of sight. The ability to touch, or grasp, differs among lower and higher order species; for example, it is clear that a hippopotamus cannot grasp a tree limb as a simian can. In the case of humans, the use of the fingers, thumbs and hands occurs within the field of vision, greatly enhancing human tactile abilities. Touching, holding, pushing, grasping, shaping, or throwing come easily to human beings. Humans take these activities and possibilities for granted. Most lower order animals can not perform these tasks.

Display rules suggest that how people touch one another conveys important and specific meanings. The question has been asked whether there is a right touch. (Jones, 1994). There are power touches, professional touches, intimacy touches and so on, each having social codes attached. Laws protect citizens from inappropriate touch, as in rape or beatings. In short, touching must be acceptable and appropriate. At one extreme lies touch aversion; that is, some people fear the touch of others, based on their negative experiences. At the other extreme, there is supportive touch. It is said that some cultures promote touch starvation; that is, the natives seem to be starved for affection, which they may not get in interpersonal situations (Jourard, 1966).

In sum, research about the five senses and how they interact in the daily lives of human beings is increasing. Research is showing how these sensory mechanisms, sometimes referred to as nonverbal channels, work together, how they are used in gendered ways, how they vary between cultures and ethnic groups and so on. It is obvious that humans need to know little about these mechanisms even though they rely on them for information. Research suggests that in the Western world especially, the eyes take primacy,not surprising in an age of television and film; nor is it surprising that engineers have created machines that hear, speak, listen, and send odors.

Framing the "Sixth" Sense

Returning to the topic of the sixth sense. Is there a sixth sense? Do people know things other than through use of the corporal senses? Considerable research has been conducted on human subjects, in an attempt to determine whether telepathy, aura reading, precognition, clairvoyance, remote viewing, the moving of objects by kinetic energy and other phenomena are legitimate aspects of human experience; if so, how are they to be interpreted? The field of parapsychology has serious scholars researching and working on the many issues involved. Again, many scholars dismiss entirely the claims of parapsychologists.

One major issue is whether results of experiments can be replicated; another major issue deals with the nature of the experimentation itself. Subjects, who are thought to have some telepathic ability, often called psychics or sensitives—terms that are often used pejoratively—complain that laboratory situations restrict their performances. For example, Ganzfeld experiments require the subject to be deprived sensorily by placing blinders over the eyes while the eyes are kept open. White noise is used as a mask throughout the experiment. The subject is asked to receive a message telepathically from the sender outside the cage while these sensory impediments are in place. This bizarre experimental method seems to be faulty on the face of it because subjects claim that it interferes with their psychic senses. How can one access the alpha state when machines impede and interfere? Could a psychic, or any subject, relax under these laboratory conditions?

A third issue seems to be centered on the effect of belief. If one is a believer, perhaps she or he is more likely to claim that unusual experiences are psychic experiences. Research about psychic phenomena, the world of parapsychology, seems to be interesting to most people; yet, the sixth sense does not seem to be established clearly enough to give it the sixth sense label. This is not to say that people who experience psychic phenomena are to be disregarded. Indeed, future research may reveal much more than is presently known. Perhaps new research paradigms will yield better results; the models used until now seem to fail.

Physical Attributes and Kinesics

Humans are fond of watching one another (Morris, 1985); the body, of course, is gendered. Women and men present themselves to others, whether their body action is confined to the eyes, the entire head, the trunk of the body or the entire body. Body behaviours have been given considerable attention in the research literature, as has somatyping, the idea that body shape and size are correlated with certain kinds of behaviours. Endomorphic, mesomorphic or ectomorphic shapes have been described. In early research it was believed that ectomorphs, the tall, thin people, had delicate personalities; medium sized people, the mesomorphs, were generally outgoing or athletic. The endomorphs, very heavy people, were thought to be languorous and slow.

Correlation is not causation, although it is often interpreted as causational. Biological structure may influence attitudes, but it does not predetermine attitudes; attitudes are created by the owner of the body, who in turn is influenced by her or his society. The importance of perceptions and stereotypes associated with body size and shape cannot be overstated, especially in Western countries, where body ideals are promoted by the media, a powerful force in Western societies. Everyone knows, generally speaking, what Miss America should look like, even though the criteria for winning it changes over time. Never should she be too heavy or too short!

Body Language

Body communication has been studied under the general name of kinesics. People often associate the idea of bodily communication (Argyle, 1983) exclusively with the use of gestures, but the field of study is now much broader. A body lexicon used to describe body behaviour was created in early research including words like kines, morphs, kinemorphic constructions and other words, created to enhance the study of nonverbal behaviour.

A kine is the smallest unit of body expression, such as a facial movement; a morph may express the movement by two or more head motions; and, a kinemorphic construction may refer to the movement of the entire upper torso—all in synchrony with the verbal stream.

Using this body language system, researchers have attempted to show how the verbal and the nonverbal streams work together in synchrony. Dancing, for example, reveals the integration of the body (Farnell, 1995) and how it manifests action signs.

Paralanguage

Semioticians focus on the ways that spoken language is tied into human behaviour and they are able to differentiate between male and female language use. Within spoken language there are paralinguistic features. Paralinguistic studies focus on how humans use language, rather than with what they actually say. Emotional elements are expressed in everyday conversation; gender and social class markers are found there. For example, older people, males and females and members of various ethnic groups, use different voice pitch, loudness or range of tonality, compared to one another. Females typically have a higher vocal range than do males as is commonly observed. This difference, of course, is not absolute. To a large extent, it is a learned difference.

The word *genderlect* has been used to the distinctive ways that males and females express themselves, as learned through socialization. Not only do males and females differ in the patterning of vocal sounds, but they tend to use different sentence phrasing, different conversational styles and different conversational floor patterns, including different conversational turn-taking styles. Animated vocalization has been associated with extroverted personalities, while interrupted speech patterns have been associated with mental and emotional disturbance. Attempts have been made to associate psychological and personality traits with vocal patterns and various paralinguistic styles. As one can hear that the vocal patterns, or voice set, of older people, are very different from the vocal patterns of young children.

People from Latin America may differ substantially in their vocal patterns, or their voice set, compared to Whites or Blacks in North America. Cubans and Native Americans may differ substantially between groups. These are learned and practiced ethnic differences. Japanese "manage the floor" in conversations differently from Americans.

Environmental Influences

It is obvious that humans move about in space; less obvious, is that their ways of moving about vary considerably, based on the ways they have been socialized. Smaller in body, females need less space generally speaking than do males. The ways that the British, the Japanese, the Arabs and others from other areas of the world use space differ, sometimes substantially. Americans tend to feel crowded when people enter their personal space closer than three feet, the desired norm. Arabs, on the other hand, feel quite normal when they are close to one another in dyads or groups.

It has been said that the ways humans use space is governed by a hidden language; hidden codes exist, guiding people, although they are not aware of them. Humans become aware of the norms of space when that space has been violated. Spatial zones of interaction have been devised, varying by cultures. For example, intimate distance, personal distance, social distance and public distances vary considerably.

The concept of zero proxemics implies that there is no space between bodies, a condition, which, in most instances, makes humans feel uncomfortable.

In loving situations, of course, one expects to be touching, body to body. A mother who does not touch her child is said to be cold and reserved. On the other hand, in other situations, space violations occur, as in rape, physical abuse and other demeaning activities. In general, extreme body closeness is shunned from culture to culture but there is considerable variation between cultures.

The concept of territoriality, a concept borrowed from the ethological study of animals, suggests strongly that humans, like other species, share normative expectations about how their space is claimed. Humans mark their spaces, perhaps by putting a purse on the table to define their space in their absence, or by putting fences between them and their neighbors. Lower order species, by contrast, mark their territory by urination or body rubbing. When students enter classrooms, they tend to choose their seats in accordance with their perception of comfort, barring other reasons, as sociometrists have shown.

The use of space varies enormously from situation to situation, from culture to culture; nevertheless, humans follow hidden display rules and context codes as they determine how they will use space.

Chronemics

Chronemics is the study of the human invention and use of time. In some societies, it is clear that humans are almost cultish about time; they follow a cult of the clock. Researchers suggest that humans have built-in physiological, psychological and social clocks and that there are biological rhythms which vary according to age and sex. For example, some people work best in the morning while others work best at night, like sparrows and owls. Time, of course, is a human conception. It does not have fixed dimensions. Early Native Americans relied upon seasonal changes for their sense of time, as do many members of traditional cultures in various parts of the globe. Today, some modern Navajo members may live away from the Reservation working in an industry that is governed by the hourly clock, returning at night to the Reservation, where different meanings for time are used.

The sense of time is related even to emotional and body health. Seasonal Affective Disorder (SAD), a form of depression, has been reported to be associated with the dark months of winter. Speed in walking, talking and behaving vary highly between and among regions of the United States based on the underlying hidden codes for the region. Some cultures are past-oriented; others are present or future-oriented. It is said that American youth tend to be future-oriented while older citizens tend to be past oriented. These generalizations appear to have some validity; but, of course, humans are free to change the way they think and behave.

Other Background Influences

The environment influences nonverbal communication. Colours in the background are thought to influence moods and behaviours. For example, the soft colour of green is often painted onto library walls furnishing a quiet, restful context. Bright red would seem to destroy the study mood. Unfortunately, the study of colour and its influence on human behaviour is only beginning to receive solid research attention. Anecdotal and popular notions seem to be pervasive. Yet, from a practical view, it seems that humans choose colours in clothing, in their houses, or for their cars because they like them or feel comfortable with them. Not just any colour will work for them. Humans don warm clothing in the winter and shed it in the summer. Clearly, humans create behaviours that are influenced by background variables. The physical environment, like the social environment, is a powerful influence on human behaviours, although the research is not substantial.

Humans create architectural environments which reflect cultural values. As mentioned, the famous Frank Lloyd Wright designed houses to blend into the landscape, creating a prairie style. His houses were designed to let the outdoors in, by using large windows, subdued lighting, skylights and overhangs. Earthy colours were used to blend the buildings into the landscape. This great American architect influenced generations of later architects. He built his houses to fit into the environment, as no prior architect had done, showing Americans how to live more meaningfully within the environmental context. On a less appealing side, American architecture, referring especially to public buildings, has been referred to as "hard architecture" (Sommer, 1974), meaning that it conforms little to comfortable human use, being designed for the faceless public person. Railroads, prisons, banks and other buildings are said to be hard, rather than soft, and to restrict rather than to open. Modern architecture and ergonomic development attempt to build better structures, more accommodating to the comfort of the users.

Architectural variations throughout the world reflect the values of their builders. The buildings of slash and burn cultures are necessarily temporary; the open courtyards of the Spanish built structures, found in South America and Spain, reflect the need for space, using courtyards. The tribal Navajo member had a sense of place and space that used open pastoral scenes, that incorporated traditional views of the four major directions, that oriented the natives to natural phenomena, such as the sun and the moon. Architectural structures and patterns arise from symbolic meaning of space, time and place found in each culture.

Sources of Knowledge About Nonverbal Communication

Darwin, the father of evolution, was interested in how humans emerged and how they expressed themselves. In recent years, ethologists still follow that interest. Biologists have solved the genetic code, the Book of Life; it now appears that humans are much closer to other species, such as chimps, in genetic make-up than has been previously assumed. The Great Chain of Being, a theoretical-religious view, placed all species, including humans, on an ordered hierarchy in order of importance, a species high on the ladder being more important than one lower down.This belief system is now eroded. It is now known that the common mouse and the chimpanzee share many of the genes that are found in humans and that some genes may have arisen from bacteria, hardly conceivable to early scholars.

It was once believed that male white men were higher on the Great Chain of Being than were women, Blacks and other people of colour. It is now understood that there is very little physical difference between these groups; there is nothing to justify the superiority of one colour or gender over the others. The study of genetics has given the ethologists new understandings about the inter-relationships of species, especially of higher primates. Self-awareness and self-validation seem to be characteristics that humans share, perhaps with chimpanzees, although this is not clear. It is, however, widely debated. The ability to take the role of the other, an important concept in SI, is part of the awareness of self that sentient creatures, such as humans, have evolved. Human aggression seems to be shared among most species whether they are higher order primates or not. For example, the concept of white supremacy, was behind White aggression against colored people, the Blacks, the Chinese and Native Americans. Whites in the past often referred to darker skinned people as colored.

Ethologists are evolutionists who study both humans and lower order animals. Human ethologists are interested in universal behaviours such as infant attachment, emotion, dominance, nonverbal behaviour and ritual. Comparative study of animal behaviours furnishes a means to put human behaviour in context. For example, research on chimpanzee behaviour in which the major stars have been Lucy, Washoe and Koko, suggests that humans and chimps are not terribly far apart in their evolutionary development, although there are important key differences. The claim is made that chimps can acquire substantial nonverbal vocabularies when they are raised among trainers. It has been shown that chimps can use tools to do work or to reach food and that, by watching their elders, young chimps can learn to do what their parents do. Chimps, parrots and other animals appear to learn things, somewhat like young human children.

Animal communication, as a field of study, is now taught in universities. Parrots are shown to have remarkable "thinking" ability; some songbirds, like finches, can learn new songs, thriving in a song-rich background. A debate rages about whether higher order creatures truly think, as do humans, or whether their behaviour is basically instinctive with some modifications. Some evidence shows that dolphins and chimps can recognize themselves in a mirror, presumably a first step in self-awareness. Unfortunately, the issues are confused by the persistent, almost unavoidable, anthropomorphizing of findings, in which scientists interpret animal behaviour using human models and assumptions. Human beings are able to be the objects of their own thoughts, unlike most or all other animals. The implication of this ability is that humans can create a sense of self and identity. They can talk about themselves and others and construct meaningful relationships. They can make sense of their social worlds.

Sociobiologists and physical anthropologists are interested in how behaviour arises. Is it tied into genetic codes? Is it learned? How does it vary by context? Are animals socialized? Which animals seem to think? How do humans differ from higher order primates? The general field called ethology is yielding important information which can be used to compare human and primate behaviours. Perhaps it is safe to say that there is a balance between nature and nurture that furnishes most of human physical and social growth.

Linguistics and Anthropology

Although the study of linguistics and anthropology have changed considerably in the past few years, spawning many subfields of inquiry, such as sociolinguistics or bio-anthropology, they were studied together for decades. Linguists, like anthropologists, know that the use of language is a key to human studies, as is the study of nonverbal communication. Early theorists assumed that language expressed unconsciously patterned social processes and that culture and language are one and the same. This linguistic relativity hypothesis was challenged in more recent times. More recently, issues have been raised about the universality of human nonverbal communication. The concept of minimum universality has been promoted relative to the display of emotions. Anthopologists refer to acculturation and assimilation, two ways by which culture gets into human heads. Humans acquire their values, symbols, beliefs, customs, technologies and habits through these twin processes. Human nonverbal ways of behaving are deeply influenced by cultural processes. Anthropologists are interested in ceremonial behaviours, in rites of passage and in how gender, ethnicity and aging are construed in various cultures.

Early anthropologists, perhaps quite unlike modern ones, often used the case study method to study villagers, often in remote places. By studying one or two villagers, it was believed that one could understand the general make-up of the entire village because the subject had assimilated the knowledge, expected behaviours and cultural ways of the villagers at large. The subjects were the carriers of culture, influenced by the acculturation process. Anthropologists studied chronemics, the time orientation of cultures, ritualistic behaviours and ceremonies and the folkways of a given culture, referring to folk cultures.

The general point to be made is that anthropologists know that the cultural background of the inhabitant of a given culture deeply influences the nonverbal behaviour of that person and the ways in which humans tend to interpret life.

The lifeworld of each inhabitant is created by the person, but the influences on that creative expression are powerful. A person living in a highly tooled and technologically oriented culture may not know how to survive in the jungles of the Amazon, as the local natives do. Their fund of tacit technological knowledge is not useful in a very different pre-technological culture. Tribal natives from the Amazon basin would not know how to survive in New York City.

Sociology and Social Psychology

The concept of socialization is well known to most readers. Starting from birth, perhaps even before, in its daily exposure to human society, the newborn becomes a fully functioning being. The individual is not determined by society to be anything in particular; rather, the individual must learn to make sense of what he experiences in everyday life. The colours blue and pink in American society are associated with the birth of boys and girls and, throughout life, as humans pass through the various stages of growth, from youth through the gerontological age, humans semantically tag themselves and are tagged by other members of society. They are genderized, ethnicized and aged in this construal process. Ethnicity, gender and age are concepts that are created and applied to groups and individuals. Constructed too narrowly, they serve to isolate their members; constructed too loosely, they fail to serve the members well. The main focus of this book is upon identity adaptiveness or the ability of humans to engage positively with others who are different from themselves. How people think influences what they do.

Standpoint theory suggests that humans are heavily influenced by their birthplace in society. The wealthy have very different expectations for their offspring than do people who live in the ghetto. They learn different ways of behaving. Social codes and the expectations of social class become imbedded in hman thinking. Social class, power and influence, ethnicity, gender and the theme of aging deeply affect how humans communicate nonverbally. These master themes, or variables, are deeply imbedded in daily life. They are revealed in the clothes that people wear, in their characteristic patterns of social conduct and in their expectations. In short, each individual must learn to make sense of the social milieau, to take account of the stuff of society, responding to it, interpreting it, and acting out roles.

Communication

Human identity is rooted in the interpretation and perception of the self, a psychological activity. In interaction with others and in conversations with the self, humans create their identities. They learn that there is an I and a Me in the self and that both are observable in human action. The I is active; the Me is responsive, both being key parts of the sense of self and identity. Self-concepts, identity and the construal of the meanings of human behaviour is the work of psychologists, communicologists and others.

The concept of face is closely allied with the concept of identity. Not to be confused with the physical face, it is symbolic. Humans present themselves to others symbolically, using their bodies and their words. People learn how to save face or to promote a confident face. They learn to ingratiate themselves with others. The face gets construed and scripted. People learn to avoid embarrassment and to create positive impressions in the minds of others, who act as audiences. Psychologists reveal that humans use action language, creating plans for action, both simple and omplex, to accomplish goals. They look back on their activities and make sense of them, building upon them, acting coordinatively with others in joint activities. They evaluate their own success or failure as they interact with others. A complex action may involve days, months or weeks of planned activity, such as those involved in courtships; or, they may be very simple, such as the brushing of the teeth in the morning. Each activity is meaningful to the participant.

A variety of communication models are used in the study of the general field of Communication and, more specifically, in the subfield called Non-verbal Communication. Each model, or approach, has advantages or disadvantages. For example, a sender-message-receiver model is popular in Communication, a linear view. This approach has been widely used in quantitative studies. The symbolic interactionist approach, has a number of advantages not shared by the SMR model, including the view that humans are creative, taking part in an interactive setting in special ways, not necessarily predictable. Nonverbal communication is not a linear process. It is a contingent process; humans build one action upon another, reflecting upon what they have done in preparation for the next episode. They negotiate and modify their actions as needed.

Nonverbal Communication Research

Human, gendered identity is constructed and achieved; it is created in a long-term process, influenced by complex, often poorly understood elements in society. It is implied sometimes that identity, personality and character are fixed, unchanging concepts; contrarily, they are dynamic, yet fairly enduring clusters of focused concepts. Socialized from birth, humans choose, often unwittingly, how they will define themselves. Even though they are born with explicit sexual characteristics, they will genderize their identities. Many scholars who hold an essentialist view of sex tend to show how males and females differ categorically; however, they fail to take into account that humans can and do define and redefine themselves as they choose, changing the ways they act in different circumstances. In saying this, it is not meant to imply that the creation of identity is a thoroughly rational process in which all of the elements are clearly known or depicted. Indeed, quite the opposite is often the case. Humans are often confused as they try to come to terms with self identification, especially in a society heavily saturated by the media.

There are biological differences that clearly influence gendered behaviour; men do not give birth or have menstrual periods, although it is claimed by some researchers that men have their own pronounced biological shifts. Women in general have smaller bodies than do men. Even this comparative smallness is amenable to alteration. Women can and do become physically powerful. The concept of gender is a powerful, modern concept influencing nonverbal communication.

Ethnicity

Race and ethnicity are powerful themes in Western society; indeed, they are universal themes, meaning different things in different cultures. It is no accident that some cultures place people on the social class ladder based on their colour alone. Like gender, concepts about race and colour are learned. People are born into a colored world but they create the meanings of the world for themselves. Humans construe the meaning of skin colour. In relatively simple and static societies, people know where they stand socially, based on skin colour; in complex, change-oriented societies, people may move about in society and create new meanings about ethnicity, race or skin colour. Unfortunately, in the United States, a country that espouses an egalitarian ethos, where all people are to be treated equally, entire populations of colored persons have been—in many cases still are—treated as strangers by the dominant and prevailing white class, based almost entirely on the colour of skin, although other factors come into play. This stranger-making process is complex and it varies according to the groups being studied.

In this book, four ethnic groups are discussed; each has different historical origins and experiences with early mainstream White Americans. Native Americans, or the Navajo, Black Americans and Chinese Americans are studied along the lines of how they achieved their identity in a white world. Identity is the key nonverbal concept and in the case of each of the above, the stuff of history has forced them to deal with their place in a white society. The presence of Cuban Americans in the United States arises from a very different social motif; usually, they have been treated as friends who fled a hostile home country to find a sense of place in the United States. Broad themes emerge in this struggle for inclusion. How can a society move from a stranger-making process to a friendship-making process, ignoring differences and building on similarities? This is the modern struggle in a society that is becoming colored more and more, according to the Census 2000 report.

Age

The study of aging, as opposed to the idea of *ageism*, is about changes in the ways that humans symbolize themselves over a the lifetime. Although biological and genetic factors are influences on the aging processes, they do not determine aging in an absolute sense. Biology influences but does not determine how people age. Stage theorists emphasize the ways that humans are influenced at various stages in their lives. Stages are not fixed and individuals vary greatly among themselves in the ways that they age. Successful aging, a concept that is emerging in modern research, is described in positive ways. Some aspects of aging do not seem to be under human control, such as the loss of acuity in vision, or the ability to see the colour blue. Yet, with technological changes and new medical techniques, the shift from the deficit concepts associated with aging have changed to positive concepts about aging. Present day models of the aging process reveal that aging need not be deleterious! The new paradigms emphasize the role of the aging person, as an active, dynamic person, acting on his or her own behalf to sustain a successful life style.

Technology and Mediation

People in highly developed technical societies live in environments that are highly saturated by the media. Television in particular deeply influences members of these societies. Technological change is profoundly altering the social landscape of advanced countries.

New Media Environment

It appears that print and broadcast media are merging; that there is media abundance, rather than media scarcity. It is now possible to tailor media content to specific, targeted audiences. Interactive media is taking the place of one-way media. The Information Superhighway is controlled in the main by large corporations or businesses, who use it for their own purposes. At the same time, individuals can construct their own websites.

The internet appears to provide unlimited channels to communicate; it can be used to build communities, to create commerce and for a variety of activities that tend to blur the lines between providers and consumers. Mediation in modern societies is a powerful influence on nonverbal communication. The inventor of the internet referred to his invention as a world brain, indicating that the internet functions almost like a neurological net spanning the globe. Other technologies, such as the telephone, e-mail, television, movies and modern satellites have become so common in daily life that they form an embedded social web of which people are largely unconscious. National boundaries are changed and traditional cultures are influenced, adapting to new technologies. The new technologies are producing new, symbolic boundaries, new networked, global communities.

Oral culture retains nonverbal, face-to-face situations, employing the full range of the human sensorium; but, as sophisticated communicative technologies emerge, the face-to-face character of oral culture disappears. In short, the technological context influences nonverbal communication, both in assumption and practice. The computer and television have most dramatically altered the social landscape, with more than half of American households owning computers and more than ninety percent having television sets, many owning more than one. Embedded now in the social landscape, television and the computer have dramatically altered how humans perceive things and how they make sense of their worlds. Human nonverbal communication is dramatically affected.

Research Perspectives

The SI research perspective, with issues and problems that arise from that perspective. Although the SI perspective is used in this text, it is broad enough to include research from many disciplines, as noted above. Much of the research cited here is, in fact, taken from research that has been incorporated from other research models. There is, however, a distinctive and large body of research to be found within the SI perspective, an approach that contains many different points of view.

Self-Assessment and Nonverbal Skills

Although this book is designed primarily to provide a way to integrate the study of nonverbal communication, it may be useful to people who wish to enhance their skills. People are not born with skills; they must learn how to become skilful, to become good performers on the various social stages they occupy. They are found at various stages of this growth process. An analysis of problems that interfere with the development of skill. It contains self-assessment tools to help learners become more proficient and insightful about human nonverbal communication.

Non-Verbal Communication

When Demosthenes was asked what was the first part of oratory he answered, "'action"; and which was the second, he replied, "action"; and which was third he still answered, "action." People tend to believe actions more than words!

Have you ever heard anyone say, "His actions spoke so loudly I couldn't hear what he said?" Have you ever wondered whether anyone has said this about you? What we do is a means of communication, subject to interpretation by others. Did you ever stop to think that even failure to act is a way of communicating? Today, many researchers are concerned with the information sent by communication that is independent of and different from verbal information; namely, the Non-verbal communication. Verbal communication is organized by language; Non-verbal communication is not.

Communication is the transfer of information from one person to another. Most of us spend about 75 percent of our waking hours communicating our knowledge, thoughts, and ideas to others. However, most of us fail to realize that a great deal of our communication is of a Non-verbal form as opposed to the oral and written forms. Non-verbal communication includes facial expressions, eye contact, tone of voice, body posture and motions, and positioning within groups. It may also include the way we wear our clothes or the silence we keep.

In person-to-person communications our messages are sent on two levels simultaneously. If the nonverbal cues and the spoken message are incongruous, the flow of communication is hindered. Right or wrong, the receiver of the communication tends to base the intentions of the sender on the Non-verbal cues he receives.

Static Features

Distance

The distance one stands from another frequently conveys a Non-verbal message. In some cultures it is a sign of attraction, while in others it may reflect status or the intensity of the exchange.

Orientation

People may present themselves in various ways: face-to-face, side-to-side, or even back-to-back. For example, cooperating people are likely to sit side-by-side while competitors frequently face one another.

Posture

Obviously one can be lying down, seated, or standing. These are not the elements of posture that convey messages. Are we slouched or erect ? Are our legs crossed or our arms folded ? Such postures convey a degree of formality and the degree of relaxation in the communication exchange.

Physical Contact

Shaking hands, touching, holding, embracing, pushing, or patting on the back all convey messages. They reflect an element of intimacy or a feeling of (or lack of) attraction.

Dynamic Features

Facial Expressions

A smile, frown, raised eyebrow, yawn, and sneer all convey information. Facial expressions continually change during interaction and are monitored constantly by the recipient. There is evidence that the meaning of these expressions may be similar across cultures.

Gestures

One of the most frequently observed, but least understood, cues is a hand movement. Most people use hand movements regularly when talking. While some gestures (e.g., a clenched fist) have universal meanings, most of the others are individually learned and idiosyncratic.

Looking

A major feature of social communication is eye contact. It can convey emotion, signal when to talk or finish, or aversion. The frequency of contact may suggest either interest or boredom.

The above list shows that both static features and dynamic features transmit important information from the sender to the receiver.

Tortoriello, Blott, and DeWine have defined Non-verbal communication as:

"... the exchange of messages primarily through non-linguistic means, including: kinesics (body language), facial expressions and eye contact, tactile communication, space and territory, environment, paralanguage (vocal but non-linguistic cues), and the use of silence and time."

Let's review these non-linguistic ways of exchanging messages in more detail.

Kinesics

Lamb believes the best way to access an executive's managerial potential is not to listen to what he has to say, but to observe what he does when he is saying it. He calls this new behavioural science "movement analysis." Some of the movements and gestures he has analyzed follow:

Forward and Backward Movements. If you extend a hand straight forward during an interview or tend to lean forward, Lamb considers you to be an "operator"-good for an organization requiring an infusion of energy or dramatic change of course.

Vertical Movements. If you tend to draw yourself up to your tallest during the handshake, Lamb considers you to be a "presenter." You are a master at selling yourself or the organization in which you are employed.

Side-to-Side Movements. If you take a lot of space while talking by moving your arms about, you are a good informer and good listener. You are best suited for an organization seeking a better sense of direction. Lamb believes there is a relationship between positioning of the body and movements of the limbs and facial expressions. He has observed harmony between the two. On the other hand, if certain gestures are rehearsed, such as those made to impress others, there is a tendency to separate the posture and the movements. The harmony disappears.

Studies also indicate that communication comes about through our degree of body flexibility. If you begin a movement with considerable force and then decelerate, you are considered a "gentle-touch." By contrast, if you are a "pressurizer," you are firm from beginning to end. The accuracy of Lamb's analyses is not fully known. However, it is important that corporation executives are becoming so sensitive to the importance of Non-verbal messages that they are hiring consultants, such as Lamb, to analyze Non-verbal communications in their organizations.

Facial Expressions

Facial expressions usually communicate emotions. The expressions tell the attitudes of the communicator. Researchers have discovered that certain facial areas reveal our emotional state better than others. For example, the eyes tend to reveal happiness or sadness, and even surprise. The lower face also can reveal happiness or surprise; the smile, for example, can communicate friendliness and cooperation. The lower face, brows, and forehead can also reveal anger. Mehrabian believes verbal cues provide 7 percent of the meaning of the message; vocal cues, 38 percent; and facial expressions, 55 percent. This means that, as the receiver of a message, you can rely heavily on the facial expressions of the sender because his expressions are a better indicator of the meaning behind the message than his words.

Eye Contact

Eye contact is a direct and powerful form of Non-verbal communication. The superior in the organization generally maintains eye contact longer than the subordinate. The direct stare of the sender of the message conveys candor and openness. It elicits a feeling of trust. Downward glances are generally associated with modesty. Eyes rolled upward are associated with fatigue.

Tactile Communication

Communication through touch is obviously Non-verbal. Used properly it can create a more direct message than dozens of words; used improperly it can build barriers and cause mistrust. You can easily invade someone's space through this type of communication. If it is used reciprocally, it indicates solidarity; if not used reciprocally, it tends to indicate differences in status. Touch not only facilitates the sending of the message, but the emotional impact of the message as well.

Personal Space

Personal space is your "bubble"-the space you place between yourself and others. This invisible boundary becomes apparent only when someone bumps or tries to enter your bubble.

How you identify your personal space and use the environment in which you find yourself influences your ability to send or receive messages. How close do you stand to the one with whom you are communicating ? Where do you sit in the room ?

How do you position yourself with respect to others at a meeting ? All of these things affect your level of comfort, and the level of comfort of those receiving your message.

Goldhaber says there are three basic principles that summarize the use of personal space in an organization: The higher your position (status) in the organization,

(a) the more and better space you will have,

(b) the better protected your territory will be, and

(c) the easier it will be to invade the territory of lower-status personnel.

The impact of use of space on the communication process is related directly to the environment in which the space is maintained.

Environment

How do you arrange the objects in your environment-the desks, chairs, tables, and bookcases? The design of your office, according to researchers, can greatly affect the communications within it. Some managers divide their offices into personal and impersonal areas. This can improve the communication process if the areas are used for the purposes intended. Your pecking-order in the organization is frequently determined by such things as the size of your desk, square feet in your office, number of windows in the office, quality of the carpet, and type of paintings (originals or copies) on the wall. It is obvious that your personal space and environment affect the level of your comfort and your status and facilitate or hinder the communication process.

Paralanguage

Is the content of your message contradicted by the attitude with which you are communicating it? Researchers have found that the tone, pitch, quality of voice, and rate of speaking convey emotions that can be accurately judged regardless of the content of the message. The important thing to gain from this is that the voice is important, not just as the conveyor of the message, but as a complement to the message. As a communicator you should be sensitive to the influence of tone, pitch, and quality of your voice on the interpretation of your message by the receiver.

Silence and Time

Silence can be a positive or negative influence in the communications process. It can provide a link between messages or sever relationships. It can create tension and uneasiness or create a peaceful situation. Silence can also be judgmental by indicating favour or disfavor-agreement or disagreement.

The Power of Non-verbal Communication in Relationships

What is a relationship without communication? It is similar to trying to swim without water. What is a relationship without Non-verbal communication? That is similar to trying to swim through a cube of ice. In order to have a good relationship, good communication is number one on the list of things that two people must have. Communication is a given in anything that we do, but not all of it is acknowledged and recognized for what it is. Of course, we all know and recognize when someone is speaking. It is very obvious. Lips are moving and breathing is choppy, but that is only the small of it.

The best example of Non-verbal communication is the sort that goes along with verbal communication. When we speak, it is not only our mouths that move. Our eyes shift, foreheads crinkle, hands flail. Some pace around because they can not sit still, while others have to take a seat in order to get it all out. All of these actions are Non-verbal and are the things that really open up the lines of understanding. Verbal communication is still very important because we are human. We have a knack for automatically expecting the appropriate response to sudden silence, or a glare, or walking away. A lot of the time, this is where miss communication occurs. We expect one response to our actions, yet we get another, and it is then that the situation escalates. Without words, it can be hard to decipher one feeling from the next, even though words are the minority of the two. Non-verbal communication happens to be the most utilized form of communication of the two, and it is why it plays such a big role in relationships.

5

Executable Model Verbal and Non-verbal Communication

Introduction

Communication is often modelled exclusively as a process of information exchange, abstracting from the physical realisation of the communication process. This approach is based on the more general perspective that a strict separation between the level of *symbols* (symbolic processes) and the *material* level (physical processes) has advantages in modelling. Following this perspective, the communication process is not embedded in the physical environment. In particular, for the case of embodied Non-verbal communication, for example on the basis of body language or gestures, a strict separation of communication processes from interaction at the material level can be rather artificial. On the other hand, describing communication processes only in physical terms may be too restrictive as well. In the model of communication presented in this paper both the material level and the level of information, as well as the interaction between the levels are taken into account in one generic process model.

At the symbolic level a distinction can be made between information representing the subject matter of the communication, and information that refers to the *process* of communication, for example, information on the communication protocol that is followed, or the current stage of the communication process within the protocol. Thus, three semantic or representation levels are introduced:

- the material level (for the physical world),

- the symbolic object level (for symbolic manipulation of information on the physical world), and
- the symbolic meta-level (for symbolic manipulation of the dynamics and reflective aspects of the agents).

Each of these three levels uses representations of structures of one of the other levels: the symbolic object level uses representations of the material world, the symbolic meta-level uses representations of the symbolic object level, and the material level uses representations of the symbolic object level. The three levels are explained, process semantics is defined by means of multi-levelled traces based on triples of three-valued states, formalised by partial models.

An executable generic process model is introduced in which a number of processes within a communication process are distinguished. Different types of interaction between Non-verbal communication and verbal communication processes are identified; it is shown how the generic process model can be applied to model both verbal communication and Non-verbal communication, as well as different types of interaction between these forms of communication, in one semantic framework. One example model is presented in which the communication protocol of a verbal communication process is modelled as reflex-based Non-verbal communication (one gesture triggers another one by stimulus-response behaviour), and an alternative model in which the Non-verbal communication in the communication protocol is guided by conscious deliberation.The implementation of the model is described. Summarizes and compares this approach with other work. In Appendix A a trace of the process is given in symbolic notation, demonstrating the stimulus-response case.

Semantic Levels in Communication

The semantic model is built by identifying the semantic levels involved, making the representation relations between them explicit, and by determining the state transitions at the different levels during the communication process. Three semantic levels are used in the semantic model of communication presented in this paper. The first is the *material level*: of the world itself, the physical reality. The second level is the level of symbolic representation of the world state: the *symbolic object level*. Within the agents, symbols are used to represent information regarding the world state. The third semantic level is the symbolic level where the agent reasons about aspects of its own state, e.g., its own knowledge and actions it intends to perform in the world: the *symbolic meta-level*. Symbolic expressions at this level do not represent information about world states, but instead are an explicit representation of information about the state of the process, of an agent's related mental aspects, such as its state of knowledge, its goals, and its intentions.

A Simple Example Communication Process

All examples in this paper are about a lecture, which is finishing. The chair person, agent A, puts up a slide expressing where to find tea and coffee. A thirsty person in the audience, agent B, interprets this information. However, the communication may be affected by an event in the material world, for example, somebody erroneously standing between the projector and the screen. In the example, agent A has a representation of the world information that pot 2 contains tea, represented at the symbolic object level by the symbolic expression contains(pot2, tea). By upward reflection to the symbolic meta-level it establishes that it has the positive belief that pot 2 contains tea. The agent A reasons at the symbolic meta-level and concludes that this world information should be communicated to agent B. Using knowledge of the meaning that can be associated to certain material configurations, it discovers that if at position p0 in the material world pattern 3 is visible then this world situation represents that pot 2 contains tea (e.g., a written text on a visible place). Moreover, still reasoning at the symbolic meta-level, it finds out that an action 'put slide 3' exists, which has as an effect that pattern 3 is at position p0. Therefore it concludes at the symbolic meta-level that the action 'put slide 3' has to be performed. The action is performed, and the intended effect is realised in the world state at the material level. In the example, the two agents are assumed to have a common ontology on the world including the names of all objects in the world, like pot 2, pattern 3, and the names of the positions. Agent B performs the observation that pattern 3 is at position p0 (which provides information at the symbolic meta-level, namely the meta-fact that this has been observed), and represents the information acquired at the symbolic object level by at_position(pattern3, p0) (the agent B's world model). Note that agent B cannot observe directly the world information that pot 2 contains tea or that slide 3 is on the projector, but it can observe that pattern 3 is at position p0.

Knowing at the symbolic meta-level that to this world situation the interpretation 'pot 2 contains tea' can be associated, it now concludes at the symbolic meta-level that it has been communicated that pot 2 contains tea.

This information is then stored by B at the symbolic object level in its representation of the world state. Note that after this process, the representation of the world state at the symbolic object level includes information that was acquired by observation (pattern 3 is at position p0), and also information that was not obtainable by observation, but acquired by the communication process (pot 2 contains tea).

Formalisation of the Semantic Model

In the semantic formalisation a state-based semantics is chosen. Each of the states is formalised by a partial (or three-valued: with truth values *true, false* and *undefined*) model. The signature (the lexicon) for these partial models is partitioned according to the three semantic levels. To define semantics of the whole communication process, partial temporal models are used. Within this approach the semantics of a process is formalised by a set of (alternative) partial temporal models, i.e., sequences of partial models. For an example of such a partial temporal model. Within each of the states in such a temporal model the three semantic levels can be distinguished. Representation relations are defined in the sense that symbolic expressions at the object level (such as contains(pot2, tea)) refer to the state of the material level, symbolic expressions at the meta-level (such as belief(contains(pot2, tea), pos)) refer to states of the object level, and the material level configurations (such as pattern 3) refer to object level information (that pot 2 contains tea).

Only the following types of transitions between two subsequent states are allowed in these temporal partial models:

Single Level Transitions

- *world change transition*

  A change in the state of the material level
- *object reasoning transition*

  A change in the state of the symbolic object level
- *meta-reasoning transition*

  A change in the state of the symbolic meta-level

  Level interaction transitions
- *upward reflection transition*

  A change of the meta-level state under influence of the object level state.
- *downward reflection transition*

  A change of the object level state under influence of the meta-level state.
- *action execution transition*

  A change of the material level state under influence of the meta-level state
- *observation transition*

  A change of the meta-level state under influence of the material level state

  A levelled transition is a transition of the overall (three-level) state which is induced by a transition of one of the types distinguished above. The transition types depicted in the first part of the trace are, subsequently:
- meta-reasoning; three times:

  -deciding that contains(pot2, tea) has to be communicated,

  -selecting the goal at_position(pattern3, p0) to be achieved,

  -determining the action put_slide3 to achieve the goal
- action execution.

  The transition types depicted in the second part of the trace are, respectively,
- observation (of at_position(pattern3,p0)),
- downward reflection (including at_position(pattern3,p0) in B's world model),

- upward reflection (identifying at_position(pattern3,p0) as a belief),
- meta-reasoning (interpreting at_position(pattern3,p0) as a communication of the information contains(pot2,tea)),
- downward reflection (including contains(pot2,tea) in B's world model),
- upward reflection (identifying contains(pot2,tea) as a belief).

The formal definitions are given below. The elements used to describe the states (the ground atoms) are expressed in a language defined by an information type.

Definition 1 (information state)

An *information type* Ó is a structure of symbols defining a set of *ground atoms* At(Ó). An *information state* for an information type Ó is a mapping M : At(Ó) '! {0, 1, u} from the set of ground atoms At(Ó) to the set of truth values {0, 1, u}; i.e., a *(partial) model*. The set of all information states of information type Ó is denoted by IS(Ó).

An information state M : At(Ó) '! {0, 1, u} is called a *two-valued* information state if M(a) " {0, 1} for all a " At(Ó). The set of two-valued information states for Ó is denoted by IS2(Ó). An example of a structure that defines an information type is a tuple of (sub-)sorts, constants, functions, and predicates of an order-sorted predicate logic. Each of the three levels has such an information type.

Definition 2 (transition)

A *transition between information states* is a pair of partial models; i.e., an element < S, S′ > (also denoted by S '! S′) of IS(Ó) x IS(Ó). A *transition relation* is a set of these transitions, i.e., a relation on IS(Ó) x IS(Ó).

Behaviour is the result of transitions from one information state to another. If a transition relation is functional then it specifies deterministic behaviour. By applying transitions in succession, sequences of states are constructed. These sequences, also called traces (and interpreted as temporal models), formally describe behaviour.

Definition 3 (trace and temporal model)

A *trace* or *partial temporal model* of information type Ó is a sequence of information states (Mt)t " Í in IS(Ó). The set of all partial temporal models is denoted by IS(Ó)N, or Traces(Ó). A set of partial temporal models is a declarative description of the semantics of the behaviour of a process; each temporal model can be seen as one of the alternatives for the behaviour. Next these notions are applied to the three levels distinguished in a communication process.

Definition 4 (levelled information state)

Levelled transitions and traces adhere to the levelled structure of the states: a levelled transition describes a levelled information state that changes in time. Following the levelled structure, only some types of transitions are allowed. For each of the levels a transition limited to this level (leaving untouched the other levels) is possible: a *world change*, an *object level reasoning* step, or a *meta-level reasoning* step. Two examples of transitions involving interaction between levels are *upward reflection* (information from the symbolic object level is lifted and incorporated in the symbolic meta-level), *downward reflection* (information from the symbolic meta-level influences the information at the symbolic object level). Other examples of transitions involving interaction between levels are *observation* (material level influences symbolic meta-level information), and *action execution* (symbolic meta-level information influences the material level). The following definition postulates that only these types of transitions are possible.

A Process Model for Communication

Within a communication process, a number of more specific symbolic processes can be distinguished:

- observation generation
- information interpretation
- communication initiation
- action generation
- maintenance of world information

Together with the physical processes in the material world that realise action and observation execution, these processes are used as building blocks to compose an executable generic process model of communication. Within the DESIRE approach each of the processes is modelled by a component. The interaction is modelled by information links. Agent B is identical in composition to agent A.

The component observation generation determines the observations the agent initiates. In the example, agent B is initiating observation of the projection screen and agent A, and agent A observes agent B. The component information interpretation produces the information conveyed in the observation results, using specific interpretation knowledge (which involves, among others, knowledge on material representation of information). The component maintain world information constructs and maintains the agent's world model. The component communication initiation makes the decision to communicate and does some preparation of the communication; it uses knowledge about when to communicate information, and the selection of goals in relation to the material representation of information. The component action generation produces the actions to be performed, using knowledge of the effect of actions.

The component external world takes the observations and the actions initiated by the agents and produces the observation results for the agents. It maintains the state of the world and takes care of the changes to the world state.

Combining Verbal and Non-verbal Communication

During real-life communication processes several types of communication play a role, among them are verbal and Non-verbal communication. Furthermore, combining verbal and Non-verbal communication can sometimes be done in a stimulus-response manner in contrast to consciously. Different types of interaction between verbal and Non-verbal communication are distinguished and explained. It is shown how differences between reflex-based (also called direct stimulus-response) reactions and conscious reactions on Non-verbal communication can be modelled.

The example communication process, only verbal communication. The verbal type of communication is the type that is normally exclusively considered in research in multi-agent systems in which all agents are software agents. However, in real life situations, often the Non-verbal communication is as important as verbal communication. Non-verbal communication is addressed and classified into three different types of interaction with verbal communication. In the classification one of the distinguishing criteria is the nature of the processing of the communication: based on reflex reactions, or on conscious reactions. For each of the types of interaction between verbal and Non-verbal communication an example is presented.

The following kinds of interaction between Non-verbal and verbal communication are distinguished:

A. Interaction of Non-verbal communication with the content of verbal communication:

1. Non-verbal communication provides information additional to the content information transferred by the of the verbal communication:

- the subject of the Non-verbal communication has no connection with the subject of the verbal communication
- the subject of the Non-verbal communication is related to the subject of the verbal communication

2. Non-verbal communication affects the interpretation of the contents of the verbal communication; modified interpretation

B. Interaction of Non-verbal communication with the process of the verbal communication:

1. the verbal communication process is affected by reflex-based reactions to the Non-verbal communication

2. the verbal communication process is affec ted by conscious reactions to the Non-verbal communication Notice that Non-verbal communication of type A. will lead to conscious reactions of the recipient; as the interpretation of observations as being communicated information is a conscious process. Combinations of the different types of interaction can occur during one communication process. In the examples it is assumed that the agents share a common ontology for world information. Simple examples of the different types of Non-verbal communication are:

A. *Interaction of Non-verbal communication with the content of verbal communication* :

1. *Additional information*

a) *No connection.* Agent A communicates verbally to B that tea can be found in pot 2. Agent B observes that agent A smiles to him and concludes that agent A recognises him. This observation does not influence the communication process concerned with where the tea can be found. Furthermore, agent B does not change his interpretation of the verbal communication on account of noticing that agent A recognises him.

b) *Related.* Agent A communicates verbally to B that tea can be found in pot 2. During the communication Agent A points to position p3. Agent B observes the direction that agent A is pointing in and concludes that agent A is telling it that tea can be found in pot 2 that can be found at position p3.

2. *Modified interpretation*

Agent A communicates verbally to B that fresh tea can be found in pot 2. However, agent A makes a face that indicates she is disgusted at the moment the verbal communication process takes place. Agent B combines this Non-verbal communication with the verbal one and, therefore, interprets the communication as follows: tea can be found in pot 2, but it is definitely not fresh. Modification of the interpretation of the verbal communication appeared to be necessary, based on the Non-verbal part of the communication.

B. *Interaction of Non-verbal communication with the process of verbal communication* :

Agent A initiates the communication process by walking to position p1. She notices that agent B is looking at her and she starts her communication to agent B that tea can be found in pot 2, by putting the correct slide (slide 3) on the projector. However, after performing this action agent A observes that agent B is looking in another direction; in reaction (either by reflex or consciously) she breaks off the communication process by removing the slide, and (to get attention) starts tapping the microphone. Agent B observes the noise of the microphone and (either by reflex or consciously) reacts by looking at agent A with interest. Agent A waits until she observes that agent B is looking interested, and then resumes the verbal communication process by putting the slide on the projector again. In such a case the information transferred by verbal communication is not affected by the Non-verbal communication, but (the control of) the process of communication is.

Implementation

A demo has been developed which allows the user to view the process step-by-step. They can also take matters into their own hand and select the types of behaviour for each agent, or even select specific actions by hand, taking the role of one or both agents.

In the area of agents, communication processes play an important role. In this paper a semantic model has been proposed for combined verbal and Non-verbal communication processes and their interaction. The semantic model distinguishes three semantic or representation levels; it has been formalised on the basis of three-levelled partial temporal models. These partial temporal models formalise both the material and mental processes and their relations. The relations between the levels can be defined as (partly circular) representation relations.

Moreover, using the compositional development method DESIRE, an executable generic process model has been designed that can be used to simulate different types of combinations of verbal and Non-verbal communication processes. In an example it has been shown how a Non-verbal communication process can be modelled that adds and modifies content to a verbal communication process, but also provides a protocol for the (control of the) verbal communication process. In this example different types of behaviour with respect to the communication protocol have been modelled: stimulus-response behaviour and variants of deliberate behaviour. The first type of behaviour has the advantage that it is very direct, but the second type of behaviour may be more flexible in unforeseen circumstances. The distinction made between stimulus-response behaviour and deliberate conscious reasoning in communication is also made. Three levels of cognitive control are distinguished, corresponding to the stimulus-response level, the conscious level and a heuristic-based level in between these two. The heuristic-based level, used in familiar, although not entirely routine, situations, can be expressed in the proposed model by rules guarded with beliefs and concluding actions. The manner in which in the example the Non-verbal communication process modifies the meaning of the verbal communication can be used as a more general approach to model irony for another approach to irony, based on an application of default logic to speech act theory.

The generic model for verbal and Non-verbal communication presented here makes the communication process vulnerable to the effects of (other) causal patterns in the material world. This may occur as a negative aspect, as often communication is assumed ideal. However, in situations in which this assumption is not fulfilled, the approach introduced gives the possibility to explicitly model the interaction between the communication process and other material processes, and to take into account causality within the communication process, situated in the other processes. Moreover, this approach can be a starting point for simulations of the development of communication from an evolutionary perspective on communication.

A substantial part of research on communication takes speech act theory as a point of departure. Agent communication languages such as KQML have been proposed. Semantics of such languages is still an issue to be investigated further. Speech acts are used to designate the effect an agent wishes to bring about in the world by communicating. Sometimes they are labelled as 'promise' or 'threaten', or more precisely 'put receiver clear about employer-employee relationship, and use this to force decision' or 'appeal to receiver to reconsider decision in light of new information'. Speech act theory treats these things in great detail. The theory, however, only considers the content of the communication, abstaining from the material realization. The limitation is that these approaches focus on communication at a verbal or symbolic level, and do not cover Non-verbal communication processes in which the physical aspects play an important role. In conclusion, speech act theory aids us when determining the content of any communication, but when the material level is important (as in Non-verbal interaction), it is less applicable. In [Cassell et al] a model is presented that does integrate verbal and Non-verbal communication, however, the model is restricted to only gestures (with the arms). The gestures are modelled in a naturalistic fashion, as the authors take great care to generate realistic verbal and Non-verbal behaviour. The interaction is limited to only one kind, type A1, where the Non-verbal information content complements the verbal content. Several types of complementary gestures are distinguished, but the overall model is less refined and a formal semantics is not presented.

6

Non-verbal Communication Skills

Power of Non-verbal Communication and Body Language

Good communication is the foundation of successful relationships, both personally and professionally. But we communicate with much more than words. In fact, research shows that the majority of our communication is nonverbal. Nonverbal communication, or *body language*, includes our facial expressions, gestures, eye contact, posture, and even the tone of our voice.

The ability to understand and use nonverbal communication is a powerful tool that will help you connect with others, express what you really mean, navigate challenging situations, and build better relationships at home and work. Nonverbal communication, or body language, is a vital form of communication. When we interact with others, we continuously give and receive countless wordless signals. All of our nonverbal behaviours—the gestures we make, the way we sit, how fast or how loud we talk, how close we stand, how much eye contact we make—send strong messages.

The way you listen, look, move, and react tell the other person whether or not you care and how well you're listening. The nonverbal signals you send either produce a sense of interest, trust, and desire for connection—or they generate disinterest, distrust, and confusion. Nonverbal communication cues can play five roles:

- Repetition: they can repeat the message the person is making verbally
- Contradiction: they can contradict a message the individual is trying to convey

- Substitution: they can substitute for a verbal message. For example, a person's eyes can often convey a far more vivid message than words and often do
- Complementing: they may add to or complement a verbal message. A boss who pats a person on the back in addition to giving praise can increase the impact of the message
- Accenting: they may accent or underline a verbal message. Pounding the table, for example, can underline a message.

Nonverbal Communication

It takes more than words to create fulfilling, strong relationships. Nonverbal communication has a huge impact on the quality of our relationships. Nonverbal communication skills improve relationships by helping you:

- Accurately read other people, including the emotions they're feeling and the unspoken messages they're sending.
- Create trust and transparency in relationships by sending nonverbal signals that match up with your words.
- Respond with nonverbal cues that show others that you understand, notice, and care.

Unfortunately, many people send confusing or negative nonverbal signals without even knowing it. When this happens, both connection and trust are lost in our relationships.

Consider the Case of Arlene

Arlene is attractive and has no problem meeting eligible men — it's keeping them that is the problem! Arlene is funny and a good conversationalist, but even though she laughs and smiles constantly, she radiates tension. Arlene's shoulders and eyebrows are noticeably raised, her voice is shrill and her body stiff to touch. Being around Arlene makes many people feel uncomfortable. Arlene has a lot going for her that is undercut by the discomfort she evokes in others.

Arlene is articulate, attractive, and well-intentioned, but she struggles to connect with others because she isn't aware of the nonverbal messages she's communicating. But she can break this pattern if she learns to pay attention to the wordless signals she sends and receives:

Arlene notices that her date is tapping his fingers and that she has been swinging her leg and foot. He looks bored, and she feels tense all over. Taking a long, deep breath and a swallow of wine, she feels her shoulders drop and her jaw relax. Arlene leans across the table and breaks into a warm smile. Her date smiles back, and their eyes meet and hold. She has also used her new observational skills at work and is now much more comfortable interacting with others in that setting.

Types of Nonverbal Communication

There are many different types of nonverbal communication. Together, the following nonverbal signals and cues communicate your interest and investment in others.

Facial Expressions

The human face is extremely expressive, able to express countless emotions without saying a word. And unlike some forms of nonverbal communication, facial expressions are universal. The facial expressions for happiness, sadness, anger, surprise, fear, and disgust are the same across cultures.

Body Movements and Posture

Consider how your perceptions of people are affected by the way they sit, walk, stand up, or hold their head. The way you move and carry yourself communicates a wealth of information to the world. This type of nonverbal communication includes your posture, bearing, stance, and subtle movements.

Gestures

Gestures are woven into the fabric of our daily lives. We wave, point, beckon, and use our hands when we're arguing or speaking animatedly—expressing ourselves with gestures often without thinking. However, the meaning of gestures can be very different across cultures and regions, so it's important to be careful to avoid misinterpretation.

Eye Contact

Since the visual sense is dominant for most people, eye contact is an especially important type of nonverbal communication. The way you look at someone can communicate many things, including interest, affection, hostility, or attraction. Eye contact is also important in maintaining the flow of conversation and for gauging the other person's response.

Touch

We communicate a great deal through touch. Think about the messages given by the following: a firm handshake, a timid tap on the shoulder, a warm bear hug, a reassuring pat on the back, a patronizing pat on the head, or a controlling grip on your arm.

Space

Have you ever felt uncomfortable during a conversation because the other person was standing too close and invading your space? We all have a need for physical space, although that need differs depending on the culture, the situation, and the closeness of the relationship. You can use physical space to communicate many different nonverbal messages, including signals of intimacy, aggression, dominance, or affection.

Voice

We communicate with our voices, even when we are not using words. Nonverbal speech sounds such as tone, pitch, volume, inflection, rhythm, and rate are important communication elements. When we speak, other people "read" our voices in addition to listening to our words. These nonverbal speech sounds provide subtle but powerful clues into our true feelings and what we really mean. Think about how tone of voice, for example, can indicate sarcasm, anger, affection, or confidence.

It's not what you say, it's *how* you say it

- Intensity. A reflection of the amount of energy you project is considered your intensity. Again, this has as much to do with what feels good to the other person as what you personally prefer.
- Timing and pace. Your ability to be a good listener and communicate interest and involvement is impacted by timing and pace.

- Sounds that convey understanding. Sounds such as "ahhh, ummm, ohhh," uttered with congruent eye and facial gestures, communicate understanding and emotional connection. More than words, these sounds are the language of interest, understanding and compassion.

Using Body Language and Nonverbal Communication Successfully

Nonverbal communication is a rapidly flowing back-and-forth process. Successful nonverbal communication depends on emotional self-awareness and an understanding of the cues you're sending, along with the ability to accurately pick up on the cues others are sending you. This requires your full concentration and attention. If you are planning what you're going to say next, daydreaming, or thinking about something else, you are almost certain to miss nonverbal cues and other subtleties in the conversation. You need to stay focused on the moment-to-moment experience in order to fully understand what's going on.

Tips for successful nonverbal communication:

- Take a time out if you're feeling overwhelmed by stress. Stress compromises your ability to communicate. When you're stressed out, you're more likely to misread other people, send off confusing or off-putting nonverbal signals, and lapse into unhealthy knee-jerk patterns of behaviour. Take a moment to calm down before you jump back into the conversation. Once you've regained your emotional equilibrium, you'll be better equipped to deal with the situation in a positive way.
- Pay attention to inconsistencies. Nonverbal communication should reinforce what is being said. If you get the feeling that someone isn't being honest or that something is "off," you may be picking up on a mismatch between verbal and nonverbal cues. Is the person is saying one thing, and their body language something else? For example, are they telling you "yes" while shaking their head no?
- Look at nonverbal communication signals as a group. Don't read too much into a single gesture or nonverbal

cue. Consider all of the nonverbal signals you are sending and receiving, from eye contact to tone of voice and body language. Are your nonverbal cues consistent—or inconsistent—with what you are trying to communicate?

Common Mistakes

- You're not subtle. Be objective about your own observations to make sure you aren't offending others by broadly mimicking their speech or behaviour. Remember, most people instinctively send and interpret nonverbal signals all the time, so don't assume you're the only one who's aware of nonverbal undercurrents. Finally, stay true to yourself. Be aware of your own natural style, and don't adopt behaviour that is incompatible with it.
- You bluff. Thinking you can bluff by deliberately altering your body language can do more harm than good. Unless you're a proficient actor, it will be hard to overcome your body's inability to lie. There will always be mixed messages, signs that your channels of communication are not congruent. It's a prime example of leakage, and something others will detect, one way or another.
- You rush to accuse based on body language alone. Incorrect accusations based on erroneous observations can be embarrassing and damaging and take a long time to overcome. Always verify your interpretation with another communications channel before rushing in. You could say something like, "I get the feeling you're uncomfortable with this course of action. Would you like to add something to the discussion?" This should draw out the real message and force the individual to come clean or to adjust his or her body language.

Improving your Nonverbal Communication Skills

Before you can improve your nonverbal communication skills, you need to figure out what you're doing right and where there is room for improvement. The most effective method is to observe yourself in action:

- **Video camera** – Videotape a conversation between you

and a partner. Set the camera to record both of you at the same time, so you can observe the nonverbal back-and-forth. When you watch the recording, focus on any discrepancies between your verbal and nonverbal communication.

- **Digital camera** – Ask someone to take a series of photos of you while you're talking to someone else. As you look through the photos, focus on you and the other person's body language, facial expressions, and gestures.
- **Audio recorder** – Record a conversation between you and a friend or family member. As you listen to the recording afterwards, concentrate on the way things are said, rather than the words. Pay attention to tone, timing, pace, and other sounds.

As you watch or listen to the recordings, ask yourself the following questions:

Evaluating your Nonverbal Communication Skills

Eye contact: Is this source of connection missing, too intense, or just right in yourself or in the person you are looking at?

Facial expression: What is your face showing? Is it masklike and unexpressive, or emotionally present and filled with interest? What do you see as you look into the faces of others?

Tone of voice : Does your voice project warmth, confidence, and delight, or is it strained and blocked? What do you hear as you listen to other people?

Posture and gesture: Does your body look still and immobile, or relaxed? Sensing the degree of tension in your shoulders and jaw answers this question. What do you observe about the degree of tension or relaxation in the body of the person you are speaking to?

Touch: Remember, what feels good is relative. How do you like to be touched? Who do you like to have touching you? Is the difference between what you like and what the other person likes obvious to you?

Intensity: Do you or the person you are communicating with seem flat, cool, and disinterested, or over-the-top and melodramatic?

Again, this has as much to do with what feels good to the other person as it does with what you personally prefer.

Timing and pace: What happens when you or someone you care about makes an important statement? Does a response—not necessarily verbal—come too quickly or too slowly? Is there an easy flow of information back and forth?

Sounds : Do you use sounds to indicate that you are attending to the other person? Do you pick up on sounds from others that indicate their caring or concern for you?

The point of this exercise is to develop your nonverbal awareness. As you continue to pay attention to the nonverbal cues and signals you send and receive, your ability to communicate will improve.

Nonverbal communication is one of the five key skills of emotional intelligence.

The Five Skills of Emotional Intelligence

Skill 1: Quick Stress Relief

Skill 2: Emotional Awareness

Skill 3: Nonverbal Communication

Skill 4: Playful Communication

Skill 5: Conflict Resolution

The ability to communicate nonverbally is the third of five essential emotional intelligence skills. Together, the five skills of emotional intelligence help you build strong relationships, overcome challenges, and succeed at work and in life.

The fourth key skill of emotional intelligence is the ability to use humor and play to deal with challenges. Playful communication helps you bounce back from adversity, boost your energy and your spirits, come up with creative ways to solve problems, and keep your relationships fresh and exciting.

Individual Presentation

1. Decide on your audience: Once you have chosen a topic for your presentation, you must consider carefully your audience. What is the age range? What sort of information

do you think they will want to get from this presentation? Where do you intend to get your data from?

2. Decide on content: What textual content are you going to use. Remember the text needs to be *original* and not just copied from another source. What images are you going to create or obtain from other sources? What sounds are you going to use? You should consider recording voiceovers for a few slides and using pre-recorded sounds on other slides. Remember, you are not expected to use all three features on every slide.
3. Decide on the user interaction: How is the user going to move through the presentation (interact with it)? The best way to show this is to create a design plan. This will show the data to be contained on each slide and will show how the user can get to each slide.
4. Prepare production scripts: For each slide draft out the data that you are going to display – the text you are going to use, where the image(s) are going to go, what form the hyperlinks are going to be (textual or hotspots) and where they are going to go. These rough drafts will form part of your design notes.

Preparing your Presentation

1. Design your slides: Using PowerPoint, decide on a colour scheme or background layout and prepare each of your slides. It is a good idea to take *screen shots* at each stage of development for *one* slide, to use as evidence of how you designed the presentation, when you do your report.
2. Put in animation, where appropriate.: Remember that animation is not expected for every piece of text or picture, and will actually detract from a presentation, if overused. However, used appropriately animation can make an important contribution to any presentation.

Testing your Presentation

Once you have prepared the presentation, you must test that it actually works in the way you intended. It is a good idea to get someone else to use it and ask for their comments on it. It may be that not all the hyperlinks work properly, or that the user gets to a dead end and cannot get out of it. Assuming the presentation works perfectly, you may still want to revise the presentation in the light of comments you receive. For example, you may find that two colours used for text and background do not contrast sufficiently. If you are looking for a merit, you should be able to provide evidence that the presentation has been checked and revised.

Writing your Report

Obviously, it is expected that, in your presentation, you will meet all the requirements in the pass criteria outlined earlier, in terms of original text, images and sounds. Your report should contain the following features:

- A clear description of what your presentation is expected to do, what audience it is intended for and what information the audience could get out of it
- An outline (design plan) showing the user interaction. This may be a flow chart or a tree diagram.
- Your rough notes showing the layout for each slide
- A word-processed account of how you created the presentation, showing a slide being built up from scratch, with screen shots as evidence, and an explanation of how hyperlinks were inserted.
- Evidence that you have checked your work
- A printout of all the slides used in the presentation. They do not need to be on separate pages, but can be joined together, six slides to a page, with hand-written annotations around them
- An evaluation of how well you completed your work, with suggestions for improvement and a description of any problems you encountered.

Major: Communications Studies/Speech Communication and Rhetoric

Ratings prove that television audiences prefer laugh tracks over silence. Now and then a new show will go experimental, opting to can the canned laughter, only to be promptly cancelled.

So why do we want to laugh on cue? Why are shows funnier when a studio full of people laughs with us? You may soon have the answers as a major in communications studies/speech communication and rhetoric. In this program, students learn how certain messages influence individual and group behaviour—and why—as well as how our reactions reflect the underlying values of society. You'll spend a significant amount of time studying different kinds of speaking and writing and the strategies speakers and writers use to make their points and drive them home. You'll take a look at verbal and nonverbal messages, audience reaction, and the varied effects of different communication environments. Communication theory will play a part too, as you delve into monumental speeches, revolutionary political campaigns, radical social movements, and the trends in styles of news reporting.

Rhetoric itself is about putting together good arguments—communication for the means of persuasion. Fiery personalities, quick wits, and the cunning will take pleasure in a major that includes rhetoric—mastering different types of appeals and how to craft those appeals and make them situation-specific, audience-tailored, and sharp as all get out. Your studies will range from classical forms of rhetoric, like great Roman orations, to modern day places where it rears its head, like websites, film, and television.

A major in communications studies/speech communication and rhetoric makes for solid pre-professional training. It will prepare you for a wealth of careers in business, public relations, advertising, human resources, government, education, media, and social services. You won't come away with specific skills—like putting together an ad campaign or producing a television show. It will, however, give you a strong foundation from which to launch any number of careers and aspirations.

Connection-oriented Communication

In telecommunications, connection-oriented communication is a data communication mode in which the devices at the end points use a protocol to establish an end-to-end logical or physical connection before any data may be sent. In case of digital transmission, in-order delivery of a bit stream or byte stream is provided. Connection-oriented protocol services are often but not always *reliable* network services, that provide acknowledgment after successful delivery, and automatic repeat request functions in case of missing data or detected bit-errors.

Circuit mode communication, for example the public switched telephone network, ISDN and SONET/SDH, are examples of connection-oriented communication. Circuit mode communication provides guarantees that data will arrive with constant bandwidth and at constant delay. Packet mode communication may also be connection-oriented, which is called virtual circuit mode communication. Due to the packet switching, the communication may suffer from variable bit rate and delay, due to varying traffic load and packet queue lengths.

A connection-oriented transport layer protocol, such as TCP, may be based on a connectionless network layer protocol (such as IP), but still achieve in-order delivery of a byte-stream, by means of segment numbering on the sender side and data packet reordering on the receiver side.

In a connection-oriented packet switched data link layer or network layer protocol, all data is sent over the same path during a communication session. The protocol does not have to provide each packet with routing information (complete source and destination address), but only with a channel/data stream number, often denoted virtual circuit identifier (VCI). Routing information may be provided to the network nodes during the connection establishment phase, where the VCI is defined in tables in each node. Thus, the actual packet switching and data transfer can be taken care of by fast hardware, as opposed to slow software based routing.

The alternative to connection-oriented transmission is connectionless communication, also known as datagram communication, in which data is sent in form of packets from one end point to another without prior arrangement or signaling. This mode operates without guarantees of delivery according to a best-effort policy. Each data packet must contain complete address information, since packets are routed individually and independently of each other, possibly transmitted along different network paths. Connectionless protocols are usually described as stateless because the end points have no protocol-defined way to remember where they are in a "conversation" of message exchanges. Because they can keep track of a conversation, connection-oriented protocols are sometimes described as stateful.

Examples of connection-oriented packet mode communication, i.e. virtual circuit mode communication:

- The Transmission Control Protocol (TCP) is a connection-oriented reliable protocol that is based on a datagram protocol (the IP protocol).
- X.25 was a connection-oriented reliable network protocol.
- Frame relay is a connection-oriented unreliable data link layer protocol.
- GPRS
- Asynchronous Transfer Mode
- Multiprotocol Label Switching

Effective Communication Skills for Sales

How many times do you have a conversation with someone who just 'doesn't get it'? How about someone who doesn't listen to you? Or worse off, how about someone who says very little and simply nods their head? There are plenty of examples of ways in which people are poor communicators. Unfortunately, these kinds of people will never be successful salespeople or managers. Effective communication is part of a person's selling skills, and is often times left out of sales training. This is problematic if communication skills are the most important factor in running a successful business, making sales, or simply living your life.

Becoming an Effective Communicator

Being an effective communicator requires that you know how to listen, know how to engage, know how to be a critical thinker, know how to retain information, and know how to articulate information properly. This article will break down effective communication into three categories. These categories include oral communication, written communication, and body language. All three are integral in mastering before you can achieve effective communication skills. Why do you need to be a good communicator in order to be successful? If you're a salesperson, you need to be familiar with successful selling techniques and you need to be able to articulate those techniques to your clients. If you're a manager, you need to be able to develop strategic sales plans or sales management strategies that require a heavy amount of written communication. It may also entail presenting information to colleagues or strangers. All communication derives from our ability to speak with others and interact with others. How can some people be better speakers than other people?

Oral Communication

Oral communication is the basic interaction through speech, between human beings. Being an effective speaker requires you to be knowledgeable of whatever you may be speaking about. You must have a purpose in speaking. In the business world, you may be trying to present a business plan to investors. At home, you may be trying to get your children to do something. In both cases, there is purpose in why you are speaking. In fact, every time you speak there is a purpose behind what you say. You need to ensure your purpose in speaking is always positive. This means going into a speaking engagement with only positive intent. If you begin speaking with negative intent, your audience will feel uneasy and will likely not listen to you. This positive intent is part of the basic sales skills any business person will need to acquire. As a speaker, you will want to speak in varying volumes and tones. This adds variance to your voice and keeps your audience connected. If you speak in the same tone, and at the same volume level, you will be speaking in monotone.

This will quickly put your audience to sleep. Variance is especially important during longer speeches or presentations. Feel free to add some tasteful humor in an effort to rejuvenate your audience. Eye contact is the most important aspect of oral communication. Eye contact with your audience allows a layer of trust to be established between speaker and audience. Through eye contact, both sides believe they are engaged and are listening intently. Finally, effective speakers also pace themselves through their material. They do not race through what they have to say. They calmly address all of their points to their audience. This will make your audience feel more at ease with you, and be more interested in ultimately believing what you have to say. If you're uneasy, your audience will be too.

Body Language

Body language is often times the most forgotten aspect of effective communication skills. You may have the most exciting or important thing to tell somebody, but if you're hunched over and yawning while you try and articulate your points, you will assure that they will not be very interested in what you have to say. They see you uninterested in your own material, giving them very little reason to be interested either. The other big no no's of body language include twitching, yawning, excessive posturing, and avoiding eye contact. Be as mindful of what comes out of your mouth, as you are with the way in which your body appears to be behaving during a speaking engagement.

Written Communication

Written communication is more of a developed skill than it is anything else. To be effective at writing, you must understand punctuation, grammar, sentence creation, and spelling. How many times have you read an e-mail or letter by someone that did not proof read what they had written? It's messy, unprofessional, and very telling of how serious you value what it is you're writing about. As a writer, you need to write like you would speak. Write with positive intent, professionalism, and be calm as you write. Professional means addressing people appropriately, and having someone edit what you have written so that it flows and that it makes sense. Important sales plans and business plans cannot be submitted to potential investors or managers if it's full of spelling mistakes and errors. Your readers will spend more time trying to figure out what you're saying than actually trying to understand your point.

The Effective Communicator

The culmination of oral and written communication, alongside positive body language is integral to ensuring you are an effective communicator. If you lack the ability to write well, do not be ashamed to teach yourself or find a tutor to assist you in learning the basics of writing. It is a very transferrable skill that will help your career or life tremendously. Similarly, if you're scared of speaking in front of crowds or are unable to effectively speak to others – take a course on public speaking. Clients of mine have spent hours talking to themselves through a recorder, just so they can replay it and make sure it flowed well and made sense. Further, I've had clients speak to themselves in the mirror to ensure their body language was positive and unobtrusive.

Communication Skills Training in Corporate

Are you a concerned supervisor or manager who wants to give the best training to your subordinates? Do you feel your staff need additional communication skills training including corporate and sales training? Does your company value impeccable communication skills of people?

A good corporation should be able to boast of people who have undergone extensive communication skills training and are well-versed in doing corporate training and sales training. Communication skills & Presentation Skills are very important in sending important messages across to large groups of people. It is likewise useful in maintaining a professional decorum in the workplace. Moreover, corporate training and sales training are aspects of corporate life that need utmost focus and concentration. Well-trained staff and personnel reflect a very good impression about the company and its management.

Where to Start

The company needs to lay out an effective communication skills training program. An effective communication skills training program encompasses all areas of communication:

- Verbal communication
- Oral communication skills
- Public speaking skills
- Confidence building
- Establishing rapport
- Nonverbal communication
- Body language

- Written communication skills
- Gestures that build audience impact

Training and Development

A well trained group of staff begins with accurate training needs analysis (TNA) based on personnel needs and weaknesses. A TNA is the core of corporate training and development. Once training needs are determined, the company can initiate a corporate training program which can include both communication skills training and sales training for all employees of the company.

Communication skills training is a basic course that all employees need to undergo. This is to ensure that the company employs people who can express themselves confidently and effectively in social and corporate situations. The same goes for sales training which is considered to be the core program for marketing and sales staff of the company. Aside from these two basic programs, there are various corporate training programs available for different areas of development:

- Teambuilding workshops
- Personality development programs
- Management and supervisory programs
- Leadership training
- Stress management programs
- Basic accounting and finance
- Training for Trainers
- Human resource functions

People as Valuable Resource

Companies who value their people do set aside a substantial amount in the company's budget to cover corporate training and development programs. The premise for this is that employees who are happy and satisfied with their growth and development in the company tend to stay for many years and serve the company well. In turn, this behaviour saves the company a lot of money since there is minimal need for re-training because employee turnover tend to be on the low side.

Moreover, people who receive ample training tend to be

happier and more energized in doing their jobs and daily tasks. The long term effect of effective corporate training is very promising to the company overall. The ability to provide basic training programs like communication skills training and sales training will result to having highly-effective and ultra-motivated people working in the company.

Training Partner

For corporations whose strength doesn't lie in providing excellent training programs, the best move is to employ the services of external training providers whose primary objective is to supply the corporate training needs of various companies. There is a wide array of training programs available worldwide which includes communication skills training, sales training and general corporate training. By working hand-in-hand with the company, training providers can customize programs based on the actual training needs of employees.

Employing the services of an external training provider can prove to be a very good move based on the following benefits:

- No need to reinvent the wheel when an expert can provide the necessary training programs needed by the company
- Savings on labour since the company need not employ additional manpower to do the actual training for the staff
- Cost-effective on a per person basis because the company only needs to provide a budget per person instead of worrying about added costs of training materials and trainer time
- No added anxiety or stress on the company side on post training analysis since the external training provider can take care of all post training requirements.

7

Non-verbal Communication: Making Sense of Gender

Gender is one's personal sense of maleness or femaleness. Cultural, sociological and psychological processes influence gender. Clearly men and women differ biologically, one from the other, and they are socialized differently, both factors influencing their nonverbal communication. A considerable body of research has focused on their differences; many popular books and discussion programs focus on their differences as well. For example some researchers have been interested in feminism and psychoanalysis; others are concerned that gender concepts are misstated, mismeasured. Scholars are re-thinking and redefining gender. But, it is clear that gender studies are on the rise; it is a popular topic in the media as well.

Competition seems to exist between researchers who espouse an essentialist model versus those who espouse an interactionist model. Essentialism suggests that differences between the genders are located in a relatively fixed, stable inner core while interactionists believe that gender is dynamic and somehat modifiable, depending on the context.

Some confusion exists between the meanings of the word sex and gender. In this text, as in many, sex is regarded as a biological term describing male and female body characteristics at birth. Genetic and biological processes unfold in the creation of sex. Gender, on the other hand, is a learned identity created in socialization. Gender describes a more fluid condition than does sex. Although biological factors influence the development of gender, it does not determine gender, although there is an interaction between biological, psychological and social processes. From an SI perspective humans, whether male or female, enact nonverbal behaviours based on their identities, the identities themselves being constructed by humans. It has been suggested that gender is an arrangement between the sexes, a type of institutional reflexivity. Nonverbal communication establishes a sense of relationship between people. Yet, the reader must remember that identity and gender are terms that describe a complexity of concepts; males and females learn to play multiple roles, some of which are played the same way by both genders; others are performed by one gender and not the other.

Social Construction of Gender

Gender is a concept complex in meaning, more complex than the concepts of sex and it changes over time (Woods, 1994). As mentioned, in the Great Chain of Being theory, now considered mythical, women and Blacks were not considered as high on the hierarchal chain as were white males. The best human model was the white, European male. To this day, by and large, women are excluded from doing science, although the situation is improving. The fully developed human was a white male; women were thought to be a deviation from the norm.

Humans define themselves in multiple ways. However, it is only in recent years that women have been able to define themselves without male interference. In many societies, even today, a female's relationship to a male is one of subservience; women may even be owned by men, sometimes taken as slaves. The predominance of male power still exists in many countries. The establishment of women's rights and ensuing affirmative action in the United States created more favorable conditions. Women can now effectively resist the "ale thing" although egalitarianism is not complete.

The concept of gender is broadly open, affording many options for individual interpretation of self. When behaviours are rigidly typed as male or female, they are usually typed in error. Gendered behaviours are learned and flexible. Contexts vary and the ways in which gendered behaviours are manifest in varied contexts is a matter of self construal. For example, black women in academia must make sense of the context. They face different influences than do white women, who themselves may face uncertainties that males do not. Patterned behaviours, often based on stereotypes, still prevail between the genders, as the following illustrates.

Stereotyped Gendered Voice

Gender is sensed, not merely by how the voice sounds, but by an integration of the senses, a multi-channeling process. The human voice, male and female, has been heavily stereotyped. For example, when a male person is "breathy" he is believed to be young and artistic; if a female's voice is breathy, she is thought to be feminine and pretty, but shallow. If the male voice is tense, he is thought to be older, unyielding and cantankerous; if a female's voice is tense, she is thought to be emotional, high strung and less intelligent. If the male voice has a higher pitch and is highly varied, he is thought to be dynamic and feminine; if a female's voice is higher pitched, she is thought to be more dynamic and extroverted.

In research that is supposedly free of stereotypes, it is suggested that women's speech fosters connections, support, closeness and understanding, while the male speech patterns tend to establish status, independence and control. Women tend toward inclusiveness in their speech and men toward dominance which can lead to misunderstandings between the genders.

In a rapidly changing world, it is hard to determine what is stereotypical and what is not, but there are research findings that appear to be solid. For example, to resolve conflicts in games it is shown that girls tend to end the game, while boys elaborate the rules to end the dispute. Girls, it appears, learn to cooperate; boys learn to compete. Girls play in smaller, more intimate pairs, often in private places, while boys seek out competition.

As people make choices, make sense of their lives and act out behaviours in context, they become socialized and oversocialized both directly and indirectly. Imitation and modeling are features of this socialization, concepts that are useful throughout life. Each person becomes male or female or something in-between, with a wrinkle or two. In short, there is an arbitrariness to the construction of gender. The socialization of gender is not a linear, exact process; there is unevenness.

Clearly, women and men think in genderized terms. Society contains thoughts and themes about gender and gender roles may seem somewhat fixed and inflexible. For example, guns are used more by males and dolls are used more by females, but these are not fixed behaviours; they are learned, malleable and flexible. The colours pink and blue have been associated with females and males at birth; these illustrations suggest that there is relative stability in the ways that humans perceive the place of gender.

Males and females tend to express themselves differently. Males tend to use more dominant, commanding gestures and movements, to take up more space than do females, to mask their emotions, and to smile for different reasons than do women. Women tend to wear a smile, as part of the expectation that they be pleasant. Women are said to be "rapport" builders and men are "report" givers, or knowledge experts, alluding to popular stereotypes. Women appear to display their emotions more readily than do men. Women seem to be able to give and interpret nonverbal messages better than men can.

Thus far the discussion has focused on gender differences. But, is gendered behaviour really extremely bipolar or does it exist at various points on a range? Various analyses of gender differences seem to be overdrawn, there being fewer differences between males and females than there are similarities. Various metanalyses suggest that gender is best interpreted as a point on a range, each gender able to occupy most of those points. It is best to discuss differences as tendencies rather than as absolute differences.

Gendered Identity

As discussed, the gendered body is not a fixed corpus; rather, each culture establishes metaphors for the body, which are taken into account by individuals in order to make sense of self. Body metaphors and themes are found in all cultures. For example, in oral societies, men were associated with the sun and energy;

females were associated with the mysterious moon. Men were thought to be rational and women intuitive. Women were considered mysterious because of menstruation, birth and lactation, leading to darkness, irrationality, the moon and magic.

All societies distinguish between males and females, although some may have a middle category, such as the berdache of the Cheyenne tribe or the mahu of the Tahitians. The guiding ideals differ from culture to culture but there are similarities between cultures. Some scholars believe that culture provides a veneer covering an essential universality of gender dimorphism. All male primates produce semen and all females give birth, but variations in behaviour occur after that. Humans engage in the love making process, full of symbolic meaning, unlike non-humans who simply mate without symbolization. The ability to symbolize and to give meaning to maleness and femaleness distinguishes humans from lower order animals. Indeed, in humans, the genders seem to require each other as the legend of Adam and Eve suggests.

In traditional cultures, it would appear that gender roles are fairly clear; in modern American society, there appears to be a blurring of the roles, high speed change being the norm. Some cultures place more value on the birth of the male than on the female, as in India and China. In China, where population pressures have led to the control of how many children are permitted, the birth of the male is referred to as the birth of the Little Emperor. Other cultures emphasize the more powerful role of females, as in the Tchambuli tribe. For example, as Margaret Mead showed, in the Tchambuli society, women do the fishing and control the economic life of the community; they also take the initiative in courting and sex activities between the sexes. The cultural pattern is different from that found in the United States, where men traditionally are supposed to be the initiators, the breadwinners and so on. Again this role is becoming blurred, as post-modernists indicate.

In the United States females tend to be drawn to fields of employment that involve sensitivity, an example being Social Work or Early Childhood Education. These differences, however, are due to socialization, to choices made throughout life, as people make sense of who they are. They may also reflect power and relational differences, males generally having more economic and political power than do women. Unlike the experience of the male in the Tchambuli society, men in the Western world tend to be competitive in everyday life while females tend to use compromise strategies. Men tend to act self-sufficiently, emphasizing work as the major theme in their lives; women tend to enact interdependent attachment styles. Women tend to be more reflexive and inward; men appear to be more outward and non-reflexive. Again, these tendencies are not to be rigidly interpreted.

Despite their perceived differences, it is usually in the union of the gendered bodies that a sense of wholeness is achieved, as in the story of Adam and Eve or of Yin and Yang in Taoism, where male and female are brought together to form a middle way. To get genders, Plato said, Zeus decided to cut all beings in two. The word gender comes from genus, which means race or kind, seemingly having little to do with biological sex.

Birthing and Socialization

Unlike many other cultures, in the United States the child is put out of the bedroom at the start, into her or his own bedroom, weaned by age one. As mentioned, the gendered labelling process begins when the child is dressed in pink or blue. Pink, of course, is associated with softness and blue is associated with rougher things. Gradually gender differences become apparent. Girls, for example, tend to be closer to their mothers, touching and receiving touch more than do males. From the start, the personal space bubbles are smaller for girls than they are for boys. Girls tend to learn language faster than boys and perhaps they learn to use nonverbal displays faster than boys. For example, the stereotypical limp wrist found among ages in females is displayed at about age five.

Children, of course, must learn how to speak, act and present themselves appropriately. By about the age of five in American life, children begin to know who they are; they have begun to understand the varied meanings behind gender and what it means to be masculine or feminine (Wood, 1994). Gender constancy begins to appear. In short, young children begin to develop working theories about who they are. They begin to create gender scripts as they mature.

Attachment and Segregation

Gradually, boys and girls become segregated in their social lives. A chronological table of change suggests that about 1-2 years, young children are attached to mother and they have fun with their father; at about age 12-24 months, children start to exhibit same sex preferences and at about 30 months, most children spend most of the time with same-sex others, given a choice. By about age 4-5, boys affiliate with the same sex. For girls, same sex affiliation seems fairly developed by age three. Mixed play continues for both sexes, however.

By about age five, elaborated play involves pretending, such as playing doctor or nurse. Sequential scripts are created and followed. These basic patterns seem to occur in Africa, India, the Phillippines and Mexico as well. By ages 6-10, three quarters of time is spent with the same sex, which seems to be a pattern that may be universal. At about ages 8-11, same sex preference peaks, perhaps even cross-cultually. Slowly, the child learns what genderization means through these self-segregating behaviours.

The culture of play is co-constructed. Playstyles are taught by parents just as lower order animal parents teach their young to chase, to exhibit playful biting and so on. Boys may get access to a group by shoving and girls by verbal bargaining and negotiation. Boys will ram bikes and act with rough and tumble, shooting one another and playing dead, which can lead to anger and agonistic behaviours. Fighting seems to be done by boys; girls seem to take turns more than do boys.

Females tend to aggress by alienating others or interfering with friendships. Boy themes tend to be heroic using guns and swords and girl themes tend to be nurturant emphasizing family interactions, such as parenting. Boys do not usually watch girl movies, but girls watch both girl and boy movies. Boys tend to use imperatives in their speech and girls tend to emphasize social relationships. Boys separate from mothers more quickly than do girls. Again, these are to be interpreted as tendencies.

The roles that are played by each gender are interchangeable and inflexible, although even today a girl may be thought of as being a tomboy when she acts like a boy and a boy may be labeled a sissy when he acts like a girl.

Middle Childhood Discourse Styles

One must be careful to stay away from stereotypical thinking. On the other hand, it is clear that children develop genderized patterns and tendencies. In middle childhood discourse, girls tend to display anger indirectly, compromising when possible, but boys tend to be assertive, daring others, playing scaredy cat, calling others stupid, sissy or faggot. Boys tend to be more direct and they tend to establish boundaries more quickly. Girls talk more than do boys, except when talking to boys. Indeed, mothers talk more to girls than they do to their boys.

Girls learn to think that boys are mean and noisy while boys may think that girls cry too much. Some cross-gendering occurs but gender segregation continues. Borderwork, or cross-gendering occurs early on, at about ages 5-6, but boys are likely to tease girls when they like them. Contact appears to be accidental and incidental and, of course, at that age, courting is denied. Thus, children acquire a fund of gender knowledge, in a type of self-socialization, and they are motivated to act in accordance with genderized expectations, stereotypical or not, feeling confident that they belong to a group of likeminded children.

Gender constancy, which occurs at about age 6 or 7 years, is in the forefront in later ages. Children know their role expectations and the cultural norms for their genders. Gender metaphors, perhaps stereotypical, have developed, with boys being rough and girls being soft, boys being angry and girls being happy. It is suggested by research that girls tend to suppress themselves in adolescence, beginning to disguise the self, perhaps fearing the loss of connectedness, trying to fit in. Perhaps they develop a politeness bias.

Female and Male Self Presentations

All people present themselves to others in interaction and they act out their sense of self, their symbolic face, in the presentations.

Framing a Feminine Presentation

Women learned to discipline their bodies well before they began their professional lives; for example, women learn to throw a ball like a girl, they learn to sit, stand, walk and tilt their heads, to gesture and to carry objects, like a girl. It is argued here that young girls are far more constrained than are males through socialization. They must learn to be fragile and to comport themselves along stricter lines. These behaviours follow women into the work world, where various issues are presented. As one woman describes projecting a presence in the professional work place, she must learn to "turn on a switch", shining in front of an audience, usually a male audience. The female presentation style in the professional workplace has had but a few years to be embellished, given the relatively quiescent role of women in America, historically. Females in the United States, as in other societies, have had a muted voice.

A popular view of males and females might go as follows: There are Don Juans and there are Carmens; there is an Adonis complex and there is a Jennifer complex. People imitate television heroes and follow trendy fashions. Women learn to flirt, to be sexy and provocative in their apparel, perhaps searching for strong and prestigious men; men seem to want young and beautiful women and present themselves accordingly. The media, of course, play up these stereotypical notions so powerfully that popular culture influences the body presentations of individuals.

Research suggests a different train of thought. For example, women tend to develop a sense of identity through connectedness with others. Their sense of self comes from building and maintaining relationships, not through differentiation and separation. Women are empowered by their participation and development of others. They are connected knowers who have the ability to think maternally. Women tend to have a caring ethic. Work, thought and feelings are bound together by this ethic. Malehood is defined differently in different societies and cultures. In some cultures, the achievment of malehood is a prize to be won, involving sanctions, trials of endurance and various ritualistic practices. In the United States, malehood is almost taken for granted, whereas in Latin countries, one learns the macho ethic, as in Cuba. It is reported that in the Truk Islands men do daring deep sea diving for sharks, youth fight in weekend brawls, drink excessively and seek sexual conquests. Laceration, whipping contests and physical abuses are inflicted on males to determine their inner strength in some countries. Flinching under pain is a sign of weakness. Thus body flagellation is still important in the islands.

The role of the hero is important to the socialization of the male in the United States. Freud drew out the characteristics of Moses as a hero and Otto Rank placed stress on myth and the birth of the hero; Jung believed that heroes were archtypal. The stereotype of the male is that he is young and aggressive, sexually powerful and able to solve confrontational problems. Heroes solved the Oedipal Riddle and cut the Gordian Knot. These ideas, of course, are tied to the past but thematically consistent with the present.

Perhaps in the modern Western world there are competing models for manhood. Instead of throwing javelins and rescuing damsels in distress, the modern anti-hero theoretically gives peace a chance, listens and is sensitive to others. If aggression is inherent in the male system it appears to be withering or taking on new forms. The emerging anti-hero tends to be androgynous.

Perhaps the demands of modern society call forth not a ruggedness in mentality but a caringness in the workplace, a sensitivity to others, unlike the demands on manhood in rural America. What seems clear is that the polarized ideas of maleness and femaleness seem to be blending in the middle, androgynously. Women may be learning to be more assertive; males may be learning to be more sensitive. At least some scholars believe this to be an ideal. Yet, it is males by and large who engage in acts of violence, in high schools, on the internet and in the family.

Gendered Lenses, Androgyny and Stereotypes

Gender enculturation lens theory suggests that gender is embedded into our discourse in such a way as to influence a child to think in male and female terms. However, because communication about gender is usually tacit, a child may not actually know what the options are. A fish is not aware of the water in which it swims!

As mentioned, some scholarship about gender rests on an essentialist perspective. That is, the researchers approach gender as though it is an entity with a fixed core, a fixed set of traits and characteristics, relatively unbending and unchanging over the course of a lifetime. Other scholars and researchers take a dynamic, situational approach. That is, they realize that under some conditions, males and females will act one way; under others, they will act differently. These different assumptions make a difference in how comparative gender research is performed.

Varieties of research tools are used to indicate how people think about gender. A high score on both the male and female BSRI gender tool indicates that one is favourably disposed to androgynous conceptualizations of behaviour. Research suggests that females who score better on the male portion of the BSRI may increase their chances of being effective leaders, although there may be fewer advantages for American males. Assertiveness, typically thought to be a male characteristic, may be learned by females. Males may become more sensitive. Yet, it seems clear that androcentrism, the emphasis upon male dominance, is still a major factor in the United States. Perceived as a social problem, the remedy is to focus on the concept of androgyny, as some researchers suggest. But male and female differences should not be overdrawn. As one example, there seems to be no solid evidence to indicate that there are strong categorical speech differences between the genders. Popular stereotypes of gender differences may actually influence research making the differences more pronounced than they are. However, if the following frame accurately describes the early conceptualization of males and females, there appear to have been very wide differences between them.

Framing Gender Stereotypes

In early American society, females were defined as submissive, less competitive, excitable, more emotional than men and so on. If women showed assertiveness or behaviours like those of men, they were considered mentally unstable. They were said to exhibit hysterical personalities. Indeed women reported more emotional problems, sought more psychiatric help and went to the hospital more frequently than did males. Femininity was correlated with high anxiety, low self-esteem and low social acceptance. Following stereotypical thinking, perhaps women unwittingly followed the prophecy, getting sick and acting as lesser beings!

Sexual Behaviours and Human Body

Gender is a fixed category

Gender is created in communication; it does not exist as a fixed, essentialist category, separate from growth processes. Mead believed that people were actors, not reactors, although they respond to influences. Humans go through stages, such as the preparatory, play and game stages. People gradually integrate themselves over time, achieving identity, whether male or female.

All males are alike; all females are alike

Although humans share interpersonal, social and cultural contents intersubjectively, each individual is unique because of the special experiences of that individual.

Sex and gender are the same concepts

Sex is a biological phenomenon while gender is a socially constructed phenomenon. However, there is an interaction between sex and gender. Women may bear children; men can fertilize the egg.

Perceptions of gender are always accurate

Men may condemn a behaviour that they see women doing but approve of it when they see or hear men doing it. Swearing is one example. Perceptions may be stereotyped. For example, it is believed that females do not make good managers, but recent research suggests that they do very well in management positions.

Males and females have the same access to opportunities

The "man-thing" has meant that there is a male bias in society, which provides males with more opportunities than it does females, especially when the females are ethnic minorities. This problem is slowly eroding.

Biological Factors

The Genetic Male and Female

Research shows that sex hormones may sex-type the brain, thereby influencing body identification creating a biological biasing effect.(1) Just how this may play out is not clear. It is obvious that both sexes can perform similar biological functions and activities, such as coitus and the intake and digestion of food. They differ about menstruation, levels of testosterone, and other physical factors, men being generally larger in body size than women. The male and female sexual parts differ substantially; as humans mature, their genetic differences generally become even more distinct and clear, especially with the onset of puberty and early adolescence. Older people may complain about loss of sex drive and cognitive acuity but even this process occurs differently in the sexes. Some research suggests that the male-female sexual distinctions present a false dichotomy because to an extent each sex resides in both male or female bodies (Hargreaves & Colley, 1987). As the study of genes continues it may reveal the extent to which humans are "hardwired" or shaped by the XX or XY genetic patterns.

Socially, of course, humans symbolize their physical identity; they gradually become genderized. Smaller at birth and throughout most of their lives, females adjust to the implied power difference associated with size. Both genders adjust to body changes. For example, male and female children start out with a similar larynx, but gradually, the male develops a huskier voice.

The innate ability of the female to produce eggs to be fertilized by the male influences how women relate to children and to family members. X and Y chromosomes affect deeply how the sexual male and female will develop. According to some research, men are more susceptible to physical problems than are women throughout the stages of life, as their earlier death rate suggests. However, the aging process presents a different sets of problems for each sex; researchers have suggested that older age is a woman's problem.

Male and Female Hormones

Chronobiology, mentioned earlier, is a newly emerging field of study; it reveals that men, like women, have hormonal cycles that influence behaviour. Men from 39-70 years of age, having higher levels of testosterone, also appear to have increased levels of aggression. In lower order male animals, the presence of androgens has been linked to aggressiveness as well. For example, studies show that hens, when fed testosterone in an early stage of their development, acquire male-like features, such as the comb and the wattles; they act more like roosters than like hens. One might ask whether pronounced levels of testosterone in the human male leads to agonistic behaviour, an aggressiveness that attentuates later in life. Does the comparatively lower level of testosterone in the female lead to a more compliant, nurturant nonverbal style than men display? Maccoby suggests that the male agonistic style of nonverbal behaviour is learned early and that it is carried throughout life in some measure, modified over time. Social behaviours overlay physical processes.

The ability of women to to conceive and menstruate influences their behaviour considerably. Even their body temperatures change in circadian and monthly cycles. The study of circadian rhythms in both males and females is receiving more attention in modern research. Perhaps the body changes from morning to evening influencing behaviours, as popularly believed.

Sexual Behaviours and Physical Attractiveness

It is known that pheromones are tied into the mating habits of lower order animals, differing substantially from species to species. The way in which these odors attract the sexes vary considerably, but both sexes may mark their territory. Whether humans have pheromones that attract both sexes is less clear, although research continues. Americans are fond of covering up their body odors with perfumes.

Framing the Attractiveness Syndrome

What is attractive in one society may not be attractive in another. In the United States, a cursory examination of the ways that people try to be attractive yields a compelling picture. For example, many women are constantly thinking about losing weight. Studies reveal the majority of the female subjects reported that losing weight was more important to them than having success in work or love. Dieting starts among women as early as fourth and fifth grades; in High School, most women are concerned about their weight.

In a youth conscious society, where the concepts of the ideal male and female physical specimens are played up, it is no surprise that both males and females are preoccupied with weight loss and muscle toning, however unhealthy the process may be. Indeed, there seems to be a relationship between body image and self-esteem. Some women diet to increase their self-confidence, thinking that they will be more feminine if they are thin. This norm is constantly reinforced by the media, where having the "perfect abs" is played up to both genders. In comparison to white women, African-American women may be less concerned with weight, dieting or being thin. Perhaps they have a more realistic view of losing weight. Some evidence suggests that many Black females believe that the slightly heavier body is more attractive than is a thin one.

Genetic fitness is an adaptive evolutionary concept, the fit animal being more adaptable than the nonfit. Genetically fit males, whether human or of other species, can mate again and again with different females. Male seals, for example, are harem masters and male roosters copulate with many hens. In humans, polygamy has occasionally been practiced in the United States, a monogamist country, but polyandry is often the norm in other countries. Beliefs and customs determine how the sexual drive of men and women is to be channeled. Demographic pressures and patterns bear on sexual practices.

Men are sexually aroused more quickly than are women. This fact, combined with the tendency for men to have more physical power than women have may explain the existence of porn, prostitution and other shunned social activites, mostly male interests. Evolutionists suggest that sexual differences influence social differences. For example, women generally desire to have a loving and comfortable environment; is this due to their genetic make-up? Do men tend to be less concerned about a loving environment due to their easily aroused sexual tendencies and their aggressiveness? It has been said in a popular vein, that for men, "sex sometimes results in intimacy; for women, intimacy sometimes results in sex".

Physical attractiveness and beauty exist in the human mind, but they do not put food on the table. Nevertheless, physical attractiveness is necessary for human reproduction. In other words, it acts as a catalyst inspiring a male to copulate with a female. Physical beauty makes humans attractive to one another. It is interesting that delinquents, people who are in trouble with the law, tend to have less attractive bodies. There is an interaction between physical shape and social expectations, as this example shows.

Cultural norms vary across cultures; it is not surprising that different cultures produce different attraction displays. Perhaps there are few universal standards of sexual attractiveness. Indeed, in the arrangment of marriages, there may be little focus on attractiveness. When choice, not arrangement is involved, research suggests that women tend to choose men who are skilful, who have prowess; men tend to choose women who are beautiful. This appears to be a universal tendency. The understanding of what is skilful or attractive, of course, varies by culture.

Research suggests that men in the United States prefer big eyes, full lips, small noses in women, but women may not share in those predispositions. Brazilian men seem to like big butts and small breasts; darkness in skin colour is problematic in Brazil. It is clear from an evolutionary and ethological view that sexual attractiveness is important to sexual copulation. Culture interacts with biology in producing offspring.

Brain and Neuronal Differences

The use of recent imaging technologies reveals the complexity of the human brain, and, to an extent shows how males and females differ. A popular belief is that males and females have significant lateral differences, each sex tending to use different sides of the brain. Early research suggested that males tended to use the left side of the brain because it is associated with linear, logical and analytic thinking, while women, who tend to have more developed right lobes, tend to be more holistic, imaginative and intuitive than are men. Recent research suggests, however, that pronounced laterality may not characterize the differences; rather, the areas of the brain associated with selected activities, such as language and spatial concepts, largely determine how the sexes use the brain, with women tending to use more of the brain Some research suggests that the neuronal structure of the languaging portion of the brain is more dense in females, possibly leading to greater verbal dexterity in women. PET scan technology can trace the flow of blood in the brain as various tasks are performed, indicating that long awaited answers to questions about the localization of activities in the brain are forthcoming.

Sensate Differences

The baby is born with the human sensorium intact, yet the various senses grow in variously staged patterns. For example, the neonate responds to touch and can detect the odor and taste of its mother's milk. Given sour things to taste, the very young child will pucker, perhaps even cry; the ability to taste is well developed from birth. The child's eyes, however, require more time to become focused and the child's ability to grasp, to reach and to touch is only gradually developed.

As young people become adults the body changes. Women tend to have a higher sweat threshold than do men, men sweating more quickly under the same conditions. The dermal response to cold is quicker for women than it is for men and they seem to be more sensitive to pressures put on various body parts. Although it may be a learned phenomenon, females tend be more expressive about feeling pain than are men. Men are often taught to suffer pain in silence, which may account for the differences.

Men seem to be better at detecting pure tones up to about age 30 but males show some loss, due perhaps, to differential noise at the place of work. It has been shown that women may suffer some change in hearing ability due to changes in estrogens and progesterone levels.

Taste abilities vary between the sexes as well, but there may be confounding effects due to socialization and cultural influences.

For example, women tend to have lower thresholds for sweet, sour and salty tastes and higher thresholds than men do for sucrose, and sodium chloride. Pregnant women prefer stronger concentrates of sweet, sour, bitter and salty than do men.

The results of the smell study performed by National Geographic, suggested that women differ from men in several ways both within cultures and across cultures. Again, the confounding effects of social expectations, of culture, make it unclear whether physical or cultural differences are at play. Different cultures emphasize different smell and taste codes so one might expect the ability to smell to be affected. The importance of these studies to a symbolic interactionist approach to nonverbal communication may seem unclear to the reader. The SI approach suggests that humans interpret and give meaning to physical and social events in their lives. Biological differences may lead to social practices; for example, men buy women chocolates when they are courting them. This long honored practice signals the relationship between biology, or taste, and social practice.

Male Sexual Life Cycle

In a popular book about the changes that males go through over their life span, their growth patterns have been described in sexual terms:

- Ages 15-30, males "race" the sexual act as if they were in the Indy 500.
- Ages 30-40, males perform dutiful sex with their wives.
- Ages 55-70, males surf sex, developing fantasies about sex.
- Ages 70 plus, men like a snuggling version of sex.

The author concludes that the male menopause begins in the fifties or sixties; there is some lapse in virility and vitality. Sheehy's analysis applies to men in the United States.

Gender, Standpoint, Power and Place

Gender is asymmetrically powered in American society and throughout the world. In many ways, males do not have to earn their status, at least in comparison to females (Wood, 1994); That is, in the United States and elsewhere as well, males enjoy a privileged status. Even when holding hands, it appears that the male hand is on the top of the females. Males and females are born into societies that reflect dimensions, such as gendered power. Gender is played out in matriarchal societies differently than it is in patriarchal ones. For example, in Libya, a patriarchal society, women are permitted only enough space in their garment to peer out with one eye.

In the modern United States, the power base has typically reflected the "man principle", indicating that, traditionally, males in the United States held power. The modern concept of the "glass ceiling" indicates that while women know about upper echelons of power and may aspire to getting upper level jobs, they are not empowered to do so. The face of America's workplace is changing but there may be forces of resistance that work against women, particularly if they are women of colour, in a matrix of domination. There are efforts to get beyond the glass ceiling by females, but it appears that the problem is different for women of colour. It has been suggested that women of colour are "twice struck", having to deal with being female in a male dominated society and with being colored in a white dominated society.

Power is patterned in specific behaviours, such as in verbal interruption patterns shown below. Theoretically, because males have more power in American society than do females, men are free to interrupt them in conversations, whether it be in the workplace, on television or in everyday situations. Recent research suggests, however, that this phenomenon may be overdrawn as noted below.

Framing Gendered Interruption Patterns

In a society in which males are dominant, where they hold power, it has been assumed in some research that they will feel free to interrupt females in various social circumstances. This analysis, however. appears to be too simplistic. A meta-analysis of studies on interruptions shows that a number of situational factors must be taken into account, such as the number of persons in the situation, their genders, and their relationships to one another.When the type of activity is taken into account, gender differences in interruptive patterns disappear. For example, when girls and females choose expressive activities, they tend to act in an affiliative manner; conversely, when boys and men select task-oriented activities, they may be more assertive, acting in an instrumental manner. In sum, the essentialist model of gender differences, which suggests that there are ongoing differences between the genders that lie at the core of gender does not help explain interruption as well as a contextualist-interactive model does.

Indeed, gender asymmetry, by implication power asymmetry, is weak in many circumstances, as the following description shows. The theory is that higher status people will touch lower status people more readily than the reverse case. But, in this study, higher status people tended to touch lower status people, initiating affectionate touches on the shoulders or arms, while lower status individuals tended to touch higher status individuals in more formal ways, such as in handshakes. Gender asymmetry seems to be weak, although males tended to initiate touch more than females.

This research suggests that it is the status, not the gender, that leads to differential touching behaviours. Touching, of course, in this context, is assumed to be associated with power, status and power being closely associated. The studies cited above, of course, are mere tips of the iceberg. Power is institutionalized and patterned in the United States, favouring white males, as it has for decades. It is now changing as the following frame shows.

Framing Women as Managers

It is reported that women make better managers than do men because they tend to be skilled in more areas that are required in management. For example, women tend to be more collaborative in their decision making than are men; women are socialized to cooperate and collaborate, while men tend to use an autocratic style. Two thousand, four hundred and eighty two managers at all levels from more than 400 organizations in 19 states were used in the study.

Few people would argue that American society is not changing, although many may argue that it is changing for the worse. Whatever the values of the individual, the ways in which gendered roles are played out in contemporary America are vastly different today, compared to the past. From the farms to the factory during the Second World War to full participation in all levels of non-professional and professional work, women are born into a new world, which increases their opportunities.

As mentioned, family sizes and family patterns are shifting radically and the roles of females are shifting along with them. For many Americans, the large, extended families of the past are gone; replacing those families are the new versions that range from the nuclear family to the laissez faire family. One parent families are becoming common. Multiple marriages which include children from two or more past marriages are not uncommon. In short, male and female parenting roles are changed dramatically in many situations.

The glass ceiling in the workplace has been broken, if not shattered, and women are now able to do what men have done in power positions before them, which is to be able to climb to the top. In modern times, women can be the Secretary of State, Senators or CEOs without raising eyebrows or being labeled bitches. In short, one is witnessing a shift in power distribution between the sexes. Affirmative action helped both minorities and women enter the economic mainstream. The idea of subcultures, perhaps a demeaning term to ethnic minorities because it can imply inferiority, is being replaced by the term co-culture, a less demeaning term. Obviously, the social system does not operate perfectly, but it is substantially more open to women and minorities than it has been in the past. Of course there are serious problems remaining.

Gender, Ethnicity and Age

Those who are defined as ethnic, especially women, are "twice-struck"; that is, they have been traditionally disprivileged and disempowered in the United States because of their gender. Black, Cuban, Chinese and Native American males have been disprivileged, as well, but females of colour have been doubly disprivileged because of colour and gender. The themes of gender and ethnicity entertwine to strike these members twice.

The aged in American society are sometimes considered victims of ageism, which is rooted in stereotypical notions about older people aging has been called a 'woman's problem' in that she has enjoyed fewer opportunities in the past than males have and continues to be more dependent on others as she ages. Often outliving their male partners. women face more uncertain futures as they age, according to this view.

Gender and the Media

Television has joined the family dinner table. Children may eat their dinner in front of the television set, munching on fast foods, picked up by their working parents who often chose the fast way to have dinner. There has been a dramatic shift in the perceived and enacted roles of the contemporary parent in America. "Soccer moms" and "latchkey kids" are buzzwords attesting to the shift. Moms may be the sole breadwinner and television and the internet may be the babysitters!

The media, especially television, are powerful socializing agents, influencing the playing out of gender in American society. Whether it is a program on MTV, a channel emphasing music and displaying sexual fantasy apparently designed to appeal to young ethnic people, or programs that promote religious messages, one finds in television a shaping lens. The image of the "perfect" male and the "perfect" female are constantly promoted by the media and by advertisers who want to sell products. As mentioned, there are few ugly people on television!

It is popular to promote gender differences on television and in books where stereotyped concepts like the Mars-Venus relationship are simplistically proclaimed.

Talk shows play up, often in very negative and demeaning ways, the problems that men and women have with each other. Less obvious an influence on gender identitiy is the internet. Nevertheless, the digital divide influences the gendered, the aged and members of ethnic groups differentially; access to the use of the internet varies by gender, ethnicity and age.

Styles and Levels of Intimacy

It is clear that relationships are created, that whatever

differences there are between the genders come into play in relationships, whether they are intimate or friendship based. Relationships are symbolic babies! Nonverbal behaviour is deeply involved in relationships. Body orientations in particular are involved. Relationships are coded; that is, there are underlying assumptions that are made about the nature of the relationship. People who are able to observe and listen empathically, are perhaps more adept at creating healthy relationships. To the extent that males exert control or focus on independence; to the extent that women want to have relationship talk, these conditions can act to produce "ships passing in the night". Males and females frequently talk past each other in these kinds of relationships. Empathic listening, difficult to achieve, helps create a balance. People of both genders have needs for self-esteem and affection.

People construct meanings for their relationships. For example, they may describe their partners as sexual, intelligent or attractive, easy, difficult or otherwise. In an intimate relationship when a person says "I love you", it calls up all of the meanings that the other party has for love, which vary considerably, based on the experiences of the person. Past baggages and successes are often brought to a new intimate relationship, influencing the character of the relationship. People do not "fall" in love as much as they "construct" a loving relationship, but when negative past baggage is brought to the relationship, both parties are challenged. Self reflection, of course, is a key to understanding; it is in this meta-process that humans confirm or deny themselves. Self-monitoring is a way to follow the relational process.

A number of scholars have focused on relational development and the processes associated with it and a variety of theories exist. The SI approach suggests that humans construct their relationships, although it is not a linear process;indeed, it may be a recursive process. That is, people arrive at one point and then return to another before moving ahead. One behaviour is contingent upon another. The values of American society, of course, frame the meaning of relationships. Because females have been described as relationship experts, it has been suggested that a female yardstick measures the success of the relationship. Males, raised to be somewhat independent, may not so easily enter into self-disclosing aspects of relationships.

Framing Romantic Myths

In youth, people hear stories about Cinderella, Sleeping Beauty, and snow White, all sweet and pure maidens who find themselves in predicaments, to be rescued by a strong, handsome prince. She waits passively for the active prince. This old-fashioned stereotype seems to have its counterpart in modern America. During adolescence, the modern young lady may fantasize about true lasting love, about meeting the right man. Boys, on the other hand, tend to emphasize conquest and sexuality and, when asked how they did on the first date, they may respond, bragging about their sexual success.

Sometimes there are perceptual differences that are built into relationships. For example, it has been suggested that females are 'defined' in American societies mostly by males; that is, men refer to women as having PMS, or premenstrual syndrome, affecting their behaviour, but the males do not refer to themselves as having HTS, or hypertestosterone syndrome, suggesting an imbalance in the way that genders are perceived. It is a common perception as well that women are by nature better, sweeter, kinder, more loving and more peaceful than men? Myths about genders abound. It appears, as well, that females in the United States are held to a higher level of expectation about being attractive than are males.

Gendered encounters are daily occurrences. Sexual encounters, on the other hand, depending on the culture, are often hidden occurrences. In the United States sexual encounters, formerly hidden from view, are now more explicit and open. In more traditional times, it was considered inappropriate to discuss sexual matters openly. Indeed, before 1900, upright piano legs were covered prudently. The values and morals of highly structured Calvinistic and Victorian America called for privacy in sexual matters. Today, however, it is not uncommon to find research about sexual encounters. In short, just as researchers focus on the sexual and reproductive habits of lower order animals, they focus on the behaviours of human couples in sexual action. As any internet user knows, explicit sexual activities may be found on a number of sites. Sexual and romantic encounters are the stuff of television programs. Americans have gone through a gendered, sexual revolution.

Types of Relationships

There may be a tendency for people to think that relationships just happen. Of course, they involve considerable work and they are processual, as the following suggests.

Process in Relationships

Relationships evolve. That is, people must be in some way attracted to one another; they must explore and reduce uncertainty about one another; there must be an evolving commitment to the relationship; and, the relationship must be sustained in routinized patterns. Even when relationships dissolve or come apart there are phases of that dissolution. Sometimes conflict is involved; at other times negotiation occurs; in all cases there is the final stage of grave dressing that is required, putting an end to the symbolic baby.

Males and females differ in their perceptions of relationships. Indeed there may be tension between the views. Females tend to emphasize rapport, emotional contexts and process; males tend to control their emotions and to think episodically. Men tend to "do" things or to control them. This affects their relationships .

Given the difficulties encountered by couples in modern societies, scholars have focused on problems in relationships. Gottman, for example, believes that he can predict whether a marriage will succeed or fail by analyzing the communicative patterns of the couples. A number of scholars have focused on the nature of love. Various love styles have been described. Eros, Ludus, Storge, Pragma, Mania and Agape are words used to describe a range of styles, from physically falling in love at first sight to ethically putting the partner's welfare above all else. In short, relationships are created in many different forms. All of them are forms of behaviour. The mother-child relationship differs substantially from the father-child relationship, as does the relationship between the mother and the father. Relationships are defined and constructed. They can take multiple forms.

Overarching themes find their way into relationships. For example, it is not common for a President of a large corporation to interact with workers low on the pay scale. The common bond is missing. There must be a meeting of the minds, a middle way, a fertile ground from which the seeds of a relationship sprout. A social nexus of some type is the glue of relationships. Power, gender, sex, age, ethnicity, time, occupation and so on may play roles in relationships, setting the conditions for relationships to flourish or disallowing meaningful contact.

Further, they involve a type of work; that is, love, a word thrown about like a commodity for purchase, involves hard work to construct and maintain. The word love, so often confused with romantic thoughts, is essentially an enacted development, not one that is thrust upon a person. There may be love at first sight, but it is merely a glimpse of what is to come. Relationships have a history and a future path; they change and are modified. Often, they take as much effort to leave them as they require to maintain them. Whatever the level of the relationship, the partners must perform and nourish the relationship; otherwise, it dissipates. Relationships are, in the final analysis, social products, symbolic babies.

Courtship Patterns

Interestingly, 85 percent of all valentines are purchased by females, which may indicate that in romantic relationships, it is the woman's influence that is paramount. Friendship and romance are different aspects of negotiated relationships but it appears that love, or romance, is feminized in many ways. Friendship, perhaps, is more spiritual and romance is more sexual, comparing one to the other. Sexual behaviours have been researched by symbolic interactionists. Although sex need not be part of love, it usually is. It is also part of prostitution, where intimacy is not a prerequisite to engage in sex. Romantic love, it would seem can only exist between two people who have meaningfully defined their ongoing relationship because it involves deep emotions that are brought out one by the other, not to be shared.In the western world love emphasizes romance distinguishing it from relationships that are socially arranged, as are found in many parts of the world.

Older Courtship Rituals

Near mid-century, the courtship patterns were distinctive. Calling them quasi-courtship cues, Scheflen, a psychiatrist, classified courtship cue behaviour into the following behavioural system. As an example of courtship readiness one wants to reduce eye bagginess and belly bulge and stand erectly. As examples of preening behaviour, one wants to fix the makeup, arrange the clothes, look in a mirror, perhaps leave the top button open on shirts and blouses and so on. As examples of positional cues, one wants to sit in such a way as to be able to talk with the opposite sex. Arms, legs and bodies must be arranged so that it is difficult for others to intervene; actions of appeal or invitation must be taken, which include flirting, gazing, exposing the thigh, showing wrist or palm, or flexing muscles. The older courtship style does not quite fit the modern approach. It is said that young Americans are a microwave generation; nothing seems to last very long. Instant everything seems to be the norm. Romantic liaisons may be quickly created and abandoned almost as quickly, both parties expecting an endpoint, such as when they graduate from college.

Perhaps females are more easily hurt in romantic relationships because it is they who tend to more readily expose their feelings than men do or because males may be threatened by intimate disclosures. Men may want to act rather than talk about feelings. As mentioned, some scholars suggest that romance is governed by a female ruler or yardstick; that is, females are more naturally disposed to building rapport and to sharing their emotions. Research suggests that the strength of romantic relationships including marriages is a direct reflection of the type of communicative attention that each party gives the other. In short, romantic relationships can display "relational health" or they can be ragged and hurtful to the parties involved. There is a semantic difficulty in the way romance is described. The word love is used in a general way to cover all manner of relationships, including same-sex relationships. But people couple together for a variety of reasons, ranging from the need for security to the need for sex; the word love may be used to describe any relationship. Arranged marriages, common in many countries, may not even include the notion of romance; rather they are arranged for socioeconomic reasons, to bind together members of social groups.

Intimate cross-gender relationships proceed in stages, although not in linear fashion. That is, some relationships may dive into a deeper stage, not waiting for a full-blossoming of the intimacy to take place, there being no commitment to permanency. In the more thoroughly gendered romantic relationship the emotions are engaged very deeply and a level reached in which both genders commit themselves exclusively to the relationship.

In the commited, dyadic cross-gender relationship, the voices of the past emerge. Thus, each gender brings scripted and schematized ideas into what she or he thinks the relationship is or should be; each person brings both the positive and negative baggage of other past relationships into the present; each person brings parental views into the relationship. In short, many voices are "heard" in romantic relationships. Together, the gendered couple create a symbolic baby, their shared version of the relationship, taking on a life of its own.

Theorists from the games school of thought, suggest that each party has a game strategy in mind. Thus, the male may play daddy and the female may play the role of the mother or even the helpless one. She may play the role of the knowledgeable relational expert and he may play the role of the dumb jock. Both, however, play multiple roles. Their relationship may become somewhat pathological and co-dependent, or it may become mature and growth-oriented. Cultures define male-female relationships in highly varied ways. In some present day cultures, such as Iraq, couples are attached only by parental permission. Polygamous relationships are encouraged in many cultures, not based on romantic love; concubinage still exists in many societies; females are treated as owned goods. Even in the United States, the emergence of femalehood is relatively recent, the process continuing today. Relationships are deeply influenced by socio-cultural processes. Modern romantic relationships are subject to many influences and social constraints. To be a permanently coupled "item" is more and more difficult in American society, as statistics reveal. Perhaps these statistics reflect the problems involved in the achievement of identity in a highly changeable, mediated society.

Violence in Relationships

Recent movements have influenced gendered power relationships in the United States. NOW, the National Organization for Women, has given females a new voice. For example, in Roe v. Wade, women won the right to control their bodies, to decide about issues related to their reproductive health. At the present time, debates continue about Roe v. Wade, as it does about Affirmative Action, both affecting men and women in white and other ethnic groups. Since the 1980's, journals devoted to masculine, or male concepts and behaviours have emerged. On the one hand, various magazines encourage males to become more sensitive; on the other hand, they have encouraged them to become "real", more manly, as in the past. Similarly, magazines and programs exist that encourage women to become body builders; others want women to become more feminine. In short, gender roles are being redefined, sometimes blurred.

In violent relationships it appears that males are the ones who use their power against their partner more than the other way around. Indeed, the courts many times seem to blame the victim of rape, often a female, as much as they blame the rapist, a process that would seem to reinforce the *status quo*. It appears that the law expects a woman to behave like a man; in other words, she should try to defend herself as men would. But, of course, there is a difference between consent and coercion. Some scholars see the male rape bias as an extension of earlier times when women were considered the property of men; even reasonable standards of justice seem to be biased in favour of men. The *New York Times* (May 12, 2001, online) reported that Dartmouth expelled a fraternity because members of that fraternity described in their newsletter patented date rape techniques, even deriding some of the women who had sex with the fraternity members.

Acts of violence cut across age, class and ethnic groups. It is estimated that 28 percent, perhaps as much as 50 per cent of women, experience some form of violent abuse, physical or verbal from their partners. Less than five percent of abusive actions are done by women. It would appear that American ideals, linking the male psyche to aggression, strength and control, influence how men act in violent male-female relationships.

A number of myths about violence prevail. For example, contrary to common thought, violence can happen in any relationship; both males and females inflict violence on their partners; violence need not be cyclical and alcohol need not be involved.. The SI approach to violence suggests that people do what makes sense to them, based on how they have framed the situation, usually influenced by how they have behaved in the past. The enactment of violence, of course, is an extreme form of the use of power, one that inhibits personal and interactive growth. Some males use their power mindlessly forcing sex in a relationship. Females who tolerate this behaviour and others like it, have been described as co-dependent; that is, they unwittingly take part in the action.

8

Basic of Language and Communication Skills

Introduction

Language educators have long used the concepts of four basic language skills:

- Listening
- Speaking
- Reading
- Writing

The four basic skills are related to each other by two parameters:

- the mode of communication: oral or written
- the direction of communication: receiving or producing the message

We may represent the relationships among the skills in the following chart:

	Oral	Written
Receptive	Listening	Reading
Productive	Speaking	Writing

The following modules will briefly describe some characteristics of each basic skill.

Listening comprehension skill

Listening comprehension is the receptive skill in the oral mode.

When we speak of listening what we really mean is listening and understanding what we hear. In our first language, we have all the skills and background knowledge we need to understand what we hear, so we probably aren't even aware of how complex a process it is. Here we will briefly describe some of what is involved in learning to understand what we hear in a second language.

Listening Situations

There are two kinds of listening situations in which we find ourselves:

- interactive, and
- non-interactive.

Interactive listening situations include face-to-face conversations and telephone calls, in which we are alternately listening and speaking, and in which we have a chance to ask for clarification, repetition, or slower speech from our conversation partner. Some non-interactive listening situations are listening to the radio, TV, films, lectures, or sermons. In such situations we usually don't have the opportunity to ask for clarification, slower speech or repetition.

Micro-skills

The following are the micro-skills involved in understanding what someone says to us. The listener has to:

- retain chunks of language in short-term memory
- discriminate among the distinctive sounds in the new language
- recognize stress and rhythm patterns, tone patterns, intonational contours.
- recognize reduced forms of words
- distinguish word boundaries
- recognize typical word-order patterns
- recognize vocabulary
- detect key words, such as those identifying topics and ideas

- guess meaning from context
- recognize grammatical word classes
- recognize basic syntactic patterns
- recognize cohesive devices
- detect sentence constituents, such as subject, verb, object, prepositions, and the like

Speaking Skill

Speaking is the productive skill in the oral mode. It, like the other skills, is more complicated than it seems at first and involves more than just pronouncing words.

Listening Situations

There are three kinds of speaking situations in which we find ourselves:

- interactive,
- partially interactive, and
- non-interactive.

Interactive speaking situations include face-to-face conversations and telephone calls, in which we are alternately listening and speaking, and in which we have a chance to ask for clarification, repetition, or slower speech from our conversation partner.

Some speaking situations are partially interactive, such as when giving a speech to a live audience, where the convention is that the audience does not interrupt the speech. The speaker nevertheless can see the audience and judge from the expressions on their faces and body language whether or not he or she is being understood. Some few speaking situations may be totally non-interactive, such as when recording a speech for a radio broadcast.

Micro-skills

Here are some of the micro-skills involved in speaking. The speaker has to:

- pronounce the distinctive sounds of a language clearly enough so that people can distinguish them. This includes making tonal distinctions.

- use stress and rhythmic patterns, and intonation patterns of the language clearly enough so that people can understand what is said.
- use the correct forms of words. This may mean, for example, changes in the tense, case, or gender.
- put words together in correct word order.
- use vocabulary appropriately.
- use the register or language variety that is appropriate to the situation and the relationship to the conversation partner.
- make clear to the listener the main sentence constituents, such as subject, verb, object, by whatever means the language uses.
- make the main ideas stand out from supporting ideas or information.
- make the discourse hang together so that people can follow what you are saying.

Reading Skill

Reading is the receptive skill in the written mode. It can develop independently of listening and speaking skills, but often develops along with them, especially in societies with a highly-developed literary tradition. Reading can help build vocabulary that helps listening comprehension at the later stages, particularly.

Micro-skills

Here are some of the micro-skills involved in reading. The reader has to:

- decipher the script. In an alphabetic system or a syllabary, this means establishing a relationship between sounds and symbols. In a pictograph system, it means associating the meaning of the words with written symbols.
- recognize vocabulary.
- pick out key words, such as those identifying topics and main ideas.
- figure out the meaning of the words, including unfamiliar

vocabulary, from the (written) context.

- recognize grammatical word classes: noun, adjective, etc.
- detect sentence constituents, such as subject, verb, object, prepositions, etc.
- recognize basic syntactic patterns.
- reconstruct and infer situations, goals and participants.
- use both knowledge of the world and lexical and grammatical cohesive devices to make the foregoing inferences, predict outcomes, and infer links and connections among the parts of the text.
- get the main point or the most important information.
- distinguish the main idea from supporting details.
- adjust reading strategies to different reading purposes, such as skimming for main ideas or studying in-depth.

Writing Skill

Writing is the productive skill in the written mode. It, too, is more complicated than it seems at first, and often seems to be the hardest of the skills, even for native speakers of a language, since it involves not just a graphic representation of speech, but the development and presentation of thoughts in a structured way.

Micro-skills

Here are some of the micro-skills involved in writing. The writer needs to:

- use the orthography correctly, including the script, and spelling and punctuation conventions.
- use the correct forms of words. This may mean using forms that express the right tense, or case or gender.
- put words together in correct word order.
- use vocabulary correctly.
- use the style appropriate to the genre and audience.
- make the main sentence constituents, such as subject, verb, and object, clear to the reader.
- make the main ideas distinct from supporting ideas or

information.

- make the text coherent, so that other people can follow the development of the ideas.
- judge how much background knowledge the audience has on the subject and make clear what it is assumed they don't know.

guidelines for a Language and Culture Learning Program

These guidelines have been created to help you design and plan your own language and culture learning program. They are organized according to three parameters:

- The stage of learning
- The basic language skill being developed
- The aspect of communicative competence in focus

Each guideline has the following parts:

- a list of objectives considered appropriate for learners of that stage in relation to the aspect of communicative competence in focus
- a list of strategies the learner can use to achieve these objectives
- a list of language learning techniques to implement the strategies
- a list of language learning activities to implement the strategies

Aspects of Communicative Competence

Communicative competence is a concept introduced by Dell Hymes and discussed and redefined by many authors. Hymes' original idea was that speakers of a language have to have more than grammatical competence in order to be able communicate effectively in a language; they also need to know how language is used by members of a speech community to accomplish their purposes.

The modules in this section identify eight aspects of communicative competence. They are grouped together in two groups of four:

Linguistic Aspects

- Phonology and orthography
- Grammar
- Vocabulary
- Discourse (textual)

Pragmatic aspects

- Functions
- Variations
- Interactional skills
- Cultural framework

Communication Skills

"We all use language to communicate, to express ourselves, to get our ideas across, and to connect with the person to whom we are speaking. When a relationship is working, the act of communicating seems to flow relatively effortlessly. When a relationship is deteriorating, the act of communicating can be as frustrating as climbing a hill of sand."

The Three Components of Communication

On a daily basis we work with people who have different opinions, values, beliefs, and needs than our own. Our ability to exchange ideas with others, understand others' perspectives, solve problems and successfully utilize the steps and processes presented in this training will depend significantly on how effectively we are able to communicate with others.

The act of communicating involves verbal, nonverbal, and paraverbal components. The verbal component refers to the content of our message, the choice and arrangement of our words. The nonverbal component refers to the message we send through our body language. The paraverbal component refers to how we say what we say-the tone, pacing and volume of our voices.

In order to communicate effectively, we must use all three components to do two things:

1. Send clear, concise messages.

2. Hear and correctly understand messages someone is sending to us.

Communication Involves Three Components:

1. Verbal Messages-the words we choose
2. Paraverbal Messages-how we say the words
3. Nonverbal Messages-our body language

These Three Components Are Used To:

1. Send Clear, Concise Messages
2. Receive and Correctly Understand Messages Sent to Us.

Sending Messages

Verbal Messages

Our use of language has tremendous power in the type of atmosphere that is created at the problem-solving table. Words that are critical, blaming, judgmental or accusatory tend to create a resistant and defensive mindset that is not conducive to productive problem solving. On the other hand, we can choose words that normalize the issues and problems and reduce resistance. Phrases such as *"in some districts, people may..."*, *"it is not uncommon for..."* and *"for some folks in similar situations"* are examples of this.

Sending effective messages requires that we state our point of view as briefly and succinctly as possible. Listening to a rambling, unorganized speaker is tedious and discouraging-why continue to listen when there is no interchange? Lengthy dissertations and circuitous explanations are confusing to the listener and the message loses its concreteness, relevance, and impact. This is your opportunity to help the listener understand YOUR perspective and point of view. Choose your words with the intent of making your message as clear as possible, avoiding jargon and unnecessary, tangential information.

Effective Verbal Messages:

1. Are brief, succinct, and organized
2. Are free of jargon
3. Do not create resistance in the listener

Nonverbal Messages

The power of nonverbal communication cannot be underestimated. In his book, Silent Messages, Professor Albert Mehrabian says the messages we send through our posture, gestures, facial expression, and spatial distance account for 55% of what is perceived and understood by others. In fact, through our body language we are always communicating, whether we want to or not!

You cannot not communicate.

Nonverbal messages are the primary way that we communicate emotions:

Facial Expression: The face is perhaps the most important conveyor of emotional information. A face can light up with enthusiasm, energy, and approval, express confusion or boredom, and scowl with displeasure. The eyes are particularly expressive in telegraphing joy, sadness, anger, or confusion.

Postures and Gestures: Our body postures can create a feeling of warm openness or cold rejection. For example, when someone faces us, sitting quietly with hands loosely folded in the lap, a feeling of anticipation and interest is created. A posture of arms crossed on the chest portrays a feeling of inflexibility. The action of gathering up one's materials and reaching for a purse signals a desire to end the conversation.

Nonverbal Messages:

1. Account for about 55% of what is perceived and understood by others.
2. Are conveyed through our facial expressions as well as our postures and gestures.

Paraverbal Messages

Paraverbal communication refers to the messages that we transmit through the tone, pitch, and pacing of our voices. It is *how we say something,* not *what we say.* Professor Mehrabian states that the paraverbal message accounts for approximately 38% of what is communicated to someone. A sentence can convey entirely different meanings depending on the emphasis on words and the tone of voice. For example, the statement, "I didn't say you were stupid" has six different meanings, depending on which word is emphasized.

Some points to remember about our paraverbal communication:

When we are angry or excited, our speech tends to become more rapid and higher pitched.

When we are bored or feeling down, our speech tends to slow and take on a monotone quality.

When we are feeling defensive, our speech is often abrupt.

Paraverbal Messages:

1. Account for about 38% of what is perceived and understood by others.
2. Include the tone, pitch, and pacing of our voice

The Importance of Consistency

In all of our communications we want to strive to send consistent verbal, paraverbal and nonverbal messages. When our messages are inconsistent, the listener may become confused. Inconsistency can also create a lack of trust and undermine the chance to build a good working relationship.

When a person sends a message with conflicting verbal, paraverbal and nonverbal information, the nonverbal information tends to be believed. Consider the example of someone, through a clenched jaw, hard eyes, and steely voice, telling you they're not mad. Which are you likely to believe? What you see or what you hear?

Receiving Messages

Listening

The key to receiving messages effectively is *listening*. Listening is a combination of hearing what another person says and psychological involvement with the person who is talking. Listening requires more than hearing words. It requires a desire to understand another human being, an attitude of respect and acceptance, and a willingness to open one's mind to try and see things from another's point of view.

Listening requires a high level of concentration and energy. It demands that we set aside our own thoughts and agendas, put ourselves in another's shoes and try to see the world through that person's eyes. True listening requires that we suspend judgment, evaluation, and approval in an attempt to understand another is frame of reference, emotions, and attitudes. Listening to understand is, indeed, a difficult task!

Often, people worry that if they listen attentively and patiently to a person who is saying something they disagree with, they are inadvertently sending a message of agreement.

When we listen effectively we gain information that is valuable to understanding the problem as the other person sees it. We gain a greater understanding of the other person's perception. After all, the truth is subjective and a matter of perception. When we have a deeper understanding of another's perception, whether we agree with it or not, we hold the key to understanding that person's motivation, attitude, and behaviour. We have a deeper understanding of the problem and the potential paths for reaching agreement.

Listening

1. Requires concentration and energy
2. Involves a psychological connection with the speaker
3. Includes a desire and willingness to try and see things from another's perspective
4. Requires that we suspend judgment and evaluation

"Listening in dialogue is listening more to meaning than to words...In true listening, we reach behind the words, see through them, to find the person who is being revealed. Listening is a search to find the treasure of the true person as revealed verbally and nonverbally. There is the semantic problem, of course. The words bear a different connotation for you than they do for me. Consequently, I can never tell you what you said, but only what I heard. I will have to rephrase what you have said, and check it out with you to make sure that what left your mind and heart arrived in my mind and heart intact and without distortion."-John Powell, theologian. Learning to be an effective listener is a difficult task for many people. However, the specific skills of effective listening behaviour can be learned. It is our ultimate goal to integrate these skills into a sensitive and unified way of listening.

Key Listening Skills:

Nonverbal:

Giving full physical attention to the speaker;

Being aware of the speaker's nonverbal messages;

Verbal:

Paying attention to the words and feelings that are being expressed;

Using reflective listening tools such as paraphrasing, reflecting, summarizing, and questioning to increase understanding of the message and help the speaker tell his story.

Giving Full Physical Attention to the Speaker

Attending is the art and skill of giving full, physical attention to another person. In his book, People Skills, Robert Bolton, Ph.D., refers to it as "listening with the whole body".

Effective attending is a careful balance of alertness and relaxation that includes appropriate body movement, eye contact, and "posture of involvement". Fully attending says to the speaker, "What you are saying is very important. I am totally present and intent on understanding you". We create a posture of involvement by:

Leaning gently towards the speaker;

Facing the other person squarely;

Maintaining an open posture with arms and legs uncrossed;

Maintaining an appropriate distance between us and the speaker;

Moving our bodies in response to the speaker, i.e., appropriate head nodding, facial expressions.

"To listen is to move. To listen is to be moved by the talker-physically and psychologically... The non-moving, unblinking person can reliably be estimated to be a non-listener... When other visible moving has ceased and the eyeblink rate has fallen to less than once in six seconds, listening, for practical purposes, has stopped."

Being Aware of the Speaker's Nonverbal Messages

When we pay attention to a speaker's body language we gain insight into how that person is feeling as well as the intensity of the feeling. Through careful attention to body language and paraverbal messages, we are able to develop hunches about what the speaker (or listener) is communicating. We can then, through our reflective listening skills, check the accuracy of those hunches by expressing in our own words, our impression of what is being communicated.

Paying Attention to the Words and Feelings

In order to understand the total meaning of a message, we must be able to gain understanding about both the *feeling* and the *content* of the message. We are often more comfortable dealing with the content rather than the feelings (i.e., the relationship), particularly when the feelings are intense. Our tendency is to try and ignore the emotional aspect of the message/conflict and move directly to the substance of the issues.

This can lead to an escalation of intense emotions. It may be necessary to deal directly with the relationship problem by openly acknowledging and naming the feelings and having an honest discussion about them prior to moving into the substantive issues. If we leave the emotional aspect unaddressed, we risk missing important information about the problem as well as derailing the communication process.

Reflective Listening Skills

Reflective listening or responding is the process of restating, in our words, the feeling and/or content that is being expressed and is part of the verbal component of sending and receiving messages.

By reflecting back to the speaker what we believe we understand, we validate that person by giving them the experience of being heard and acknowledged. We also provide an opportunity for the speaker to give us feedback about the accuracy of our perceptions, thereby increasing the effectiveness of our overall communication.

Paraphrasing-This is a concise statement of the content of the speaker's message. A paraphrase should be brief, succinct, and focus on the facts or ideas of the message rather than the feeling. The paraphrase should be in the listener's own words rather than "parroting back", using the speaker's words.

"You believe that Jane needs an instructional assistant because she isn't capable of working independently."

"You would like Bob to remain in first grade because you think the activities would be more developmentally appropriate."

"You do not want Beth to receive special education services because you think it would be humiliating for her to leave the classroom at any time."

"You want to evaluate my child because you think he may have an emotional disability.

Reflecting Feeling-The listener concentrates on the feeling words and asks herself, "How would I be feeling if I was having that experience?" She then restates or paraphrases the feeling of what she has heard in a manner that conveys understanding.

"You are very worried about the impact that an evaluation might have on Lisa's self esteem".

"You are frustrated because dealing with Ben has taken up so much of your time, you feel like you've ignored your other students."

"You feel extremely angry about the lack of communication you have had in regards to Joe's failing grades."

"You're upset because you haven't been able to get in touch with me when I'm at work."

Summarizing-The listener pulls together the main ideas and feelings of the speaker to show understanding. This skill is used after a considerable amount of information sharing has gone on and shows that the listener grasps the total meaning of the message. It also helps the speaker gain an integrated picture of what she has been saying.

"You're frustrated and angry that the assessment has taken so long and confused about why the referral wasn't made earlier since that is what you thought had happened. You are also willing to consider additional evaluation if you can choose the provider and the school district will pay for it".

"You're worried that my son won't make adequate progress in reading if he doesn't receive special services. And you feel that he needs to be getting those services in the resource room for at least 30 minutes each day because the reading groups in the classroom are bigger and wouldn't provide the type of instruction you think he needs."

Additional Verbal Communication Tools

A number of other verbal tools encourage communication and facilitate the goal of gaining a more thorough understanding of another's perspective:

Questioning-the listener asks open ended questions (questions which can't be answered with a "yes" or a "no") to get information and clarification. This helps focus the speaker on the topic, encourages the speaker to talk, and provides the speaker the opportunity to give feedback.

"Can you tell us more about Johnny's experience when he's in the regular classroom?"

"How was it for Susie when she rode the special ed. bus for those two weeks?"

"Tell us more about the afterschool tutoring sessions."

"What kinds of skills do you think are important for Jim to learn in a social skills class?"

"Could you explain why you think itís difficult for Ben to be on the playground for an hour?"

"I'm confused-are you worried that the testing may mean time out of the classroom for Jim or is there something else?"

Verbal Communication Tools

1. Paraphrasing-a brief, succinct statement reflecting the content of the speakerís message.

2. Reflecting Feeling-a statement, in a way that conveys understanding, of the feeling that the listener has heard.
3. Summarizing-a statement of the main ideas and feelings to show understanding.
4. Questioning-asking open questions to gain information, encourage the speaker to tell her story, and gain clarification.

Barriers to Effective Communication

"A barrier to communication is something that keeps meanings from meeting. Meaning barriers exist between all people, making communication much more difficult than most people seem to realize. It is false to assume that if one can talk he can communicate. Because so much of our education misleads people into thinking that communication is easier than it is, they become discouraged and give up when they run into difficulty. Because they do not understand the nature of the problem, they do not know what to do. The wonder is not that communicating is as difficult as it is, but that it occurs as much as it does."-*Reuel Howe, theologian and educator*

When people are under stress, they are more apt to inject communication barriers into their conversation. These barriers can exist in any of the three components of communication (verbal, paraverbal, and nonverbal). According to Thomas Gordon, author of the Parent Effectiveness Training program, people use communication barriers 90% of the time in conflict situations. For this reason, it is worthwhile to describe some of the common responses that will, inevitably, have a negative effect on communications:

Verbal Communication Barriers

1. Attacking (interrogating, criticizing, blaming, shaming)

"If you were doing your job and supervising Susie in the lunch line we probably wouldn't be in this situation, would we?"

"Have you followed through with the counseling we asked you to do? Have you gotten Ben to the doctor's for his medical checkup? Did you call and arrange for a Big Brother? Have you found out if you're eligible for food stamps?"

"From what I can see, you don't have the training to teach a child with ADHD. Obviously if you did you would be using different strategies that wouldn't make her feel like she's a bad person."

2. "You Messages" (moralizing, preaching, advising, diagnosing)

"You don't seem to understand how important it is for your child to get this help. Don't you see that he's well on his way to becoming a sociopath?"

"You obviously don't realize that if you were following the same steps we do at home you wouldn't be having this problem. You don't seem to care about whatís going on in this child's life outside of school."

3. Showing Power (ordering, threatening, commanding, directing)

"If you don't voluntarily agree to this evaluation we can take you to due process. Go ahead and file a complaint if you want to."

"I'm going to write a letter of complaint to the superintendent and have this in your file if you don't stop humiliating my son in front of his classmates. I know my rights."

4. Other Verbal Barriers: shouting, name calling, refusing to speak.

Nonverbal Communication Barriers

1. Flashing or rolling eyes
2. Quick or slow movements
3. Arms crossed, legs crossed
4. Gestures made with exasperation
5. Slouching, hunching over
6. Poor personal care
7. Doodling
8. Staring at people or avoiding eye contact
9. Excessive fidgeting with materials

All of these examples of barriers thwart communication, mutual understanding, respect, problem solving, and identifying solutions that will meet everyone's needs. They put a serious strain on relationships that ultimately need to be collaborative in order to most effectively meet the needs of our children. Use of these "communication errors" results in increased emotional distancing between the parties, escalation in the intensity of the conflict and a negative environment for everyone involved.

Language and Communication Skills

Communication begins at birth with touch, then with vision, and finally with speech and hearing or audition. Each child needs to learn the "codes of his/her culture" because the language of each culture is different. Yet, if a child is to learn about his/her world, the ability to communicate must exist. Even after a baby learns the rudiments of communication through touch, vision and hearing, those skills need to continue to be refined until, at about age 7, the brain is ready to deal with the abstracts concepts involved in reading, writing, comprehension, math "language" or concepts, and body language.

The acquisition and use of language and communication skills is at the heart of learning disabilities. These skills include speech, reading, writing and spelling, comprehension, reasoning, math language and body language. All of these skills need an intact sensory system to function appropriately.

Language acquisition is divided into several parts:

- Receptive language: language that is spoken or written by others and received by an individual, i.e. listening or reading (decoding or getting meaning from spoken words or written symbols). In order to receive language, the individual must be able to attend to, process, comprehend, retain and/or integrate spoken or written language. In order to do proper auditory processing, the individual needs to have phonemic awareness, the ability to notice, think about and manipulate the individual sound in words and phonemes (sound-symbol correspondence); and phonological awareness, sound —symbol recognition or the ability to recognize specific sounds, which is necessary for good reading and spelling. Good visual processing demands the ability to interpret visual symbols, to differential visual figure from ground, to have a functional visual memory and, for writing, good visual-motor activity.

- Cognitive language: language that is received, processed into memory, integrated with knowledge already integrated and made a part of the knowledge of the individual from which new ideas and concepts can be generated. It is a part of the creative process that shapes the thought of each person.
- Expressive language: language and communication through speaking, writing, and/or gestures, i.e. selecting words, formulating them into ideas, and producing them through speaking, writing, or gesture (encoding or the process of expressive language). Expressive language involves word retrieval, rules of grammar (syntax) word and sentence structure (morphology) and word meaning (semantics). By the time a child is five years old, speech skills should be such that the child can be understood 100% of the time. The ability to read easy words and comprehend them should be in place for most children by the time a child is 7 or 8 years old. If children are not ready to read by fourth grade, they will not be able to keep up with the curriculum designated by the state.

9

The Interview Advantage

How to Use Nonverbal Communication to Impress

When interviewing for employment you could be thinking that if you are the candidate with the best answers to interview questions, you'll get the job. In fact, that isn't typically the case.

CollegeJournal reports that, according to some studies, "Body language comprises 55% of the force of any response, whereas the verbal content only provides 7%, and paralanguage, or the intonation — pauses and sighs given when answering — represents 38% of the emphasis."

As you can see, nonverbal communication is as important, or even more important than, verbal communication. The evaluation of your nonverbal communication will start as soon as you walk into the company's lobby and continue until the interview is finished. If your nonverbal communication skills aren't up to par, it won't matter how well you answer the questions.

Nonverbal Communication Matters

If you come to an interview reeking of cigarette smoke or chewing gum, you will already have one strike against you. Too much perfume or not enough deodorant won't help either. Not being dressed appropriately or having scuffed shoes will give you a second strike. Talking on your cell phone or listening to an IPod while waiting to be called for the interview may be your final strike.

What's important, when interviewing, is to appear professional and attentive throughout the interview process. Before you leave for the interview, make sure you are dressed professionally, neatly groomed, your shoes are polished, and you haven't overdone (none is better than too much) the perfume or aftershave. There's more than one hiring manager who won't hire someone they can smell (good or bad) before they meet them face-to-face.

There are things that you should you bring with you to the interview and things that you need to leave at home:

What to Bring to an Interview

- Portfolio or pad holder with a copy of your resume and a list of references on quality paper
- Work Samples (if relevant)
- Notepad, Pen
- Breath mint (before you enter the building)
- Women: extra pair of pantyhose (keep in your briefcase or car)

What Not to Bring to an Interview

- Cell phone
- iPod
- Gum
- Cigarettes
- Candy
- Soda or coffee
- Scuffed shoes, messy and/or not-so-clean clothes

While You Wait

The way you sit in the lobby, the way you greet the receptionist and the interviewer, and the way you wait, will all have an impact on whether you are going to be considered for the job. Be friendly and pleasant, but, not overbearing. If you need to wait, sit quietly (no phone calls) and patiently. Shake hands with the interviewer. Your handshake should be firm-not sticky or wimpy. To avoid sweaty palms, visit the rest room, wash your hands, then run them under cool water prior to the interview. Keep your palms open rather than clenched in a fist and keep a tissue you in your pocket to (surreptitiously) wipe them.

Nonverbal Communication During the Interview:

- Make eye contact with the interviewer for a few seconds at a time.
- Smile and nod (at appropriate times) when the interviewer is talking, but, don't overdo it. Don't laugh unless the interviewer does first.
- Be polite and keep an even tone to your speech. Don't be too loud or too quiet.
- Don't slouch.
- Do relax and lean forward a little towards the interviewer so you appear interested and engaged.
- Don't lean back. You will look too casual and relaxed.
- Keep your feet on the floor and your back against the lower back of the chair.
- Pay attention, be attentive and interested.
- Listen.
- Don't interrupt.
- Stay calm. Even if you had a bad experience at a previous position or were fired, keep your emotions to yourself and do not show anger or frown.
- Not sure what to do with your hands? Hold a pen and your notepad or rest an arm on the chair or on your lap, so you look comfortable. Don't let your arms fly around the room when you're making a point.

Your verbal communication is important too. Remember your manners and and thank the interviewer for taking the time to meet with you. Don't use slang. Speak clearly and definitely.

What's most important, is to remember that the image the interviewer has of you when he first meets you is the one that is going to last. If you're slouchy, sloppy or messy it won't matter how well you answer the interview questions. You are not going to get the job. When practicing for an interview, work on your nonverbal communications as well as your other interviewing skills. It could be what clinches the job offer for you.

Interested in how interviewers evaluate candidates based on nonverbal communication? Take a look at How Employers Use Nonverbal Communication in Hiring. "Awareness of nonverbal communication and the messages job searchers send does influence your evaluation of job candidates – and it should."

10

Oral Communication

The first step in planning an oral presentation involves acknowledging two fundamental differences between oral and written communication.

One essential goal of oral communication is to make personal contact with the audience, and to help connect them to the content. Reading a written report aloud is not usually an effective strategy for engaging with the audience. The needs/preferences of the audience play an even larger role in oral presentations than in writing. The content of presentations should be prepared with this goal in mind.

Second, oral presentations are fleeting (or time-sensitive). If readers get lost or stop paying attention for a few minutes, they can always flip back a few pages. Listeners, on the other hand, usually can't interrupt the speaker and ask that s/he start again and go back a few minutes. Once words are uttered, they vanish. Presenters can account for the fleeting nature of oral presentations by making sure that the presentation is well organized and by making structure explicit in the talk, so the audience can always knows where they've been and where they're going.

This section outlines principles and strategies for planning, designing visuals for, practicing, and presenting your talk.

Planning your Talk

The first step in Planning an Oral Presentation involves acknowledging two fundamental differences between oral and written communication.

One essential goal of oral communication is to make personal contact with the audience, and to help connect them to the content. Reading a written report aloud is not usually an effective strategy for engaging with the audience. The needs/preferences of the audience play an even larger role in oral presentations than in writing. The content of presentations should be prepared with this goal in mind. Second, oral presentations are fleeting (or time-sensitive). If readers get lost or stop paying attention for a few minutes, they can always flip back a few pages. Listeners, on the other hand, usually can't interrupt the speaker and ask that s/he start again and go back a few minutes. Once words are uttered, they vanish. Presenters can account for the fleeting nature of oral presentations by making sure that the presentation is well organized and by making structure explicit in the talk, so the audience can always knows where they've been and where they're going.

A Speech or Notes? The first decision a presentation planner must make is whether to speak from notes or to write a complete speech. Either strategy can work. Some students are not comfortable without a prepared text to read; others can easily talk authoritatively with only notes (and sometimes without). Choose what you're comfortable with, or something in between the two options. However, if you choose to write a prepared speech, make sure that it's designed for oral delivery, that you've practiced it adequately, and that you don't read from the sheet. Using a prepared text as a security blanket is okay, but relying on it too much makes it difficult to connect or engage with the audience; be prepared to depart from your text when necessary and be flexible.

1. Purpose Statement
2. Opening Strategy
3. Main Idea
4. Overview
5. Conclusion
6. Take Away Statement.

Components: A well-planned oral presentation should contain these elements at the beginning and the end of the talk:

1. The first step in planning a talk is developing a Purpose Statement: this is the objective for the talk, or what the speaker wants to accomplish. The purpose statement is more than a statement of topic. For example, your purpose might be to explain the advantages of your design, to allay the concerns that a project is behind (or justify why it is), or to clarify a complex aspect of your work. This purpose statement, however, is not always explicitly stated in the presentation itself: you may not necessarily say "I'm giving this talk to explain why we're five weeks behind schedule" or "I'm giving this talk to sell 500 computers to you." Although often unstated, the purpose statement guides your preparation for your talk.
2. A well-planned presentation should also have an Opening Strategy that helps develop a rapport with the audience. There are a wide range of strategies available, but they all attempt to connect the audience to the content. Some example opening strategies are:
   - Telling jokes, anecdotes, bits of history, startling facts, etc.
   - Giving key information the audience needs
   - Making the listener own the problem

   Major considerations for planning opening strategies are relevance and time: make sure that the opening strategy chosen suits the context and the content of the talk, and that it doesn't take up too much time.
3. The Main Idea is how the purpose statement manifests itself in the talk: it is the explicit statement made at the beginning of the talk that identifies a) the topic and b) the end goal of the talk. Be careful when using the phrase "talk about" in your statement, because it tends to give only a statement of topic: "I'm going to talk about Project X" establishes a topic, but doesn't provide any further focus for the talk. Instead, the main idea should be based on a stronger verb. For example, given the two unstated purpose statements from above, your main idea might be:

- "We'll diagnose the problems with Project X and provide recommendations for mitigating them."
- "This presentation identifies the advantages of Bluetooth enabled computers and Local Area Networks."

These stronger verbs help to establish the goal of the presentation. Sometimes you will begin your planning by establishing this statement; other times you might start in the middle to help you figure out what you are trying to say. Regardless, you need a strong sense of purpose to motivate your talk

4. An Overview gives the listeners a mental roadmap of the whole talk, making the structure explicit at the beginning. For example, if you have three reasons why the project is behind, sketch them out quickly:
   - "Project X is behind because the raw materials for High Performance concrete arrived late, unforeseen weather delays prevented pouring on four days, and changing specifications forced us to re-design two areas."
   - "First, we'll explain what Bluetooth technology is, what it can do for Local Area Networks, and how its low cost and ease of use gives it advantages over other networking solutions."

   When developing an overview, make sure that it contains actual information that is relevant to the talk. Be careful not to provide a generic statement of structure, such as: "I'm going to explain the problem, provide several solutions, evaluate them, and give recommendations." This overview could be applied to many talks because it says nothing specific, and is not particularly helpful for the audience (especially if they are hearing more than one talk).
5. The Conclusion should provide a brief summary by referring to the presentation's main point(s). You don't usually need to go over every single point or repeat the headings stated at the beginning of the talk, but you should signal that your talk is coming to an end by using phrases

such as "in conclusion" or "to sum up" and reiterate your main idea.

- "By ensuring that our suppliers are held responsible for delays, building a sheltered mixing area, and maintaining closer communication with the audience, we should be able to smoothly get back on schedule on Project X.
- "Because it's cheap and easy to implement, Bluetooth technology can make for effective and easier to manage LANs."

6. The Take Away Statement is the last sentence that comes out of your mouth: it will also be the last thing the audience remembers and should clearly identify a) that the talk is over (and to give the audience the signal to applaud) and b) identify what the audience should take away from the talk, or what they can do with the information given in the talk. Don't finish the talk by saying "that's it" – it may signal that the talk is over, but it doesn't remind the listener of what s/he should take away from the talk. For example, a summary for the second sample talk, you could say:
   - "So, the next time you're untangling wires from printers, mice, keyboards, speakers etc. from the back of your computers, think about easy managing a network of Bluetooth enabled computers would be."

Presentation Organization

These six key components should sandwich the body of the talk. However, presentation planning also involves organizing the body of the talk. There are two steps in organizing the body 1) identify the key points and 2) use an organizational method appropriate for the presentation content and purpose. Some relevant organization structures are listed below.

- Chronological: Breaks talks into steps, organized by time; useful for process descriptions or progress reports.
- Ascending or Descending Pattern: Sorts topics based on performance in predetermined criteria, such as difficulty (easiest to hardest), size (smallest to largest), significance

(least to most important), or cost (inexpensive to costly.)

- Pro and Con: Divides talk into positives and negatives. Useful in evaluating; can be objective or persuasive.
- Cause to Effect: Breaks material up in results and precipitating causes; can be speculative (starts with causes) or analytical (starts with effects). Emphasizes ways one thing leads to another.
- Scientific Method: Follows reporting structure for lab work: purpose, methods, results, discussion, and recommendations.
- Problem/Solution: Describe situation/ explain problem (or opportunity)/explain solution (include methodology if appropriate)/justify solution.

Practising Your Talk

The second step to delivering an effective Oral Presentation is Practice. Practice is a necessary part of presentation preparation, but there are different types of practice that help accomplish specific goals.

1. Practising delivery on your own will help you to:

   (1) become familiar with the material you're delivering,

   (2) develop a proper cadence and rhythm for your speech, and

   (3) allow you to establish proper timing for your talk.

Ideal presentation delivery is not usually achieved by reading a prepared speech, but by engaging the audience through a natural, conversational style. If working from notes, use these practice sessions to develop a familiarity with the material and to develop/ memorize key sentences that will anchor parts of your talk. If you're working from a memorized text or reading a written speech, you should try not to sound like you're reading, and work on fostering natural, conversational delivery.

Timing is important in oral presentations: when you're given a time limit, respect it. In most situations – such as conference panels with a hard time limit and more than one speaker – audiences do not have the luxury or the inclination to listen beyond the given times. In fact, audiences tend to get annoyed if a speaker goes over significantly. When practicing, ensure that you time yourself. In order to get accurate timing, your practice sessions have to be uninterrupted. Times in these practice sessions aren't always accurate because they don't mimic the real conditions of delivery very well – but they will give you rough idea of whether or not you're in the ballpark.

2. Practising in front of a mirror can allow you to work on:

   (1) maintaining eye contact,

   (2) using gestures appropriately, and

   (3) making sure you're familiar with the material.

When working on eye contact, ensure that you're actually engaging the audience and sustaining the contact for more than a few seconds. In other words, make sure that you're not just looking in the general vicinity of the audience, but making actual contact with audience members. In the mirror, focus on your own eyes, and note when and how often you look away. If you need to look away (at your notes) every few seconds, you'll need to become more familiar with the content. A second or two at a time is not usually sufficient to connect with the audience. Instead, focus on maintaining eye contact for sustained periods (if you need to, look at your notes for longer periods as well).

If you have a large or full-length mirror, you can also use this technique to correct your posture and identify your gesturing techniques. Use this time to spot problems with your gesturing – too much or too little – and identify areas in the talk where you can use gestures to add emphasis or meaning to your presentation.

3. Practising in front of others is the best type of practice because it mimics the actual conditions of delivery. In this situation, you have "one go" and can time your delivery more accurately, and should be able to practice eye contact, gesturing, and generally engaging the audience. If possible, use this opportunity to test your familiarity and interaction with the visuals you plan on using.

You should also ask your friends for feedback on the content and structure of the talk, and make sure that the talk served the purpose that you identified in the planning stage.

More Practice Strategies: When working on effective vocal and physical delivery, you may want to try some of these simple practice strategies; these shouldn't be used in the actual performance, but are useful for fine tuning specific aspects of delivery. The first relates to gesture and voice, the second is an audience reminder trick, and the last two focus on enunciation :

The Bad Actor Strategy

Try performing the talk aloud (and alone behind a locked door) as if you were a bad actor (William Shatner comes to mind). Go completely over the top! Make huge sweeping gestures and overdo the words. Do this Twice. As you do it the second time, try to make mental note of two key things:

- Where your voice rises for emphasis
- Where you want to make gestures

The information you gain here shows you the natural points of emphasis. That important information can now be used in a "normal" version of the talk. Of course, one of the things you'll find is that "normal" has changed, as the speech becomes more energized.

Follow the Leader Practice

One of the most important, but most neglected, aspects of the talk is how we make transitions between points. Imagine you have an audience full of people with very poor short-term memories, but you're trying to get through to them. Deliver your talk repeating everything, and using whatever transitions you need to make that audience grasp your talk, without forgetting points. Here are some useful transition words / strategies:

"First, ... second, ... third, ..."

"Now that we understand the background to the problem ..."

"Logically, this point leads to the second aspect of my talk ..."

"After this point ..."

"Now you can understand why ..."

"In conclusion..."

"As a final afterthought ..."

"Thank you. Now, I'd be glad to respond to any questions."

The Eliza Doolittle Method

In "My Fair Lady" Eliza had the accent knocked out of her with speech lessons. We all need that. Finding our best pitch, our best tone and our best accent requires practice. Choose a familiar bit of speech and use it to hone your delivery. You're best off to start with something other than your speech, and only apply it to your speech later. Speeches by Shakespeare, Churchill, or Martin Luther King Jr. all serve well as practice points. Once you've mastered one of these, then bring the same enunciation effort to your talk. If you have an accent, you need to learn this exercise taking particular care of sounds that may trip your listeners. For example, many Chinese speakers of English struggle to distinguish "l" vs. "r" etc., so you need to work with these sounds, particularly if they appear in words that are central to your purpose.

The Mouth of Marbles Technique

This exercise is designed to work your mouth muscles to help you enunciate more clearly. It is a good trick to do as shortly before your talk as possible (as well as a regular exercise if you're doing a lot of speaking). Place two fingers between your teeth and practice this speech:

Tomorrow, and tomorrow, and tomorrow,
Creeps in this petty pace from day to day,
To the last syllable of recorded time;
And all our yesterdays have lighted fools
The way to dusty death.

After you've done it once or twice with your fingers between your teeth, remove your fingers and do it again. Take note of the sensation in your lips – those are muscles beginning to work. Do the same thing with the opening of your talk. Then deliver the whole talk.

Performing your Talk

In Performance, you're simply doing what you've practiced many times before (if you've practiced all the ways outlined in

Oral Communication/Practice). Thinking of the actual performance in this way should help to calm nerves and anxieties about giving the talk. The following page outlines some of the main goals in performance, and strategies for achieving them. Most of these you'll have had a chance to practice already; but some considerations will only come up in the actual performance.

Assuming an Appropriate Presentation Persona:

When you deliver a formal presentation, you are "performing" – as in a play – in front of an audience. While you don't want to become something artificial when you talk, you do want to play the part of a speaker. The role you are playing is "you," but it's not the same "you" as we see in informal settings. This is a persona that should look and feel quite natural, but also be elevated from the everyday person. For some, assuming a presentation persona may include costuming – wearing a suit or getting more dressed up than usual can help you assume the appropriate character.

Effective vocal delivery: includes appropriate volume, pace, and natural speech

Adequate Volume is an essential component of effective delivery. If you can't be heard, you can't be understood, and your main point will be missed. Being audible is often not enough. Even if you can be heard, speaking too softly means that that the audience expends energy to trying to make out what you're saying; this may mean that they aren't paying enough attention to interpreting and understanding what you're saying. Generally speaking, the problems that presenters have are with low volume; rarely are speakers so loud that their speech is distracting. Speak loud enough so that the further member of the audience can hear you comfortably.

The same is true for Pace. Especially when nervous, presenters tend to talk too quickly, trying to get the talk over as soon as possible. Too fast a pace results in the same difficulties that low volume presents: the audience spends most of its energy in trying to make out the words being spoken, rather than in interpreting or understanding what's being said.

Ideally, we would all be able to speak naturally, as we do when we're engaged in a conversation, during presentations. However, presenters often fall back on a "reading" rhythm and speech pattern, even if they're working from notes. What constitutes "natural speech" differs from person to person, but it is usually marked by variations in pitch, tone, and pace, with appropriate pauses, all of which add layers of meaning to the words being spoken. The best that you can aim for is the speech that you can achieve when talking to friends on a topic you're confident and passionate about, with a more little formality added in.

Effective Physical Delivery: includes positioning, eye contact, body language, and connecting to your visuals

The first step, taking your position, should be done prior to the talk: determine the best place to stand before the audience arrives. The best place is a) where you don't block anyone's view, b) where you can see the audience, and c) where you can easily operate the projector / laptop and engage with the visuals. If you are very nervous, anchor yourself with a podium or desk – but not by leaning back or sitting. That is usually regarded as too casual. Instead, stand behind it, and use the desk as a front piece. During the talk, you might consider moving around to make sure you're paying attention to the entire audience.

Eye contact is an important strategy for both connecting to the audience and getting information from them. Effective eye contact is achieved when the speaker actually engages the audience. Just because a speaker doesn't read from a speech or look at their notes often doesn't mean that they've made effective eye contact: they could be just be staring outward or at other distractions, like their visuals. Look into the eyes of audience members and confirm that they're looking back. This also requires that eye contact is sustained: looking at someone for a second doesn't achieve the same level of engagement as maintaining that contact for four to five seconds.

If you actually engage with the audience through eye contact, you can also see whether people are confused or bored. You can use that information to help you decide whether to move on, or spend more time on a particular point.

Effective body language involves both posture and gesture. Posture communicates much about confidence and attitude towards the audience and material. For example, slouching suggests a casual attitude that may not be appropriate for formal presentations; leaning forward with hands on a desk suggests an aggressiveness that may make the audience uncomfortable. An upright posture communicates confidence and formality.

Gestures and movement can be used to deliver information as well. If you practiced gestures beforehand, they will happen more naturally when it comes time to deliver. Some speech coaches advocate "standing still" and that is generally good advice, but some excellent speakers move a lot. Why? Because they are comfortable moving. If you look comfortable, your audience will be comfortable too. Therefore, the general guide to appropriate gesture is "do what makes you comfortable." Obviously, some comforting gestures can be annoying – key rattling, jingling the change in your pocket, picking your nose: these are called physical tics. However, if walking around or talking with your hands makes you more comfortable, it probably also makes you more effective.

Connecting with your visuals and managing them correctly is also a key part of effective physical delivery. If you're using overhead transparencies, don't fumble with your slides. Throw away paper separators before you present. When placing a slide on the projector, make sure that you look back at the screen to see that all is visible, and adjust the slide if necessary, but do not stare at the screen. Using a laptop with PowerPoint presents another potentially dangerous distraction: the computer. In fact, presenters are much more likely to focus on their computers than their notes. Using a PowerPoint presentation as a stand in for traditional notes is often not a good idea.

When possible, point at the relevant parts of the visual and direct your audience's attention, but don't let your gesture to the screen lure you into reading from the screen or talking to the screen. A shaky pointer blocking the view can also be very distracting. Remember to focus on your audience, not the projector or computer monitor.

Show Mastery

Showing that you have mastery over your material gives your listeners confidence in you and sets them at ease. This can be as simple as showing that you are able to operate the equipment. Another way to show you are confident in your material is humour. It can lighten dry technical talks, especially after some particularly heavy going. Cartoons can be an effective way to draw parallels with points you are trying to make, if relevant. Even short verbal asides, rhetorical questions, or anecdotes can go a long way to keeping audience interest.

You can also show mastery by taking control of the questions, during or after the talk. During the talk, interact with the audience. Ask them if they are following you, or ask them simple questions to see if they are. Liven them up a bit.

After the talk, take control by managing the question and answer period. Always finish with a strong take away statement, allow the audience to clap, and then ask for questions. Control the question period by choosing the speakers, preparing yourself to handle certain questions beforehand, and taking the time to consider questions before formulating a response. If you encounter a question that you can't answer, acknowledge that you can't answer it, and tell them that you'll consider that in the future or turn the question back on the audience.

If questions lead things astray, try to steer the topic back on track, otherwise audience participation can drive things far away from the main points of the talk. Take discussions off-line if they are consuming too much time or will not readily be resolved – suggest that you will check a fact or point and respond to the questioner by e-mail or telephone. Feel free to interrupt debates among audience members; after all, it's your talk!

Supporting your Talk with Visuals

Visuals are an important part of oral presentations: they can be used to highlight important information, explain technical concepts and details that are difficult to explain through words alone, and can help connect the listener to the content.

In planning presentation visuals, you have the same options as with writing *(options and purposes described in* Online Handbook / Components of Documents / Using Visuals in Writing), but will have to adjust your visuals for presentation on a screen, further away from your audience (than a piece of paper arms length away).

Many of concerns outlined in using visuals in writing still apply to their use in oral presentations. The following are particularly important in a presentation setting.

1. Introduce the graphic and explain its role in the presentation in words. Make sure that the graphic has a specific purpose in your presentation, and use your speech to identify its purpose and to highlight the key parts of the visual that serve that purpose. For example, when presenting a table of results, highlight (visually, through gestures, and in words) the cells that hold the most significant data.
2. Make sure that the precision of the illustration matches the precision of the speech: this is of particular concern when using graphics originally design for a written text, which is likely to provide a more detailed accompanying description, in oral presentations. Adjust the visual so that it suits the presentation content.
3. Ensure than graphics are properly titled and labeled. In an oral presentation setting, it is likely that some listeners may miss your introduction to the graphic. Readers who miss this introduction can simply flip back; listeners do not have this luxury. The title and the labels hold the key to interpreting the graphic element and its role in the presentation.

In addition to these shared issues, using graphics in an oral communication setting presents some other challenges:

Orientation of Visuals

When using transparencies, always use landscape orientation rather than portrait. This is not a constraint introduced by

PowerPoint (which limits users to landscape format), but by the fact that a landscape oriented slide fits better on a projector than portrait oriented ones. Landscape oriented slides allow you to use more of the space available on the slide, without having to adjust the slide during the presentation.

Text/Image Size/Resolution

The titles and labels need to be readable from a distance. This means that text should be a minimum of 18 point in size (24 point is typical).

18pt 20pt 24pt 28pt

While Times New Roman is typically the standard font for written documents, less print oriented fonts with harder edges and fewer curves are more suitable for presentation slides. Commonly used fonts for oral presentations include:

Furthermore, a standard approach to using images from written documents is simply to resize the image so that it fits the slide. This sometimes works, but resizing a small, low-resolution image to a larger size can result in fuzzy images that are difficult to interpret.

Text Based Slides

In an oral presentation, text based slides are common. They function to highlight the key points and reinforce the structure of the presentation. However, text based slides also encourage listeners to read, rather than listen. This is especially true if the presenter reads the text of the slide: avoid this. To use text based slides effectively, minimize the amount of the text on the slide by using note form instead of complete sentences, and leaving the details for your speech, rather than on the slide. The slide presented below is an example of a poorly designed slide, using too much text:

- The Orbiter is one key component of the space shuttle, and holds the astronauts along with all the equipment
- The solid rocket boosters are another, and provide the

initial thrust required to get the shuttle out of the atmosphere. It is jettisoned and recovered.

- The liquid rocket booster is the final component, and provides the thrust required to get the rocket into orbit. It is jettionsed after leaving the atmosphere, and burns up on reentry.

Reduce text by adding a title (Components) and using note form:

Shuttle Components:

- Orbiter:
    - Holds astronauts and equipment
- Sold Rocket Boosters:
    - Provides initial thrust to exit atmosphere
    - Jettisoned and recovered
- Liquid Rocket Booster
    - Provides thrust to achieve orbit
    - Jettisoned and burns up on reentry

The Dangers of Presentation Technologies

The devices and programs we use to produce and display our visuals in oral presentations present their own sets of dangers:

Overhead Slide Projectors / Transparencies: When using slides, make sure that you've oriented yourself with the projector, ordered and prepared your slides well – presenters can waste a significant amount of time and lose points by putting slides on backwards or upside down, flipping through their transparencies to find the right ones, and not placing the transparency on the right spot or correctly aligning their slide

Blackboards/Whiteboards/Flip Charts: The danger in using these is that you'll have to draw the diagram on the fly – this can be a good thing, if the drawing is not too technical and you can maintain your speech and contact with the audience throughout the talk. However, most presenters will wind up with their back to the audience, focused on drawing, rather than maintaining their rapport with the audience.

PowerPoint (or other presentation program): is both a godsend and a curse. It can help support presentations, but has also been blamed for hiding shoddy engineering or misrepresenting information. When using PowerPoint:

- Make every effort to ensure that the technology works, but prepare for the worst: many presenters have been humbled by an non-functioning, missing or incompatible projector, cables or laptop.
- Avoid using Clip Art and animations, unless they have a specific purpose other than decoration. Animations can slow down the pace of the talk or distract from the content. The "Appear" animation is useful when well integrated with the talk; use it to bring up points on screen when you discuss them. Clip art usually has little purpose and only distract.
- Similarly, choose a presentation template wisely. Avoid garish and low contrast colour schemes that can make text difficult to read.
- When using PowerPoint, you have two dangerous distractions: the laptop screen and the actual screen. Presenters often use the Slide Notes and Presenter View functions instead of hard copy (on a sheet of paper or cue cards) notes. However, be aware that presenters are much more conscious of eye contact when using hard copy notes: you're less likely to read off your notes than you are to read off the computer screen.

Slide timing/number

The amount of time that a slide is left on the projector is an important consideration in planning. As a general rule, slides left on screen for less than 20-30 seconds don't allow enough time for the audience to digest the material properly. Slides should also not be left on the projector after you've finished discussing the material on the slide – take off the slide after you're done with it.

A related issue is the number of slides suitable for a presentation of X minutes. A general guideline is a maximum of 2 x # of minutes in a presentation; any more and you'll be flipping through slides too quickly. Note that the figure is a maximum, not a recommended number.

Using Slides to Make Structure Explicit

Slides can help to make the structure of the talk explicit at the beginning and throughout the presentation. An overview slide is often useful while you outline the path of your presentation; slide titles corresponding to the different components (sometimes numbered) of the talk remind the audience of where they are in the talk.

Introduction to Oral Communication

Oral skills – both speaking and listening – are at the very foundation of literacy. Classroom talk helps students to learn, to reflect on what they are learning, and to communicate their knowledge and understanding. The strategies in this section provide simple but powerful tools for improving communication in every classroom and all subject areas. Whatever you teach, these tools can help you to obtain more precise information about what your students know and can do. This, in turn, can help you to provide better feedback and guidance. Students need authentic opportunities to learn how to listen and speak effectively in a variety of situations – in pairs, and in small and large groups. Students are sometimes assigned an oral activity (e.g., working in small groups) without a clear understanding of what is expected and how to be most effective. By taking the time to teach specific oral strategies in the context of your subject area, you will boost your students' confidence and performance.

Struggling students need:

- encouragement and explicit instruction to build their strengths and address their needs.
- a safe and encouraging environment to practise oral skills, if English is not their first language.
- extra practice, a peer to work with, and support from the teacher before presenting.
- well-chosen partners or team members who can model

knowledge, skills and strategies at a level that is accessible and not intimidating.

Pair Work

Working in pairs provides students with an opportunity to "think aloud" about what they know, and a process for acquiring and reflecting on information. For many students, pair work is a comfortable starting point to practise the skills they will need to participate in larger groups.

Small-group Discussions

As with pair work, the strategies for small-group discussion give students the opportunity to develop critical thinking skills, build positive relationships, work cooperatively, and participate actively in their learning. You can put your students at ease by modelling effective skills for small-group discussion and by providing many opportunities to practise these skills in a safe environment.

Whole-class Discussions

Students learn more readily in a class where they experience cooperation and a sense of belonging. By involving the whole class in shared activities, and by teaching students how to be good listeners, to respect each other and to participate without fear, you can maximize participation and minimize anxiety for all students.

Presentations

Presenting in front of a class can be a terrifying experience. Most students dread the class presentation, especially if they have not had enough instruction or practice before evaluation. By taking time to teach effective presentation skills before such an assignment, you free the student to focus on the content instead of the "performance." The quality of presentations improves with effective instruction, practice and support.

Pair Work: Think/Pair/Share In this strategy, students individually consider an issue or problem and then discuss their ideas with a partner.

Purpose Encourage students to think about a question, issue, or reading, and then refine their understanding through discussion with a partner.

Payoff

Students will:

- reflect on subject content.
- deepen understanding of an issue or topic through clarification and rehearsal with a partner.
- develop skills for small-group discussion, such as listening actively, disagreeing respectfully, and rephrasing ideas for clarity.

Tips and Resources

- Use Think/Pair/Share in all subject areas for almost any topic. For example: in Business, discuss ethical business practices; in Math, solve a word problem together to better understand the task; in Science, exchange hypotheses before conducting an experiment.
- Use it to help students with their in-class reading. Ask them to read a chapter, think about the ideas, and then take turns retelling the information to a partner.
- Use it at any point during a lesson, for very brief intervals or in a longer time frame.
- Increase the amount of time devoted to Think/Pair/Share, depending on the complexity of the reading or question being considered. This strategy can be used for relatively simple questions and for ones that require more sophisticated thinking skills, such as hypothesizing or evaluating.
- Take time to ensure that all students understand the stages of the process and what is expected of them.
- Review the skills that students need to participate effectively in Think/Pair/Share, such as good listening, turn-taking, respectful consideration of different points of view, asking for clarification, and rephrasing ideas.
- After students share in pairs, consider switching partners

and continuing the exchange of ideas.

- See other strategies, including Take Five and Discussion Web for ways to build on the Think/Pair/Share strategy.

Further Support

- Some students may benefit from a discussion with the teacher to articulate their ideas before moving on to share with a partner.

What Teachers do What Students Do

- Have students read a selection or pre-pare a topic, question, or prompt for a planned Think/Pair/Share activity.
  OR
- Choose a "teachable moment" during the class where the process of reflection and shared discussion would bring deeper understanding, and insert a brief Think/ Pair/ Share activity into the lesson at that point.

In either case:

- Consider the social and academic goals for the Think/ Pair/Share activity, and plan for pairing of particular learners that would further those goals.

Pair Work: Think/Pair/Share

- The Think/Pair/Share is based on information and ideas from a reading selection.
- Ask students to spend several minutes thinking about and writing down ideas.
- Set clear expectations regarding the focus of thinking and sharing to be done.
- Put students in pairs to share and clarify their ideas and understanding.
- Monitor students' dialogue by circulating and listening.
- Formulate thoughts and ideas, writing them down as necessary to prepare for sharing with a partner.
- Practise good active listening skills when working in pairs, using techniques such as paraphrasing what the other

has said, asking for clarification, and orally clarifying their own ideas.

- Call upon some pairs to share their learning and ideas with the whole class.
- Possibly extend the Think/Pair/Share with a further partner trade, where students swap partners and exchange ideas again.
- Consider adding a journal writing activity as a productive follow-up to a Think/Pair/ Share activity.
- Pinpoint any information that is still unclear after the pair discussion, and ask the class and teacher for clarification.

Pair Work: Take Five

In pairs, students take five minutes to orally review a concept and present it to the class, usually at the beginning or end of a class period.

Purpose

- Briefly consolidate or reinforce learning.

Payoff

Students will:

- develop a strategy that can be used to review content material in all areas.
- share responsibility for teaching and reviewing with each other.
- "talk" their way into meaning and understanding through verbal rehearsal.
- perceive continuity with content from class to class, especially when a lot of material is being covered quickly.

Tips and Resources

- Use this review-and-share strategy on a regular basis to reinforce the learning of subject-specific vocabulary.
- Have the take-five pairs present their reviews on sheets of

chart paper, which you can then post in the classroom for ongoing review.

- Try not to pair students who are too far apart in their ability or understanding of the material.

Further Support

- ESL students may benefit from pairing with a partner who speaks the same first language so that they can clarify the concepts in their first language and build more confidently on their prior knowledge.

Pair Work: Take Five

- Decide on a concept from the previous day's lesson for review and consolidation
- Arrange students in "take five" buddies, with a designated student A and student B in each pair.
- Invite students to engage in a Think/Pair/ Share with their partner on a concept, formula, term, etc., from the previous day's work, assigning a different task to the A and B students. (For example, student A recalls or checks notes to find the formula for the volume of a cone, while B does the same for the formula for the volume of a sphere. Each shares the formula with his/her partner. Or student A reviews the process of photosynthesis, while B checks the meaning of all the words/terms in the process.)
- Let students know that one pair will be responsible for reviewing the concept with the whole class.
- Review notes, texts, and other materials relating to the concept being discussed.
- Consolidate learning through sharing, discussing, and clarifying the concepts together.
- Plan how to present the concept to the class if called upon to do so.
- Ask one pair to write the formula/process or concept on the board and review it with the class.

- Repeat the process, if appropriate, by rearranging the pairs and setting another Think/Pair/Share task for review and discussion.
- Support each other as a team in recall-ing and explaining the details to the class.
- Practise and develop the skills of explaining, rephrasing, and clarifying for the class.

Pair Work: Timed Retell

In this strategy, students practise their listening and speaking skills. Students divide into pairs and take turns speaking, listening, and retelling information in timed steps.

Purpose

- Enhance critical thinking skills.
- Create an argument and be concise in its delivery.
- Develop attentive listening skills while sharing viewpoints on an issue.
- Make connections between written and oral skills.

Payoff

Students will:

- share ideas.
- develop listening skills.
- apply skills in different ways – in pairs, small groups, and with the whole class.

Tips and Resources

- Timed Retell can be informal or more formal, as described here. In the more formal approach, students require more confidence.
- Students may make notes during the brief presentations given by their partners.
- It is possible to use this activity with more extensive subject matter. In that case students will need time to properly research the topic and devise their arguments.
- Additional information about peer editing is found in

Writing Strategies: Revising and Editing.

Further Support

- The struggling student may feel uncomfortable speaking in front of the whole class. Students should be given other opportunities to share and practise speaking skills before this assignment.
- As always, consider pairs carefully.

Small-group Discussions: Group Roles Students are divided into groups of a certain size – for example, five members. Each student is assigned a specific role and responsibility to carry out during the small-group discussion.

Purpose

- Encourage active participation by all group members.
- Foster awareness of the various tasks necessary in small-group discussion.
- Make students comfortable in a variety of roles in a discussion group.

Payoff

Students will:

- all speak in small groups.
- have specific roles to fulfil, clearly defining their role in the small group.
- receive positive feedback that is built into the process.
- participate actively in their learning.

Tips and Resources

- It is important to vary the composition of small groups, allowing students the opportunity to work with many classmates of various abilities, interests, backgrounds, home languages, and other characteristics.
- It is a good idea to repeat this activity throughout the year. This will allow students the opportunity to experience different roles and to improve their skills.
- Time the exercise to keep students focused on the task.

- If research is required, involve all students in the process, regardless of their role. This activity provides an excellent way for students to share research and come to a consensus about important information.
- For role ideas, see Student/Teacher Resource, *Sample Role Cards.*
- To encourage students to reflect on their learning, use Student Resource, *Small-group Discussion Reflection Sheet.*

Further Support

- Although it's important to vary the composition of groups, it is also important to consider the particular needs of struggling students.

Small-group Discussions: Group Roles

- Choose the task or topic for discussion.
- Decide how many students will be in each group.
- Decide on the roles for each group mem-ber.
- Prepare role cards for each student.
- For example:

Leader: defines the task, keeps the group on task, and suggests a new way of looking at things.

Manager: gathers and summarizes materi-als the group will need, keeps track of time, and collects materials the group used.

Note maker: records ideas generated by the group, and clarifies the ideas with the group before recording.

Reporter: reports the group's ideas to the class.

Supporter: provides positive feedback for each speaker, makes sure everyone gets a turn, and intercepts negative behaviour.

- Understand the question/task.
- Understand their roles and responsibilities.
- Divide the class into groups.
- Present the parameters of the task.
- Explain time limits and keep track of time.
- Circulate around the room, ensuring that all students are

fulfilling their roles.

- Comment constructively on the group process.
- Fulfil the roles to the best of their abilities.
- Use active listening skills.
- Act positively and encourage other group members.
- Participate fully in the discussion.
- Adhere to the time limits set by the teacher.
- Ask students to individually complete an evaluation of the discussion.
- Put students in groups.
- Debrief with the whole class, asking students to comment on the success, benefits of the exercise.
- Plan to repeat this activity, allowing students to try each of the other roles.
- Complete the *Small-group Discussion Reflection Sheet*.
- Discuss the successes and benefits of using structures/ rules in small groups.

11

Communication Processes for Virtual Organizations

Introduction

Few topics have received more attention in the management literature of recent years than that of virtual organizations. Articles abound on the possibilities of virtual meetings, work teams, offices, factories, firms, and alliances. Given the burgeoning interest in this emerging phenomenon, it is surprising that very little empirical research exists on virtual organizations. Especially lacking are studies of communication processes within virtual organization settings. To help remedy this situation, this Special Issue provides an early window into several important communication processes that occur in virtual contexts. We are pleased to provide readers with a compendium of six articles that, collectively, advance current knowledge of communication processes for virtual organizations. Both single and multi-firm studies are included here, with analyses covering such diverse topics as communication content, communication structure and effectiveness, tradeoffs in electronic and face-to-face relationships, and the use of communication in formation of organizational identity. All of the studies include rigorous analysis and careful measurement of communication, and all take place within naturally occurring organizational contexts, not laboratory settings.

The Special Issue is based on two key premises: (1) technology, organizational structure, and communication patterns are all tightly coupled, and (2) organizational form and communication systems co-evolve, which implies that the meaningful study of one requires an accounting of the other (Koza and Lewin 1998). A wealth of literature on technology and organizations has demonstrated the plausibility of these premises. Beginning with these assumptions the papers in this Issue move forward to study how communication processes and organizational design interplay in the new, "virtual" enterprise.

Virtual Organizing

A virtual organization is a collection of geographically distributed, functionally and/or culturally diverse entities that are linked by electronic forms of communication and rely on lateral, dynamic relationships for coordination. Despite its diffuse nature, a common identity holds the organization together in the minds of members, customers, or other constituents. The virtual organization is often described as one that is replete with external ties, managed via teams that are assembled and disassembled according to need, and consisting of employees who are physically dispersed from one another. The result is a "company without walls" that acts as a "collaborative network of people" working together, regardless of location or who "owns" them. This entity is a new global network created by linking together extant networks of smaller, regional banks. Customers of the regional banks now have the feel of being a part of a large global bank because electronic media bring them the worldwide services of Barclay, though they remain members of the smaller, regional banking entity. In this way, tensions between global and local are reconciled, and smaller groups or firms can exist within larger entities and realize their advantages.

Relationships within the virtual form are tenuous. In fact, a key implication of virtual organizing is that these forms are more reconfigurable, their boundaries are considerably more blurred, and their relationships are more likely to be contractual than traditional forms. Greater switching of tasks, roles, or work assignments is also typical in virtual organizations. This calls "combinatorial freedom," or the ability to dynamically allocate work across people or subgroups depending on workload demands. In some cases, the entities composing the organization may participate in several virtual organizations simultaneously and the virtual organization may not have legal existence. The implications of the virtual form: "unlike its contemporary predecessors, the virtual corporation will appear less a discrete enterprise and more an ever-varying cluster of common activities in the midst of a vast fabric of relationships."

Figure 1. Summary of the attributes of virtual organizing

The component entities of a virtual organization are:

Geographically distributed

Electronically linked

Functionally or culturally diverse

Lateral (versus hierarchically) connected

Making the following organization designs possible:

Highly dynamic processes

Contractual relationships

Edgeless, permeable boundaries

Reconfigurable structures

To summarize, the components (individual workers, teams, departments, units or firms) that make up a virtual organization are geographically distributed, functionally or culturally diverse, electronically linked, and connected via lateral relationships. These attributes enable the organization to dynamically modify business processes to meet market demands, to coordinate via formal and informal contracts, to define the boundaries of the firm differently over time or for different customers or constituencies, and to re-arrange relationships among components as needed. The attributes of virtual organizing and the implications for organization design. It is important to note that these attributes can be applied to employee-employer relationships, to teams, to firms, and to inter-organizational arrangements.

Few pure virtual forms exist today. Instead, aspects of virtuality occur in many business enterprises. For example, although most companies still maintain a divisional structure, they increasingly are forming external relationships with other firms in the form of strategic partnerships, alliances, and outsourcing contracts. Likewise, cross-organizational teams are still rare, but teams inside firm are becoming more geographically distributed and cross-functional. In addition, rapid advancements in telecommunication technologies have enabled more telecommuting and cooperation among physically distributed employees. These trends suggest that firms are acquiring more virtual characteristics than in the past. Even firms that may not look virtual at the surface are organizing selected activities and processes virtually.

Because purely virtual firms are still rare, the processes for developing virtual organizations and the eventual impacts of virtuality are still unknown. Proponents of virtual organizing extol the benefits in terms of greater adaptability, faster response time, and task specialization, while critics argue the potential downsides, including greater conflict, decreased firm loyalty, and higher probability of catastrophic effects. From a communication perspective, both positive and negative attributes might be envisioned. For example, greater geographical reach of the firm might be enabled via electronic communication, but the firm also may struggle with maintaining a coherent identity. Similarly, more participation in discussion by larger groups of people may be possible, but information overload may be a burden to participant; and more efficient communication may be possible but so might greater alienation. Realistically, what will virtual organizing bring? Specifically, how will changes in communication processes support virtual organizations and, in turn, be changed by virtual processes? While exploring these issues, it is important to keep in mind that the virtual organization concept is bound up in our social fascination with the future ýÿ the coming of a new century and our collective imagination for new ways of doing business. The virtual organization provides a metaphor for considering an organization design that is held together, literally, by communication.

Communication in Virtual Organizations

Communication is fundamental to any form of organizing, but it is preeminent in virtual organizations. Without communication, the boundary-spanning among virtual entities would not be possible.

Electronic communication enables parties to link across distance, time, culture, departments, and organizations, thereby creating "anyone/anytime/anyplace" alternatives to the traditional same-time, same-place, functionally-centered, in-house forms of organizational experience. Electronic communication loosens constraints of proximity and structure on communication, making it possible for spatially or organizationally distant parties to exchange messages with one another. Further, electronic communication provides an opportunity to signal interest in forming connections that otherwise would be difficult or impossible to maintain.

In this way, communication is not only the *trigger* for virtual relationships but also can be the *outgrowth* of them (DeSanctis, Staudenmayer and Wong in press). New exchanges between parties, or new relationships, can occur as a result of established connections among distributed entities. Indeed, one of the hopes for virtual organizations is that new connections among entities will result from lateral boundary spanning and blending of expertise. According to this view, the real power of the virtual form is realized when relationships among electronically connected people or firms produce new and/or qualitatively different communication that yields product or process innovation.

Communication in the virtual form is expected to be *rapid* and *customized* in response to customer demands. This implies that communication content and direction are likely to be more *temporary*, as links between organizational entities are formed and dissolved over time. To the extent that lateral relationships in the virtual form substitute for hierarchical channels, *greater volume* of communication should occur, as two-way exchanges among a greater number of people are more likely. To the extent that communication volume is greater, there may be pressure to make some communication more *formal* or programmed in order to gain efficiencies and bring routine to otherwise customized work. Simultaneously, some communication is likely to become more *relationship-based*. Parties may seek a relational basis for transactions so that intimacy can be created in the face of distance, and trust can be established and maintained. Personal relationships and informal contacts are known to be more powerful than formal structures or reward systems in lateral organization designs. Consequently, a likely tension in the virtual form will be simultaneous needs for more and richer communication, on the one hand, and pressures for greater transaction efficiencies, on the other.

The exact nature of communication processes in virtual forms, their antecedents and consequences are, of course, unknown as of yet. However, it is possible to glean some insight from the rich body of literature on synchronous and asynchronous electronic organizational communication. Communication in the virtual organization certainly will become more *electronically mediated* than in the past, and the vast set of empirical findings regarding mediated communication can foreshadow how communication will change as firms "go virtual."

Implications of Electronic Communication Research

Six areas of electronic communication research provide implications for the four major aspects of virtual organization design:

(a) highly dynamic processes,

(b) contractual relationships among entities,

(c) edgeless, permeable boundaries, and

(d) reconfigurable structures.

When reviewing these six literatures, it is important to keep in mind that most findings are based on the study of electronic mail and computer conferencing systems rather than other forms of electronic communication, such as group voting, decision modeling systems, document management systems, or electronic data interchange. Further, most of the research compares electronic communication to spoken language, especially face-to-face communication, despite the fact that electronic communication has many properties similar to written language.. Like face-to-face conversation, electronic communication is interactive, but like document preparation electronic communication is typically edited. As a result, behaviour in electronic communication settings takes on characteristics of both document writing and informal speech.

Communication Volume and Efficiency

Compared to face-to-face communication, most studies find that implementation of electronic communication increases the overall amount of communication. Where research has shown that communication has decreased, the result has been explained in terms of reduction of back-channel information such as speech acknowledgements and social greetings. There is no doubt that people perceive significant differences in communication channels, but the hierarchy of preference is not clear. For example, some authors report a general preference for face-to-face and telephone over computer-based conversations, while others find that people choose media based on convenience. Assuming communication volume goes up in virtual organizations, intense pressures for communication efficiency should also occur. But the research suggests that gains in communication efficiency for a given task, especially problem solving tasks, may be difficult to achieve electronically. The literature strongly suggests that problem solving and task completion are not faster when electronically mediated. Further, face-to-face meetings are faster even where tasks are low in complexity. Voice-based modes of electronic communication, in particular, are efficient for task completion even though people use twice the number of words to communicate than in pure text. It may be that the addition of high-speed voice capability to electronic mail will yield efficiency gains for organizations in the future, but for the time being the research is not encouraging in terms of the ability of electronic communication to reduce communication volume or improve task efficiencies such as reducing product development cycles. Achieving the kinds of efficiencies that are needed in the dynamic process design of virtual organizations is going to be a challenge, indeed.

Message Understanding

Successful communication requires the establishment of mutual knowledge, and parties use physical and linguist co-presence to make inferences about one anotherýÿs knowledge. This implies that lack of face-to-face contact in electronic communication may negatively impact message understanding, but the literature is confusing on this point. Electronically mediated groups have been found to have more difficulty establishing meaning of information and managing feedback in discussion. But it has also been shown that removing visual channels from conversation does not significantly disrupt conversational control and understanding. In fact, there may be some value in reducing the visual channel in interaction. For example, the evaluations of others (e.g., interviewers evaluating job applicants) are less stereotyped and more valid when visual observation is removed from communication. The implication is that removal of visual cues may actually improve the quality of message understanding, at least in some cases, by removing the distraction of irrelevant stimuli.

The key to effectiveness in interaction is strong maintenance of mutuality of the conversational model. Some studies show individuals take longer to form impressions of one another when conversing electronically because it takes longer to decode social cues. Nevertheless, mutual understanding via electronic media is certainly possible. In addition to physical and linguist co-presence, participants in communication also use their community membership to make inferences about one another knowledge. Parties apply the norms of social context to interpret messages and respond accordingly. This means that, compared with face-to-face interaction, the social and normative context may be of even greater importance in computer-mediated communication. Given sufficient contextual information, mutual understanding can be very high in electronic communication. Parties can become highly cohesive across distances, and electronic conversation can evolve to take on the attributes of a social community. The implication of this line of research is that, despite pitfalls, electronic communication can support effective relationships among parties. The key is to identify the specific contextual conditions that facilitate effective relationship maintenance. To the extent that mutual understanding can be achieved via electronic communication, the implications for virtual organizations are positive. As virtual organizations form and re-form their business processes, they would do well to provide rich contextual information to communicating parties; this could heighten message understanding and shorten the time that might otherwise be required to establish mutuality of the conversational model.

Virtual Tasks

Researchers have invested considerable effort in isolating the conditions under which electronic communication is most effective. A number of years ago scholars proposed that as channel capacity decreases from face-to-face to telephone to computer-based systems and memos, the medium becomes less rich. They proposed that for equivocal tasks, face-to-face meetings should be used, and for unequivocal messages lean media such as written memos should be used. Their theory has not been supported by the research data, however. For example, a number of studies report no superiority of video communication (greater channel capacity), over audio or text-based media (less channel capacity); and matching channel capacity to task equivocality has not been found to improve performance. Nonetheless, the belief that face-to-face interaction is more powerful than mediated interaction continues to exist in popular writing on virtual organizations.

It is concluded from a case study that the face-to-face mode of communication was appropriate for building a shared interpretive context among parties; conversely, computer-mediated communication was more appropriate for communicating within an established context. But in many other studies the "task-medium fit" hypothesis has not been supported. The modality can influence task more than the other way around. In their study, people were more task-oriented on the telephone than face-to-face, and modality influenced the weighting of task goals. If task complexity is, in parallel fashion, influenced by medium, then the core rationale underlying the task-media fit hypothesis is seriously undermined.

About the only consistent finding in the empirical literature with regard to task and media is that groups are more effective in divergent thinking tasks when communicating electronically rather than face-to-face, especially (but not only) if the communication is done anonymously. Thinking convergently, resolving conflict, or reaching consensus, however, is better done face-to-face than electronically. In other words, electronic communication facilitates information sharing but can make consensus formation more difficult in time limited contexts. Scholars explain that face-to-face groups can more readily reach under-standing and sense-making of information than electronic groups. The implication is that certain organizational tasks, or types of work, may be more effective when performed in virtual mode than others; in particular, exchanges involving knowledge elicitation or sharing may more readily lend themselves to the virtual mode than those involving consensus formation or conflict resolution. This puts limits on the kinds of work that might be managed via external, contractual relationships among entities in the virtual network. Further, it suggests that some tasks may require more structured or formal relationships when managed across boundaries whereas others might be effective with less structured or formal relationships. There is a great need for research that isolates the task conditions that are most effective in virtual settings as well as the kinds of contractual arrangements that work best with a given type of task.

Lateral Communication

Perhaps the most encouraging result from the literature is the demonstrated capability of electronic communication to support lateral communication and broad participation across social groups. Virtual organizing presumes that coordination occurs less through hierarchy and more through transactional exchange and network relationships, thereby enabling faster, more customer-responsive information flow. Numerous studies report that parties communicating electronically are less prone to domination by high-status members than face-to-face groups; electronic groups also display greater equality of participation. Of course, these patterns are not guaranteed, and some studies fail to find the expected flattening of communication hierarchies. Still, electronic mail, in particular, has been shown to complement general work networks and provide more diverse, participative and less formally aligned relations. In one study it is reported on electronic communication patterns of technical and administrative employees within and between departments of a large telecommunications firm. They discovered high levels of lateral communication and inter-departmental communication and a notable preference for synchronous technologies to support lateral communication. Consistent with prior findings on influence of social norms, they reported more boundary-crossing communication in less hierarchical work groups. Overall, the findings of this literature support the notion that electronic communication can enable boundary spanning among culturally or functionally diverse parties of virtual enterprises.

Norms of Technology Use

Early on, researchers thought that electronic communication would be stripped of social context cues and would tend to be task-focused rather than relational, and free-wheeling rather than socially controlled. But more recent studies show that relationship-oriented communication can be high in electronic media settings and that electronic communication is heavily influenced by surrounding social norms. Numerous studies show that electronic communication patterns are less a function of the medium per se than of the norms, practices, and social conditions surrounding media use. Even low channel-capacity media, such as text-based electronic mail, can be used for complex communication if the organization encourages and supports it. In addition, individuals, groups and organizations develop certain electronic communication styles or practices.

Individuals are known to develop rhetorical styles of communication that can transfer to the electronic medium. Some styles, for example, reflect high concern about confidentiality whereas others do not; hence, some individuals are more prone to be concerned about confidentiality in electronic mail than others. Similarly, individual differences can determine who dominates electronic discussion, and these differences can overpower media effects. Groups can develop stylistic communication patterns as a function of the particular parties involved and the emergent dynamics of their interaction. As a result, there are extensive variances in the ways that people use electronic communication media, whether individuals or groups.

Many studies, demonstrate that parties project personal styles, previous experiences and social norms of interpersonal interaction into electronic conversations. The potential for conflict is substantial as communication in the virtual organization takes place across organizational and social boundaries and as the cultural and professional diversity of relationships increases. Further, the dynamic nature of the virtual organization may make it difficult for electronic communication styles to "gel" or develop new, standard norms for communicating. Participants in virtual relationships may do well to make communication norms explicit in advance and to establish procedures for reconciling differences in communication practices that emerge as they do business across multiple boundaries. As business processes are redesigned, organizations will have to simultaneously find ways to preserve the beneficial norms that have been established while promoting newer ones that are more appropriate to the redesign.

Evolutionary Effects

There is little doubt that the dynamics of electronic communication in the enterprise may be different in the long run than in the short run. New communities with potentially differing perspectives and social realities from those of today are likely to emerge as more persons read and write on computer networks. Electronic classrooms, for example, have been shown to evolve their own communication patterns that are kindred to yet substantively different from traditional classrooms. Impressions of others, impression management, and the degree and type of relational communication all change over the course of electronic interactions. As noted earlier, longer-term interactions tend to improve message understanding and deepen interpersonal relationships. The evolution of relationships in the context of electronic communication occurs both "in the small" of individual relationships and "in the large" of entire communities. A question that arises, then, is the viability of rapidly configurable, or disposable, structures in virtual organizations to sustain these longer term interactions. Organizations may have to figure out which aspects of communication they can disrupt and re-arrange and which they should allow to evolve over longer periods.

It may be that electronic communication products, such as conversations and documents stored in knowledge repositories, can provide stability to otherwise tenuous relationships. Perhaps communication histories from one setting can be carried into the communication future of other settings via evolving databases. The issues of volume, load, task, and message understanding are significant, particularly for complex information exchanges and problem solving. Future research might consider how electronic communication products might be used to support the evolutionary aspects of communication in dynamic networks and reconfigurable organizational settings. For example, it may be that transactive memory systems, the context-specific and unique communication processes that develop within a group and guide knowledge sharing, can be somehow formalized and re-applied when groups are dissembled and re-arranged.

Research Directions

There is no doubt that new developments in organizational structure, practices, and communication technology can promote the construction of new organization designs. Considerable theory and evidence shows this to be true. At the same time, the literature just reviewed reveals the complexities involved in shaping communication processes for virtual organizations. Electronic media can do much to enable highly dynamic processes, contractual relationships, permeable boundaries, and reconfigurable structures. But the challenges are many due to the complexities of achieving communication efficiency and message understanding in electronic mode; the uncertainty surrounding design of tasks in virtual mode; and the powerful role of norms, hierarchical relationships, and evolutionary effects.

Perhaps the core issue for managers is determining the actions they might take to influence what the firms of the future will become. "Genres" of communication processes in virtual organizations may evolve on their own. But what can managers do to shape the design of the boundaryless, flexible enterprise and to encourage productive and healthy communication processes? In addition to uncovering relationships among technology, structure, and communication, researchers should direct attention to specifying and evaluating strategies for organizational members. Possibilities include embedding procedural templates for communication into electronic media, goal setting and specification of desired norms for communication, or use of mediators to facilitate usersýÿ interaction with technology and to alter contexts of use. Finally, given the emphasis placed on trust, cohesion and identity in virtual forms, team building interventions may help organizations to manage communication and build mutual understanding among virtual participants.

The articles in this Special Issue address several important questions:

- How will the frequency and content of communication change in virtual organizations?
- To what extent can electronic networks substitute for personal relationships as inter-firm coordination mechanisms?
- Will formalized, programmable communication replace more informal, customized communication?
- What does it take for remote workers to be effective in their jobs?
- How will virtual organizations maintain cohesion and a sense of organizational identity?
- Can virtual teams effectively form trust? What does it take to maintain trust in virtual teams?

Grabowski and Roberts ("Risk Mitigation in Virtual Organizations") review the properties of virtual organizations and provide a series of propositions on how virtual organizations engage in risk mitigation. They argue that the content of communication in virtual organizations will include more discussion of safety issues and efforts to clarify goals, relationships and responsibilities than in traditional firms. Kraut and colleagues report on a large sample study of managers from four different industries. They find that electronic communication complements personal relationships more than it substitutes for them; their finding suggests that increased electronic communication does not necessarily lead to efficiencies in overall organizational communication. Further, the existence of personal relationships between a firm and a potential supplier predicts use of electronic networks to coordinate production. Outsourcing contracts, it seems, are based on more than evaluation of contract terms. Ahuja and Carley ("Network Structures in Virtual Organizations") examine the communication structure and content of a virtual research and development group. They find the communication structure in the group to be more hierarchical and centralized than the virtual organization literature would suggest. They also examine the relationship among structure, task routineness and performance as they attempt to uncover the reasons for lack of anticipated lateral communication in the virtual team. Staples and colleagues ("A Self-Efficacy Theory Explanation for the Management of Remote Workers in Virtual Organizations") report on a survey of remotely managed workers from 18 organizations. They find that remote worker effectiveness depends on remote work self-efficacy, experience in working remotely, and information technology capability. The competencies required to effectively manage remote workers include good listening skills, time management, information technology skills, and maintaining ample availability to remote workers.

Wiesenfeld, Raghuram, and Garud ("Communication Patterns as Determinants of Organizational Identification in a Virtual Organization") also report on a study of virtual workers. They find that use of electronic communication significantly relates to identification regardless of the degree of oneýÿs virtual status. Their study provides empirical support for the proposition that electronic communication can aid organizational identification and act to bind together otherwise scattered members of a virtual enterprise. Jarvenpaa and Leidner ("Communication and Trust in Global Virtual Teams") conclude this Special Issue with a report on global virtual teams whose members are separated by location and culture while working on a common collaborative project; their only economically and practically viable coordination mechanism is electronic communication. The teams experience a form of "swift" trust, but such trust is fragile and temporal. They find that communication related to the task activities of the project is crucial to maintaining trust in these teams and that, contrary to some claims, social communication complements rather than substitutes for task communication in teams with persistent trust. Their results are some of the first empirical insights into trust development in global virtual teams.

This Special Issue marks an important advance in the study of communication for virtual organizations. Yet considerable further development is required to achieve the kinds of scientific knowledge that will enable practical, prescriptive statements about how to manage communication for virtual organizations. This burgeoning area of scholarship needs extensive theoretical development, conceptual explication, philosophical analyses, empirical research, and substantive criticism. The articles in this Special Issue should provide significant impetus to these future endeavors.

Effective Communication in the Virtual World

Effective communication in the virtual world can be tricky. After all, you're communicating with people you don't know. Communicating effectively without knowing a person isn't easy. It's impossible to know what angle will work with a person when you don't know anything about them. Also, a huge part of communication revolves around body language and eye contact and you don't have these key points via the Internet. This puts everyone at a large disadvantage when we are tying to understand someone and they are trying to understand us.

In face-to-face communication or telephone conversations, we can rely on a person's voice to help us determine what the person is feeling. On the Internet, we don't have this advantage, either. There are ways to communicate in the right way virtually, though. It just takes a small effort to remember a few things.

Email

Be clear and concise when you use email as a way to communicate. For some reason, people feel email is looser than regular written communication. It shouldn't be. You need to use email as if it were written on paper. The old adage say what you mean and mean what you say is good advice in any form of communication. It's even more important in business emails to be just as formal and correct as you would have been on paper. If you send business emails out full of chatspeak and emoticons, you won't be taken seriously. Save the chatspeak and cutesy emoticons for your friends.

IM

Instant Messages can sometimes be hard to decipher. Is that a typo or did the other person really mean they do want to take a phone call. So be careful when using IMs. Make sure you take your time and what you meant to say is what you actually typed.

Message Boards/Forums

Be aware, some people on the Internet can be downright cruel because of the anonymous factor. So go into any message board or forum with the attitude that someone might just be rude on purpose. That said, don't ever behave this way. Just because it seems anonymous, remember there truly is another human on the receiving end of your words. And you never know what damage you can be inflicting on another person. That's not who you want to be.

When in Doubt-If you are ever unsure of what a person meant to say virtually, no matter what form we're talking about, ask! Miscommunication is so easy via Internet. People tend to read into another person's words because there are so many key communication elements missing. Instead of guessing, just come out and ask parts of any message you do not understand. That's the best way to effectively communicate in any situation.

Avoid the Pitfalls of the Communication Blackhole

The advantages of working with a virtual team and having virtual clients are many. Among those advantages are less idle chatter, no annoying co-worker popping by just when you are in a zone, and in general the quiet. That is also a disadvantage. It is much harder to build a relationship with a team member and pick up on eachother's silent cues and Non-verbal communication. The only solution is to use virtual tools and to probably in your mind, over communicate.

In the beginning-Setup and communicate with your team and with clients your best means of communication. Do you like email? Do you prefer the phone? Can you be reached only at certain hours? Make sure everyone knows how they are expected to communicate, how often, and when.

Email

While not perfect email is still the best method of communicating and documenting the work process. Make sure everyone "whitelists" you and adds you to their contact list. Make sure you add them to your contact list. Sometimes file size for attachments is an issue. Make sure you know if their service will block large files and find ways of dealing with it.

Telephone

Sometimes it is just easier to pick up the phone. I find it much easier to work out a complex question or if you feel you are not getting it, in person. Frustration comes from not having all the information or not getting the emotions behind the written communication. Schedule periodic phone check-ins, preferrably weekly, so you can get that personal interaction and just clear the air.

Instant Messenger, Chat, Texts

These are great resources to talk out situations as well if one or more of you can't be on the phone for whatever reason. It is still hard to get a handle on true feelings if it is a sticky situation but the communication is real time and may be better than a disconnected email conversation. There are several programs out there. Make sure you know which ones everyone uses and try to get a concensus on what you will use.

Snail mail and fax

While very "old school" it still is necessary at times. Check into online faxing tools like eFax and it will save you a ton of time and resources, but will give you a professional look with a real fax number.

Now that you have the tools in place, communicate with clients whenever you work on their projects. In the email include:

- What tasks you worked on
- If needed the hours spent
- What you still need to do
- Any questions you have
- Any suggestions you have

When dealing with your team virtually consider these communication tips:

- Consider a weekly team meeting, via conference call or skype.
- Get a project planning software that everyone can update and have access to. Basecamp, Microsoft Project, or another program will do the trick. This will foster greater communication and anyone can look at the project and know where it is at.
- Treat your team like clients. Make sure you are communicating with them regularly to make sure they know your piece of the puzzle is being worked on and moving forward.
- Let them know when you will be available, unreachable, and in general what your working hours will be.

Communicating virtually provides freedom and flexibility. It can cause problems if not done consistently, effectively and in a manner that really speaks to your team and your clients. Without the advantage of the spoken word and being present to pick up on Non-verbal cues, you really have to make an effort to over communicate. What feels to you like over the top may be just right for the person you are keeping in the loop.

12

Non-verbal Communication: Making Sense of Communicative Technologies

Media Ecology and Information Technologies

Myths About the Media

The Reality Myth

This myth suggests that the media present reality as it is. Reality, of course, is created by individuals in interaction with others. The media represent or mediate social reality. Cyber-reality is a visual fabrication of everyday life. It is not everyday life, although it may influence the work and play of individuals.

The Media Distribution Myth

This myth implies that the media are distributed evenly throughout society; in actuality, people have differential access to the media. Although this is changing, the aged, the poor and some members of ethnic groups do not have the same access as do mainstream White Americans.

The Uniform Influence Myth

This myth suggests that all people are uniformly influenced by the media. In actuality, the background of people, their age, ethnicity, gender and culture influence their use and interpretations, as advertisers know.

The Mediated Construction of Reality

The printing press and the telegraph were precursors to the advent of television and the computer. "What hath God Wrought?" the question asked by Morse, sent more than 150 years ago from Washington to Baltimore on the telegraph, foreshadowed the emergence of the modern, electronic society. The telegraph and the telephone, created in 1876, deeply influenced the patterning of society before the age of computers and television. Communicative technologies, such as television, radio and the internet have, in a similar way, substantially altered the ways that humans do things.

Framing the Construction of Reality

Searle suggests that there are three parts to the construction of reality. The three parts are objective reality, or the factual world, what Searle has called the brute facts; symbolic reality, such as art forms, plays, literature, media contents; and subjective reality, which is the reality constructed by the individual on the basis of objective and symbolic reality..

That the media influence human society is clear; just how they do so is less than clear. A variety of theories have been proposed in the scientific study of the media. How a television program is framed is important.

Is a program that deals with pornography framed as a problem for womens' rights; or, is it presented as pleasurable for men? The way it is framed influences how the situation is defined. Perhaps more than any other theorist, Marshall McLuhan gave the study of the media an early push, an impetus. He declared that the medium not only bears a message, but it is a message by itself. The popular phrase is that the medium is the message.

This seminal work delineated the ways in which human society is altered and influenced by the type of media that is dominant at a given time. The oral world was different from the newer print world and the print world was very different from the world of television. Each medium has its own type of influence on human behaviour. Whole civilizations have been variously influenced by their technologies. Runners bore messages in ancient civilizations. The quipu was used to count in early Incan societies. Smoke was used as a signalling mechanism by early Americans. Satellites flash messages instantly in the modern world. Technologies, created by humans, return the compliment; they are involved in creating societies, influencing human affairs.

Designs for Human Action

The media have been referred to as designs for society. Their built-in structure and the ways they are used influence and pattern human behaviours. For example, members of a pastoral sheep raising society, an oral society, having few or no communicative technologies, are likely to talk face-to-face about events in their lives. Intersubjective, shared meanings are deeply imbedded in the pastoral setting. Time slows down and the pace of events is slowed. The sheepherder's sense of place is keen. He eats no fast food. It is likely that the lives of his sheep-raising parents and grandparents were very similar; they lived the same way. If a person was identified as a sheepherder, everyone in a pastoral society knew what that meant. Daily life was routine, patterned and continuous. Seasons changed the patterns, but the sheepherder identity remained intact. All is different in modern society. Technologies intrude in human affairs, shaping and altering how people communicate. They constitute designs for human human action and behaviour.

New Forms of Sociodrama

The SI approach emphasizes the dramaturgical behaviour of humans in interaction. Humans engage in daily mini-sociodramas. They act toward others as though they were performing a role on stage; things may be going on backstage but people are attentive to what they must do to accomplish tasks or plans. Television, film, the radio and the internet have become part of the sociodrama of everyday life. True, they present artificial sociodramas, but people interact with them as though they were real. The media present symbolic messages to people who make sense of them in terms of their experiences. By comparing the media content to real world content, individuals come to terms with the meaning of the media presentation.

Television "talks" in the sense that the producers may try to send specific messages, especially through advertising. Programs bear messages. Advertisers and organizations deliberately target their messages. For example, The Health Education Council produced an anti-smoking ad showing a young child in a wheel chair smoking; the child was asked how many cigarettes he smoked. The viewer filled in the blanks. This process of filling in the blanks occurs in all visual presentations, film or television; it occurs as well in the messages that are exchanged on the internet. Each activity engages the individual in an active symbolizing process.

Perhaps American have a taste for things that are slick and colorful. Television producers sometimes seem to act as though that were the case. It has been said that if one has taste, he loses interest in television, an interesting statement from a writer who spent time on the major networks. On the other hand, it appears that television is furnishing the bridge between the 'lively classical arts' and the tastes of the everyday viewer. One can watch professional wrestling or one may watch an opera, not by sitting in an auditorium, but by sitting in her home, merely switching channels. Mediated reality is instantly available. There is no requirement that one drive or walk to a theatre or to purchase tickets in advance. As one television critic put it, we have "instant everything".

The internet is synchronously interactive, providing a forum in which imagination plays an important role. Often, one person in interaction with another via e-mail, forums or chat groups, does not know who the other party is. This aspect of the internet tends to mask identities. People can pretend to be who they are not. Masks have been used over the centuries in drama, as in China, to disguise or create new characters, but the electronic mask is modern, requiring little training to use. The internet enables a person to put on new face. The computer, like television, is a design for action.

Pervasiveness of Electronic Media

It is argued that the electronic media, including television, have created changes in physical spaces, including things as basic as shopping malls and as large as cities in dramatic ways.

Fun and pleasure, as well as crime, are associated with these places. Not only do people have telepresence, they have co-presence; that is, television sets and other communicative devices are everywhere that people are.

Television is found in nearly every public quarter. Bars and restaurants, hospital waiting rooms, automobiles, and even camps in the distant mountains have television screens. In some places, screens may be so large that they seem to engulf the audience. Humans seem not to tire of watching human behaviour. The author remembers watching a Superbowl and by switching channels, he could watch the war in Iraq! Both activities were real in that they were really happening, but they were mediated, altered by the technology of television.

Family eating patterns traditionally centered on the dining room table where face-to-face communication took place. Discussion about daily matters was important at the dinner table. Television displaced the family table; now, family members may gather around the television set located in the entertainment center, eating a fast-food take-out. In very practical ways, technologies shape human behavioural patterns; they are designs for living influencing how people relate to one another.

Human Extensions

Early scholarship focused on the effects of tool use by humans. All tools, from the use of a pencil to the use of e-mail extend the potential for human interaction, just as the bulldozer extends the ability of humans to change the surface of the earth. The effects are often taken for granted, not felt or observed in everyday life. How many people ask or think about how the use of pencil and paper created new patterns of interaction in everday behaviour? It is the business of scholars to ask these questions. Yet, the effects on the daily life of the student is obvious, even pronounced. Writing, whether on papyrus or modern paper, stabilizes society, leading to the storage of knowledge in libraries. In short, pencils, used to write, extend the fingers and the mind. All communicative technologies are symbolic extensions of human behaviour.

The printing press of course increased the speed with which

humans could exchange their printed messages. Today, the creation of new technologies or twists on older ones, many very sophisticated, is mushrooming. It is not a slow, linear process; it is, seemingly, an exponential process. The half-life of technological invention is reduced more and more, as Moore's Law suggests. In other words, technologies have always influenced human behaviour. But previous inventions came about relatively slowly. In present times new inventions are produced in very short periods of time. One of the outcomes of this shortened time period between inventions is that young people may introduce their parents to a new technology, not the other way around, as in the past.

Human Nonverbal Communication

Television and the internet diffentially influence human behaviour as discussed in the following sections.

Television and Advertising

As mentioned above, researchers want to know how human behaviour is influenced by the media, essentially television in this case. Television, of course, is a relatively recent invention, not available to the masses until after mid-century. A number of research approaches or models have been used.

Framing Research Models

The "bullet theory", a naive and simplistic theory of the power of television to influence people directly, was used in early research. The use of propaganda in WW II influenced the development of this model. Propaganda was a one-way process, designed to make people think or do things. The Americans and their Allies and the Germans and the Axis powers used propaganda extensively. The bullet theory suggested that, as in the trajectory of a bullet, the message reached its target, the audience, directly and it was received as it was sent. But media messages must fall upon "ready soil" so to speak; humans must be ready to accept them, to interpret and use them, and they do so in various ways. Messages may have little direct influence as suggested by the bullet theory.

Cultivation theory suggests that heavy users of television differ from light users in how they use television and in the ways that they are influenced by it. Heavy users may "resonate" more with the topic shown on television than do light users. Television may also produce a general climate of fear or uncertainty in some populations. For example, women may fear crime more than males do; even though both may be watching the same program, males and females may differ in the in the fear or apprehension that is triggered by the program. In short, televised programs and advertisements differentially influence viewers even though they may be watchin the televised activity.

As mentioned, one of the key ways that television influences human behaviour is through advertising. Advertising is basically about persuasion designed usually, but not always, to make money. Advertisers "construct" their audiences; that is, they aim at women or men, children or parents, Blacks, Whites, Hispanics, or other target groups. Once the audience is constructed, advertisers find ways to get the attention of people in that audience, using bright colours, sexual themes, or other ways that are known to gain attention. Persuasive communications try to tap the emotions or they try to associate well-known people with the product. They may even try to shock an audience to get attention.

Whatever persuasive technique they use, they try to build a symbolic bridge to the audience; they try to create a need in the mind of the viewer for the product. Advertisers will try to sell their product by showing how it will benefit the purchaser; they will claim that their product is superior, more beautiful, more useful or in some way better than other products, presenting this information as "fact". Unlike the use of propaganda which is essentially a one-way process designed to "brainwash" viewers, television producers try to engage the viewer interactively with their presentation. By engaging his emotions and his mind, their chances of selling their products to him are increased. Perhaps he will not go out and buy a product immediately, but the images are there for future reference. In short, advertisers know that by appealing to basic human needs, values or identities, they can tug at feelings, influence the emotions and move people to act, to purchase their product.

On the other hand, advertisements may be designed to keep

their product name in front of a target audience. They may want everybody to join the "millions" who have bought their product. The fact that MacDonald's claims to have sold billions of hamburgers influences some people to buy using the kind of reasoning that suggests that if so many people have bought them, they must be good. People who are not aware of the persuasive techniques used in these advertisements may be uncritical about the product, a situation that helps the advertiser achieve her or his goals.

Audiences, of course, are not real entities; they are constructed abstractions, used for a purpose, as in advertising. Advertisers construct the audience that they wish to target, a children's audience being very different from an adult audience. The age, gender and race are important to advertisers, who pitch their products directly at them. Although there is considerable discussion in modern American society about whether, how, or how much television and film influence young people in good and bad ways, clearly there are effects and influences; otherwise, businesses would not spend millions of dollars to sell their products nor would so much effort be spent studying their effects. Nor wood scholars be studying the impact of television on children's nonverbal behaviour. Dr. Robert S. Feldman, at the University of Massachussetts, has set up an internet site designed precisely to study how television impacts on children's behaviours. He believes that television distorts or exaggerates real life and that it draws upon limited emotions, such as anger, happiness and sadness.

Advertisers, of course, are part of the mix. They lead their customers to their products, using clever, attractive, emotional messages. Some advertisers have even used seductive ways to influence viewers, as in subliminal advertising. How much subliminal advertising really works is not clear, although popular books have been written about the process.

Subliminal processes operate below the threshold of the senses; they are said to 'work' on the subconscious mind in suggestive ways. Whether they work or not remains an issue. Their use has been the subject of legal controversy. For example, advertisers have produced subliminal messages in films seen in theaters, hoping that without realizing it, members in the audience will be motivated by the subliminal message to buy their product. Of course, theree are serious, ethical issues involved in the use of undisclosed, hidden messages, designed to make people do things. Whether the message works or not is another question, although those professionals who practice hypnotism may have a special understanding of how it works. Mead referred to humans as walking somnambulists, meaning that people at times may move about, without realizing they have done so, as in sleepwalking. On one hand, advertising presents an opportunity for businesses to present their products in responsible ways on television and on the internet.

On the other hand, another view of advertising says that it is saturated with excessive and obsessive commercialism, with sensationalism and distortion in an attempt to get to the audience, the effect being to distort the consumers's world. As has been said "there are no plain women on television," a statement attributed to John Ford, a producer; television needs beautiful women and advertisers frequently play up the beautiful body to sell a product.

Television, of course, conveys visual symbolism to people. MTV, a relatively new television format owned by Viacom, the owner of CBS Television, targets a specific audience, using youthful images and music that is appealing to mostly a Black audience. Children's programs rely upon fuzzy lifeless characters that come alive in a child's imagination, as in Sesame Street on public broadcasting networks. Indeed, PBS stations intentionally downplay advertising so that 'cultural' programs are less influenced by commercial advertising. Jock sports and extreme sports are aimed at young males. In short, symbols that appeal to different audiences are continually created to build a bridge to that audience. Not all audience members respond to the same symbolism in the same ways.

The Computer and the Internet

Internet has become a powerful socializing tool. One need only read the articles that are presented in Wired Magazine or through the Hypermedia Research Centre see the impact of the internet. Cybersociology Magazine is advertises itself as a forum for the discussion of the social scientific study of cyberspace. The internet influences human behaviour in ways that are different from the influence of television. As mentioned, people can mask their identities on the internet, but they also gain access to information, to chat groups, to friends, even to college courses on the internet. In short, the internet via the computer has radically altered behavioural patterns, some of them negative.

The computer and the internet have brought about technospeak, new words that originate with specialists and become part of the public lexicon. New words, such as emoticons, netizens (net-citizens) and netropolis (net-metropolis), cyberpunk, spamming, hyper-reality, and cyber-rapture are part of a new language used by tekkies. A netiquette is a type of coded communication used in a virtual community where geographical boundaries do not exist.

The Media as Influences

The concept of multiple selves, as a normal growth pattern, but in the blur of activities that are associated with television and the internet, young people may struggle with identity formation or suffer from chronic revision of who they are, resulting in neurasthenia or anomie. A replacement of real persons by artificial persons, the abandonment of the essential self, may occur due to the effects of television, the internet and other salient mediating technologies. In short, there may be unintended, latent and negative influences resulting from the use of modern communicative technologies. How directly television influences behaviour varies, but certainly there are copycat behaviours. As mentioned, television promotes the perfectly formed woman to viewers. To be contemporary, the media must promote a woman whose sizes and BMI index are very different from a few years ago when women were shorter and a bit heavier. Today, the models are thinner and taller, as the beauty queens attest. The image of beauty queens, projected on television, becomes a template, a looking glass, against which one measures herself. Some women, unfortunately, are negatively influenced. Women can become anorexic or buliminic as they strive to achieve the perfect BMI. Some people, of course, already have unhealthy goals; such depiction on television or in print media can increase the state of unhealth.

Given the saturation of society by the print, film and television media it has been strongly suggested that the formation of the identity process is made difficult and confusing. Media effects and influences are dynamic and pervasive. A media culture immerses every person in it. People are bathed in a society saturated by the media..

Television and Violence

American society has always been violent, varying from one period to another, as noted in the Westward movement in early America. Violence is known to all societies, some being violent more than others. The classic Marxist position is that the story of humankind is the story of stuggle, members of one class against members of another. In some ways, it appears that the media, especially television, are mere overlays of the everyday routines of society that have contributed to the structure of dominance, which suggests that the violence that is found in society will continue to be found on television.

Scholars have focused on the relationship between television and violence. Some scholars suggest that viewing TV violence has a cathartic effect; in other words, viewing violence is a way of reducing the likelihood that the viewer will be violent because it channels and diffuses violent tendencies. Others hold very different perspectives.

For example, a major study called The Great American Values Test revealed that viewers of a specially designed program changed their values after watching it; people who were dependent on television, compared to those who watched it less, changed their values more by comparison. In short, television programs can and do influence people, especially those who are dependent upon it. The issue of whether and how television influences people, their beliefs and behaviour is salient in contemporary society where young people are shown in the media shooting one another, bullying each other and increasingly engaging in crimes. The question naturally arises about the role of the media in influencing the behaviours. It was reported in 1973 that by age 12, the average child had watched 101,000 violent episodes on television, including 13,400 deaths. It would be interesting to know if the same pattern holds in present-day society.

Popular materials, such as television programs, films and internet communications, do not by themselves contain meaning. Humans create and attach meanings to them. Mediated 'reality' is not life reality; rather, it is representive of life having enough life-like characteristics to make it recognizable. When it appeals to the way that humans think and make sense of their worlds, communicative technologies are influential. Indeed, cults can form around the presentations of television and film.

Cultish Behaviours

People devote strong attachments to a person, a principle or types of fads. Often, mass media create cultish followings, such as those formed around the Grateful Dead or Madonna. Star Wars, The Empire Strikes Back, Star Trek and other film and television productions have attracted cult-like followers, showing the power of the media to appeal to the ways that people think and make sense of their worlds.

The Superbowl is celebrated with feverish passion, almost orgy-like. People are attracted to Disney World productions in great numbers. The Woodstock event in Rome, NY attracted thousands of apparently disinhibited people. People swarm to religious and social events: Do the media inspire these assemblies or do they merely serve to point them out? Clearly, most of them are sociodramas that are made possible only by the media.

Psychological Influences

The media, referring here to television and the internet due to the lack of space, play important and useful roles in society. They disseminate information, form bonds of association, and present forums for the resolution of problems. The internet is useful in business and education, in medicine and science. The beneficial uses and influences of these media are profound. Many scholars promote their virtues. They can serve to help educate a society, to make it more literate, more aware of aspects of human existence that would not otherwise be available. The downside is serious, too. Scholars, concerned about the quality of life in a society dominated by television and the internet, have focused on selected topics discussed below.

Stimulation

Humans appear to have a need for stimulation; television and the internet provide it. The need for stimulation, when extreme, as in the over-use of the internet, seems to be almost pathological, a form of cyber-rapture. Research suggests that some surfers seem to prefer porno-sex found on the net to the real thing (Couch, 1996) and that virtual reality blurs one's sense of reality. The suggestion is made that those who prefer virtual reality over everyday reality may lose their ability to distinguish the two realities. In a sense, the perception of reality, whether it has been stimulated by television or the internet, becomes reality for the person engaged. The issue seems to be that porn on the internet may promote behaviours that are not considered healthy. The obvious way that the use of communicative technologies influence nonverbal communication is shown by the amount of time that individuals engage in TV viewing or computer interaction. When people watch television, use video games, surf the net or engage others in e-mail they do so at the expense of engaging in other activities. The popular image of the couch potato and the TV as a babysitter are well known. Background music can be used while one is typing a book or running for exercise, but viewing television or using the internet are more consummate activities. In this respect, they may be forms of serious, diversionary play. Television and the internet can inform, beguile, amuse, stimulate, affect emotions and provide opportunities to pass time. Postman worries that people are amusing themselves to death.

While there is a serious work side in the use of modern communicative media—for example "knowbots" may eventually take over some of the roles now performed by librarians—excessive reliance upon TV or the internet for entertainment takes up time once used for direct personal contact. The social skills that are learned in direct interaction with others are given less time to form. Perhaps parents and researchers rightfully show concern when their children spend too much uncontrolled and unsupervised time in front of the television set or on the internet.

Disinhibition

As pointed out above, modern mediating technologies can influence everyday life pervasively, filtering reality, altering ways of doing things, setting agendas. They influence self construals, the way people dress and walk, the way humans enact lines of action and they change the ways that human activity is channeled. The internet is challenging old ways of thinking about the self, of relationships and of society. Interestingly, the internet provides an opportunity for people to act out identities anonymously, playing with alternate versions of the self in psychodrama. Moods and identities can be artificially created, possibly leading to disinhibition.

Models for Males

It has been suggested that television influences the type of men that young men will become. Do young people, especially males, lose control of their aggressiveness and impulses under the influence of television? Television can promote negative images, such as mutants with names like Magneto, Sabretooth or Toad; yet, at the same time, television can promote positive images. The Lion King, perhaps, teaches positive values and the value of hard work. At best, the influence of television on male behaviours seems to be mixed.

It is easy to blame television and the internet for inspiring negative behaviours, providing a simple answer to complex problems. Both technologies may influence people in very positive ways, too. As an example, the internet can be used for playful expressivity and artfulness by clever people. Even forms of sociodrama may be performed on the internet. Very creative work can be done on the internet; very profound presentations may be found on television.

Tekkies, Junkies and Copycats

It has already been mentioned that television and the internet provide stimulation which seems to be a pervasive need among many youth. Both television and the internet are engaging, attractive communicative media. But scholars, researchers and parents are concerned that overuse may be a sign of addiction. Indeed, in a recent court case, the defence claimed that his client was addicted to the use of the internet.

Humans have always created fantasies. People grow up reading literature about villains and heroes, about lovers and lost love, and about tragedy and success. American culture is imbued with this imagination quotient. The internet provides MUDs, or multi-user dungeons, where the imagination roams. It is easy to understand why young people are attracted to them. Young people are often passionate users of the internet because it engages the imagination. Some scholars are concerned that internet users will be abusers, become addictive, engage in hidden and dangerous exchanges and so on. All kinds of information are available on the internet, including pornographic and salacious materials, which young people can access if they wish to. Of course it and other kinds of information does not merely hang out there; it gets into the ways that people think, into their conceptualizations and their social relations. Perhaps it is extreme, but some scholars believe that the influence of the internet is pervasive enough to influence how people view nature and the universe. That is, as a technology, it is transforming the social order and how people think about their social worlds.

Human Behaviour

Face-to-face communication permits the participants to display their full bodies to others. As mentioned, the full human sensorium comes into play in face-to-face enactments. Humans in areas of the world that lack communicative technologies still rely upon primal communication.

They may represent their cultures through paintings on cave walls or other places in the landscape, and they may embellish their faces with paint, but essentially their interactivel conduct is face-to-face. In cultures saturated by the use of television, the computer and the internet, the human sensorium does not come into play in the same ways. Television is essentially a visual medium; the radio is an aural medium, each influencing viewers and listeners through these body channels.

By using modern tools, engineers are able to mimic all of the human senses. Voice, face and fingerprint recognitions systems already exist. Can smell and taste systems be far behind? Obviously not; in the print media, scratch-off perfume smells have been used. As technological development continues in increasingly sophisticated ways, the way that the real body works in face-to-face interaction, in which the full sensorium is deployed, will be mimicked. Robots will be able to see, hear, feel, taste, and touch, just as humans do. But, of course, this will be artificial reality, however useful and imaginative the robot is.

The Alteration of Place, Time and Space

The contexts of human action are shifting rapidly. Moore's Law dictates that the growth of computer technologies is seemingly exponential, with doubling effects occurring over an increasingly shorter period of time. New technologies create new contexts influencing existing human habits. As mentioned, television is used in medical buildings and malls, in restaurants, schools and bars. The telepresence leads to a new co-presence. Because television is available, new forms of association are engendered. The geography of place and space is altered. Old boundaries are eliminated and new boundaries formed. Time barriers are crossed with ease. It takes no longer to read a newspaper located nearly anywhere on the globe than it takes to go to the store to buy a paper. Friends communicate across oceans and continents instantly. No paper and pens are needed. People born into these contexts may take them for granted. Until they experience alternative realities, young people, born into these technological contexts, may not know how dramatically modern communicative technologies have altered society. The capability of modern communicative technology to increase and diffuse human exchanges seems boundless.

The Reduction of Lagtime

Lag time was a difficult problem in early communication when stage coaches delivered the mail or when couriers ran with messages. A waiting period was necessary. The country doctor may be summoned too late, the distance too far. Even with the advent of the daily newspaper, lag time is apparent when one compares online newservices with print services. The New York Times, the Washington Post or the Boston Globe or any other newwspaper, but the on-line version is available instantly, as are newspapers from around the world. News that is found in paper print is old by the time it gets delivered to the front door.

In short, the new electronic technologies reduce lag time to almost nothing. Following Moore's Law, there have been 18 doublings of the speed of microprocessors since their invention. The computer, which drives the speed of change, is becoming more and more sophisticated. The author in writing this book used four major library systems on-line, each in a different part of the United States. Although he went physically to the libraries, his search for materials was facilitated by the use of the internet, his library time dramatically reduced.

Emergent Cyborgs?

The gee-whiz aspect, the world of wonder, associated with the development of new technologies, gives new meaning to mind-body-machine interaction.

Framing Cyborgs

Cyborg-like human-machinery is being used in medicine, in research and by engineering companies. Pioneering medical devices, such as the artificial human heart, have been used for decades; modern research is now more sophisticated. Electronic gadgets may be used to increase brain power; nerve circulation can be improved electronically; the small intestine can be observed by a very small, wandering, picture-taking computer; robots simulate human activities; computers can read voices. In short, the electro-bionic human is here. No longer do people say "gee-whiz" with every new development; they are getting used to the idea that cyberculture and cyborgculture are here, giving new meaning to the term "human extension". The Cyborg factor, of course, is a fanciful metaphor; nevertheless, it gives one pause for thought.

Modern electronic media serve to provide a new looking glass, one that was not anticipated, the term, "looking glass self". Of course, people always filter reality perceptually, but television and the internet not only present filtered reality, they construct artificial realities. The bodies of the ideal man and the ideal woman are constantly presented on television. Now, the perfectly pixeled female body has been created in virtual reality.

Many people, fail to realize that TV reality is representational; it biases and filters everyday reality. For example, the major news programs which try to project the image of authority, are actually presenting highly selected news, merely a small portion of the news that could be presented. Yet, the news sets the agenda for the day for many people. The influence of television and the internet is not uniform across society nor are all people blindly influenced by them. Women, members of ethnic groups, the aged and children have differential access to television and the internet. They tend to use it differently, too.

The Diaspora

A narrow band could be drawn across the Northern Hemisphere, ranging from Japan and Taiwan through the United States into Northern and Western Europe, outlining the path of technologically developed countries. The American and European film industries distribute their wares to distribution points throughout the Southern Hemisphere. With the exception of Iran, most mid-Eastern states get about 40 to 60 percent of their television programs, mostly entertainment, from the United States and Europe. One side effect is that English is becoming the language of choice around the globe.

Communications Controversies

Is it third world development or is it yet another example of the vestiges of colonialism in which powerful countries dominated less powerful countries in the third world? In 1991, UNESCO adopted a policy supporting "free, independent and pluralistic media." Freedom, rather than control, was the issue then, as it is now. In the modern world, Japanese, European and American companies, members of the "first world" are the prime movers and shakers of the global mass media market. No longer do North Americans dominate the market as they did earlier. Members of the Third World, of course, are still dependent by and large upon the export of media and media products from the North.

Some parts of Africa, Asia, and Latin America remain outside the direct influence of these technologies. Relatively closed societies, such as China, restrict television and internet access to its citizens, although this is changing rapidly. The use of stationary satellites provides the means to broadcast television globally, potentially providing access to all members of the human race. The internet and wireless telephones are gradually being used throughout the world. A canopy of electronic activity is being put into place as suggested decades ago in a spiritual metaphor by Teilhard de Chardin, a futurist, who wrote The Phenomenon of Man.

Symbolically, the world is being hardwired. Indeed, countries with advanced military systems and space systems, use a global net of satellites for transmission. Ship to shore missiles are directed using global satellites. Traditional tribal customs are still practiced in parts of the Amazon basin, but tribal members may have short-wave radios. Traditional societies seem to be slowly blending into modern ones. How much change should be expected? How much change is desirable from the unique perspectives of various cultures? Vast technological changes are occurring in a world where most languages in oral societies have not yet been written down! Is the end to diversity in sight?.

Isolated groups found on the Islands of Oceania, in the Great Outback of Australia, in deeper parts of Africa and in Amazonia in South America and even in the severely cold climates of the Arctic Region are now able to have voices of their own. Indigenous people, many sheltered from modern technologies, are not indifferent to using television, the radio and the internet to establish their own voices.

Displacement

It has been suggested that the internet can promote new dimensions and relationships in cross-cultural affairs, in East-

West and North-south relations. But, of course, each culture, containing rules of conduct and various display rules, will use the technology differently. For example, display rules about self-disclosure vary greatly. Chinese people and Native Americans do not engage in self-disclosure as readily as do Americans generally. Will these display rules change in a faceless internet relationship? The cultural assumptions, the display rules, the cultural ways of communicating vary widely among cultures and nations.

With the arrival of new technologies, perhaps sponsored by large corporations, by governments or by religious groups the patterned ways of doing things get interrupted. For example, in a story told to the author personally, Indians who lived in the back regions of India, when shown health films were puzzled because only the heads of the actors were shown in the film. There was perceptual confusion because only part of the person was shown! In a story told by the New York Times many years ago, when the United States landed a man on the moon, a leader of an African tribe said it couldn't be so because he could not see the person on the moon. In short, these stories, not meant to demean individuals, illustrate cultural assumptions and patterns which are disturbed, or overlayed, when new media become part of the environment. This overlay would seem to benefit some people and not others.

The Digital Divide

Television and the internet can provide new political arenas for formerly disempowered people. There is a politics in what is popular; in short, many women believe that television mispresents their real interests and that the medium can be used more effectively to promote egalitarianism.

The poor are often aliens in an affluent society such as the United States. Despite the belief in the egalitarian ethos, the American occupational structure is stratified. The haves and the have-nots are on the opposite sides of a digital divide. To the extent that there is class "warfare" between the information rich and the information poor, the rich win the war. For example, only recently has the Navajo Nation been hardwired for the internet. The President of the United States visited Shiprock, New Mexico, taking computer technology to the local Indian schools. Schools for Navajo youth now use film, videography and the computer in the classroom. Yet, many tribal members on many reservations, not only the Navajo, do not have telephones and school dropout rates are very high. The digital divide is a metaphor that suggests that females, older people, Blacks, Native Americans and most members of Third World countries, do not have the same access to the computer and related technologies as do mainstream, college educated white males. The concern is that, as in education, the gulf will negatively influence their life chances. Recent research suggests that today 50 percent of the users of the internet are femalein the United States, a dramatic change from the recent past. Nevertheless, concern is expressed that the gender divide and associated problems will find their way onto the net. Internet interaction is supposedly faceless; however, gender is displayed in writing patterns, in cursive style and expressive styles. Females use a variety of phrases, styles and emphases that can "give them away."

Digital Divide

People with low incomes and little education and people who are above 60 years old are less likely to have or to use a computer, although this pattern is changing. A recent survey shows that almost all Americans under sixty years of age have used a computer; nearly 9 in 10 people say they are enthusiastic about the computer; more than two-thirds say that they need a computer at work; over half of the respondents say they are getting a multi-media system at home; it is the young people who are the most enthusiastic about using computers.

The same survey by National Public Radio suggested that Americans were concerned about many things as well. They believe that the have and have-not gap is widening, widening the racial problems; they are afraid that pornography will influence their children; and, they are afraid that their privacy will be intruded upon.

Like the telephone and television, once luxuries affordable to only a few members of American society, the computer has become an essential ingredient of American society. People need it; it is not a mere toy. It extends what people can do in vital ways.

Social Patterns

The texture of society is changing from gemeinschaft, a personal community, to gesellschaft, an impersonal community. Braudel is using German sociological concepts to depict society. The face-to-face community is personal; the mediated society is impersonal. A new pseudo-society is emerging, based not on face to face interaction, but on words and pictures located in techno-space, free of the constraints of time and place. The mediated face replaces the real living face.Virtual reality replaces everyday reality. Boundaries dissipate. Ironically, distance becomes localized. The emergent electronic folk-culture exists at the present time. People in this community are not required to associate with a country or nationality, although they may do so if they wish. There are no political boundaries and there are few established rules and customs. The people in this community speak techno-speak, they use emoticons and special markers to let others know what they mean. Later, of course, they will see one another as technology improves, as television and the internet blend. For now, however, they are faceless citizens in an electronic community.

Cyborg Factor

More and more, researchers are focusing on the interaction of modern communicative technologies and human biology. Television and the internet have been focused on the above, but there are offshoots of each technology, especially computer technology, that deeply influence human behaviours. Science fiction has shown the horrors of the robot-human connection in which humans are blended with steel to create a cyborg-like creature. Advances in science, in artificial intelligence and in robotics not only bring a sense of wonderment but a sense of fear about the possible negative, interactive consequences.

Cybernetic organisms (Cyborgs) have been around since the 1950's, says Donna Haraway. It started when a white lab rat was implanted with a pump to inject precisely controlled doses of chemicals into the rat to alter its physiological parameters. It was part animal and part machine. Humans have been Cyborgian for some time. They are becoming like mechanized machines, eating treated foods, working out in ergonomically developed gymnasiums, wearing shoes specifically designed for exercise, taking artificially created medicines, getting implants. Modern Cyborgs are information machines. Can better human beings be created by combining machines with the biological body?

The Cyborg factor is imaginative, metaphorical. Indeed, the metaphor, the concept of a Cyborg has been trashed. Yet, the metaphor suggests the potentially intimate connection between humans and the machines they created. Almost daily, people are reminded of the new technological developments in medicine, engineering and science. One generation passes new technologies on to the next almost in a blur of confusion. The technological trajectory is not clearly focused, but it seems obvious that robots that can do what humans can do are forthcoming. Is the world of the born being replaced by the world of the made? Some scholars think that body, mind and machine function best when they are interactively engaged.

The half-life of technical knowledge, or the speed by which technology changes and is adapted for human use, is brief, perhaps less than five years in many bio-chemico-engineering fields. Until the 1900s, the half-life of technical knowledge was long. Today, one generation of computers, television and other advanced technologies, leads quickly to another. Moore's Law suggests that computer technology and software change several times a year, often in major ways. Much earlier, referring to the emerging technological society, where changes were slowly appearing, Jacques Ellul, an influential social theorist referred to "technological bluff", an illusionary factor that suggests that the introduction of new media bears a price; there are losses and gains, when one system overtakes another. As it was then, it is now; there are losses and gains when one media overtakes another. Certainly there are lag effects.

At the present time, there appear to be emerging patterns in which the traditional media, such as TV, film, radio and print are blending with newer forms, such as data banks and multimedia computers; personal electronic media are becoming common, such as electronic bulletin boards, the internet and other data highways.

And this dovetailing pattern is spreading across the globe. National boundaries are disappearing; power is being redistributed; self perceptions are changing. The global information society is here. The oral, the typographic and the electronic media influence human societies in different ways, but the most powerful of these influences are found in the electronic media.

Of course, the social structure influences the growth of technology as well and the social structure is changing rapidly. If the medium is the message, as McLuhan told us, the message is complex, plural and often confusing . Cyberspace is still uncharted territory with a flavor of the Wild West.

New Netculture

We live in a new netculture where a virtual theatre exists. An imaginative carnival of wordplay is possible on the internet. People can move their players about in virtual space, puppets and images. There is a scrolling script that looks like a script of a play. Rituals can be created and recreated on the net. In effect, there is a new theatre on the net.

Humans languages are symbolic; they symbolize human consciousness. At present, languages are bounded. Perhaps the 7,000 or so dialects and languages of the world will become extinct, or greatly modified. The new global community has its own language, as mentioned, although even here there is variation. The Japanese, for example, sometimes use different sets of emoticons than do Americans. But, it seems clear that future iconography and symbolism will be very different from that which exists today. Many symbols, of course, are enduring, existing over long periods of time, such as religious symbols, but others are more fleeting, such as the symbol of the Nike sneaker, of Coca Cola, of Levi jeans, symbols that will be modifed, or perhaps extinct in a few decades.

Early emblematics used circles, such as breast representations; early pottery bore water marks; seals were used as signatures later; pictorial writing was used by the Mayas; and, now math and cyber symbols have emerged. Culture and consciousness are being transformed with a swiftness not seen before.

Symbols are powerful short-cuts to meaning. They tie

experiences together, they blend the past and the present and the future and create a new consciousness by the users. Perhaps humans are moving from a Global Village to a Global Mind. The new language reflects the symbolism of technology. To some, the dawning of a new age, predicted in the 80s, seems to be here. The new electronic, communicative technologies are in some sense an extension of humans, of the human body, of brains and emotions. The old mind-body dualism seems to be gone, or at least blurred; the emotions are engaged in new ways on the internet as well. The body of flesh and blood, of neurons and brains, of emotions and feelings, is now symbolized in new ways.

Does human consciousness change when technology impacts on society? Many theorists believe that the essential building block of human consciousness, of time, space, place and experience is noted by the fact that humans speak, they symbolize. The question is whether the new technologies have their own form of language.

In a discussion on the internet, Jennifer Cobb, a theologian, asked, non-humorously, whether God could be found on the internet. Certainly, the advent of bioengineering, of genetic research, of computer artificial intelligence, of imaging possibilities, of intra and extra space discoveries make changes in the symbolic texts of everyday life. Even a very practical thing, such as shopping on the net, changes the meaning of shopping. Even now it is possible to formfit clothing to the self by creating a virtual 'you' on the net.

Post-modernists believe that the fabric of modernity is being replaced by postmodernity. That is, the meaning of power, of gender, of ethnicity is being altered substantially under the influence of "freeing" technologies. Some argue that a new egalitarianism may more easily be formed under the new circumstances. The concept of the looking glass self, espoused by Cooley decades ago, bears upon this section. The essence of that concept is that people see themselves in society; through interaction they become who they are. Human identity is achieved by reflecting on the events and contexts of everyday life. People negotiate the meaning of life. In short, the social text informs them.

The present texture of American society is very different

compared to what it was in earlier times. A person born 200 years ago would hardly know how to live in the present society. Is there a newly emerging consciousness? If so, what is the nature of that consciousness? Answering that question is the work of people who live in that society. Human nonverbal communication is, and will be, deeply involved in the answer to the question, as the past, the present and the future seem to be blending together.

13

The Importance of Face-to-Face Communication at Work

As more communication up and down the line at work is done electronically, face-to-face discussion can easily fall by the wayside. While the speed and volume of communication increases with e-mail, voicemail and instant messaging, some of the dialogue and personal touch can start to disappear. A global survey shows that 67 percent of senior executives and managers say their organization would be more productive if their superiors communicated more often by personal discussion. While they desire more personal discussion from their superiors, however, the top personal method of communicating for these same business leaders is e-mail, based on the survey by NFI Research.

"Too many people take the easy way out and try and do everything via e-mail and in a lot of cases consume more time on both sides of the equation than they would have by simply picking up the phone or going to see the person," said one survey respondent. "I often find that when I look the other person in the eyes and ask them something I get far more than I ever would over e-mail." "Personal discussion is the foundation of communications," said another respondent. "Once this foundation is established, it enables all of the other forms of communication. Having a personal connection builds trust and minimizes misinterpretation and misunderstanding."

When Technology Does the Communicating

While the majority of business leaders say their organization would be more productive with more personal discussion, some lament that many people fall back on technology to do the communicating. "We have started to run our business by using technology instead of good old-fashioned personal communication," said one manager.

"We need to take vacations from our BlackBerrys, computers and voicemail and get out and talk to everyone in the organization. Nothing can replace open and honest face-to-face communication." Using e-mail rather than personal discussion can also delay decision-making. "I find that many executives avoid conversation because they may be forced to make a decision or express an opinion," said one respondent. "If they can keep communications within e-mail, they can continually pass the buck around or back without having to commit. Management by failure to act may be the new favoured process."

In other cases, communicating via technology can be effective. "Instant messages and e-mail are communication accelerators," said one executive. "Discussion databases are more efficient for larger groups. But there is no substitute for in-person communication when appropriate." "Our organization uses DVDs as a medium to distribute corporate messages to significant segments of the workforce and it is effective," said another.

Consider Context and Purpose

The key is to use the correct communication method at the right time. "When give-and-take is required, there is no form of communication that works better than getting out of one's chair and speaking to the person face to face," said one survey respondent. "If personal discussion is not an option, the telephone or Web conferencing is an acceptable second choice. If you aren't concerned about the response, then e-mail, text message and memos work fine for pronouncements from on high."

"We're beginning to learn that different methods of communication are more effective at certain tasks than others," said another respondent. "E-mail is great for scheduling and confirming meetings, phone is good for quick conversations that require two-way communications and a memo is preferred for long background pieces. In-person and scheduled meetings are always the best for any discussion requiring true dialogue and consensus." With so much to do at work, it's not always easy to find time for personal discussion. However, in the long term, face-to-face communication just might assure that communication is clear and understood.

Group Dynamics

Group dynamics is the study of groups, and also a general term for group processes. Relevant to the fields of psychology, sociology, and communication studies, a group is two or more individuals who are connected to each other by social relationships. Because they interact and influence each other, groups develop a number of dynamic processes that separate them from a random collection of individuals. These processes include norms, roles, relations, development, need to belong, social influence, and effects on behaviour. The field of group dynamics is primarily concerned with small group behaviour. Groups may be classified as aggregate, primary, secondary and category groups.

In organizational development (OD), or group dynamics, the phrase "group process" refers to the understanding of the behaviour of people in groups, such as task groups, that are trying to solve a problem or make a decision. An individual with expertise in 'group process, such as a trained facilitator, can assist a group in accomplishing its objective by diagnosing how well the group is functioning as a problem-solving or decision-making entity and intervening to alter the group's operating behaviour.

Because people gather in groups for reasons other than task accomplishment, group process occurs in other types of groups such as personal growth groups (e.g. encounter groups, study groups, prayer groups). In such cases, an individual with expertise in group process can be helpful in the role of facilitator.

Well researched but rarely mentioned by professional group workers, is the social status of people within the group (i.e., senior or junior). The group leader (or facilitator) will usually have a strong influence on the group due to his or her role of shaping the group's outcomes. This influence will also be affected by the leader's sex, race, relative age, income, appearance, and personality, as well as organizational structures and many other factors.

Key Theorists

Gabriel Tarde's Les lois de l'imitation (1890) (translated as the Law of Imitiation, 1903) conceives sociology as based on small psychological interactions among individuals (as in a chemical compound), the fundamental forces being imitation and innovation.

Gustave Le Bon was a French social psychologist whose seminal study, *The Crowd: A Study of the Popular Mind* (1896) led to the development of group psychology.

Sigmund Freud's *Group Psychology and the Analysis of the Ego,* (1922) based on a critique of Le Bon's work, led to further development in theories of group behaviour in the latter half of the twentieth century.

Kurt Lewin (1943, 1948, 1951) is commonly identified as the founder of the movement to study groups scientifically. He coined the term *group dynamics* to describe the way groups and individuals act and react to changing circumstances.

William Schutz (1958, 1966) looked at interpersonal relations from the perspective of three dimensions: *inclusion, control,* and *affection.* This became the basis for a theory of group behaviour that sees groups as resolving issues in each of these stages in order to be able to develop to the next stage. Conversely, a group may also devolve to an earlier stage if unable to resolve outstanding issues in a particular stage.

Wilfred Bion (1961) studied group dynamics from a psychoanalytic perspective, and stated that he was much influenced by Wilfred Trotter for whom he worked at University College Hospital London, as did another key figure in the Psychoanalytic movement, Ernest Jones. He discovered several mass group processes which involved the group as a whole adopting an orientation which, in his opinion, interfered with the ability of a group to accomplish the work it was nominally engaged in. His experiences are reported in his published books, especially *Experiences in Groups.* The Tavistock Institute has further developed and applied the theory and practices developed by Bion.

Bruce Tuckman (1965) proposed the four-stage model called Tuckman's Stages for a group. Tuckman's model states that the ideal group decision-making process should occur in four stages:

- *Forming* (pretending to get on or get along with others);
- *Storming* (letting down the politeness barrier and trying to get down to the issues even if tempers flare up);
- *Norming* (getting used to each other and developing trust and productivity);
- *Performing* (working in a group to a common goal on a highly efficient and cooperative basis).

Tuckman later added a fifth stage for the dissolution of a group called *adjourning*. (*Adjourning* may also be referred to as *mourning,* i.e. mourning the adjournment of the group). It should be noted that this model refers to the overall pattern of the group, but of course individuals within a group work in different ways. If distrust persists, a group may never even get to the norming stage.

M. Scott Peck developed stages for larger-scale groups (i.e., communities) which are similar to Tuckman's stages of group development. Peck describes the stages of a community as:

- *Pseudo-community*
- *Chaos*
- *Emptiness*
- *True Community*

Communities may be distinguished from other types of groups, in Peck's view, by the need for members to eliminate barriers to communication in order to be able to form true community. Examples of common barriers are: expectations and preconceptions; prejudices; ideology, counterproductive norms, theology and solutions; the need to heal, convert, fix or solve and the need to control. A community is born when its members reach a stage of "emptiness" or peace.

Dimensions of Group Process

Aspects of group process include:

- Patterns of communication and coordination
- Patterns of influence
- Roles / relationship
- Patterns of dominance (e.g. who leads, who defers)

- Balance of task focus vs social focus
- Level of group effectiveness
- How conflict is handled
- Emotional state of the group as a whole, what Wilfred Bion called basic assumptions.

Groups of individuals gathered together to achieve a goal or objective, either as a committee or some other grouping, go through several predicatable stages before useful work can be done. These stages are a function of a number of variables, not the least of which is the self-identification of the role each member will tend to play, and the emergence of natural leaders and individuals who will serve as sources of information. Any individual in a leadership position whose responsibilities involve getting groups of individuals to work together should both be conversant with the phases of the group process and possess the skills necessary to capitalize on these stages to accomplish the objective of forming a productive, cohesive team.

Various theories of group development exist. The model below combines elements of theories. In this model, each phase of group development is looked at with respect to group members' concerns with task and personal relations (process) functions.

	Phase Personal Relations Functions	Task Functions
1	Orientation	Testing and Dependence
2	Organizing to Get Work Done	Intragroup Conflict
3	Information-flow	Group Cohesion
4	Problem-solving	Interdependence

Application

Group dynamics form a basis for group therapy, often with therapeutic approaches that are formed of groups such as family therapy and the expressive therapies. Politicians and sales personnel may use their knowledge of the principles of group dynamics to aid their cause. Increasingly, group dynamics are of interest in light of online social interaction and virtual communities made possible by the internet.

How Face-to-face Communication

Today, most of your clients, colleagues and stakeholders are just a phone call or email away - technology has made communication that simple. However, while tools like telephones and computers score high on convenience and speed, they lack the warmth and emotion that face-to-face communication provides.

In my earlier features, I have highlighted the importance of telephone etiquette, making use of online networking and business chat etiquette. However, there are some occasions where you must revive the by-now forgotten art of face-to-face communication.

Appreciating Colleagues

In the words of Helen Keller, 'We are all walking with a signboard on our forehead which reads - 'Appreciate me'.' It seems we have replaced the pat on the back with 'Thank you' and 'Good job' emails. But there is nothing that motivates someone more than seeing their boss walk up to them and appreciate them in front of everyone.

Go to your colleague's cubicle and congratulate them on the great report they sent or the presentation they made recently. I remember one of my ex-bosses who used to call us team members to his cabin just to say 'thanks' and pat our backs. The team immediately took a liking to him as most people expect a warning or feedback when the boss invites them to their cabin.

"It's difficult to build rapport over an email; I would feel much better if my boss appreciates me in person," says Ashok Krishnan, a CA with Nestle.

Providing Feedback

When you provide feedback over an email or a phone call, the receiver may have a completely different perception about its relevance. This effect is amplified when you are not communicating face-to-face. The reader or listener may think you are cold and indifferent and that's why you avoided meeting them in person to discuss the issue. A face-to-face meeting gives you the opportunity to put your point across, while being sensitive and diplomatic at the same time.

"I have noticed that colleagues often use emails to avoid confronting the real issue. If someone fails to meet their target, I would prefer they tell me in person than offer an explanation over email," says Vidhanshu Bansal, a director with Pixel Webtech.

Assigning New Responsibility

There is a great risk of the message getting diluted when a responsibility gets delegated through email or a phone call. Don't be surprised if your team does not show a sense of ownership or complete tasks on time if you are not communicating face-to-face. Nonverbal communication, such as tone of voice, facial gestures and eye contact help individuals understand the importance of a task and the need to complete it on time.

"We rely on conference calls, video conferencing and online meetings but, from my experience, there's nothing more impactful than meeting the team in person," says Delhi-based Ashu Gosh, a manager with Aviar IT Consulting.

Damage Control with Clients

If you haven't provided the product or service the client expected, you are putting your relationship with the client at stake. An apology mail would not suffice in a sensitive issue like this. Go to the client's office, if possible, without them having to call you for an explanation, and reassure them that the confidence they demonstrated when they gave you business was not misplaced. Your client would be pleasantly surprised that you took the time to come and meet them, especially when things went wrong.

"I used to interact on almost a daily basis with a client over emails without ever figuring out whether the person was male or female. When a report I was supposed to send got delayed, I made a rude comment about a female colleague which offended the client who happened to be a lady herself," says Deepak M.L, a manager with Convergys.

Resolving Conflicts

Workplace conflicts are common in most organisations. The lack of interpersonal communication only worsens the situation.

It's important to remember that 55 per cent of meaning in an interaction comes from facial and body language and 38 per cent comes from vocal inflection. Only seven per cent of an interaction's meaning is derived from the words themselves. So, trying to resolve a conflict over email or a phone call is often a bad idea.

"A colleague complained about another colleague and copied the senior management on the mail. I was surprised to see that mail translating into a flood of mails providing and seeking explanation. The person who sent the original mail was just one floor above the person who was at the receiving end. I had to sit down with both of them in person to resolve the conflict," says Kailasam R, a manager with Lufthansa Airlines.

Your communication style says a lot about you as a professional. In the words of Ralph Waldo Emerson, 'You are always under examination by people around you, awarding or denying you very high prizes when you least think of it.' So leave the comfort of your cubicle and build trustworthy relationships by communicating face to face.

Face-to-Face Communication-Old Fashioned? Not!

It's unbelievable how dependent we've become as a society on electronic communication devices! E-mail, text messaging, PDA's, cell phones, video conferencing, blackberries, blueberries, rasberries, and more...have taken the place of good old fashioned, face-to-face communication leading to many interpersonal difficulties and miscommunications in today's workplace.

You may be thinking...Why improve my interpersonal skills when most businesses do 99% of communication by telephone, teleconferencing, videoconferencing, e-mail, and on rare occasions, snail mail. A popular way of thinking today...but, is it really the correct way? "Face-to-face communication remains the most powerful human interaction," says Kathleen Begley, Ed.D., author of Face-to-Face Communication, Making Human Connections in a Technology-Driven World. "As wonderful as electronic devices are, they can never fully replace the intimacy and immediacy of people conversing in the same room and it has worked for millions of years."

In business, we talk about "B2B" (business to business) and "B2C" (business to consumer) methods. I try to buck the trend (in a positive way!) to stress the importance of face-to-face communication.

You'll hear me talk a lot about the "P2P" (people-to-people) connections and how important it is to get beyond technology and talk face-to-face with friends, family, colleagues, customers, vendors, and the like. You may think that's a bit old-fashioned, but in my opinion, there is no substitution for the human, up-close and personal contact. Don't get me wrong, there is a place for the terrific technology tools we have today and I use it regularly, but it's not always my first or best choice.

Several decades ago, John Naisbitt, in his mega 1960's best-seller, Megatrends: Ten New Directions Transforming Our Lives, brought a new concept to the forefront called "high tech, high touch."

His idea was that "as human beings became capable of anonymous electronic communication, they would concurrently need more close-up personal interaction."

Seems to me that he was right on target! We live in a society when flocking to the local coffee shop or diner for coffee chats with business associates or friends is a testimony to our need for human togetherness, especially when most coffee lovers can make a latte or cappuccino right in their homes. Think about the fortunes coffee establishments are making on our need for face-to-face communication! The people-to-people connections...

We hear of the many children (and adults) who spend countless hours alone playing video games.

However, The Game Manufacturing Association reported in 2003 that family board game sales (like Monopoly and Scrabble) are booming and growing at 20% per year. Cranium has recently come out with a whole new line of board games for our "little people" (ages 3+). The people-to-people connections start at an early age-if you haven't heard it, ask me to tell you my "Papa Zitto" story!

Even when disaster strikes and the news media bring these events into our homes and workplaces via TV, radio and the

Internet, we seek out opportunities to share grief. I personally waited in line for almost three hours with hundreds of others to visit Ground Zero in New York when it opened to the public in December 2001. Many people also left makeshift shrines nearby to honor the victims of that tragedy.

We lead hectic, multi-tasking lives both at home and in the workplace these days and we find the need for balance even more critical than in days gone by. We understand that technology can be impersonal, but it's quick!

We know we need to make time for more people-to-people connections but, the reality of the hectic pace doesn't leave us much time for this more intimate form of communication. You may be thinking, isn't it much faster to make a quick phone call, send a brief e-mail, or hook up via video-conferencing to have a meeting of the minds?

Yes and no. It's a communications paradox...faster is not always better. So the better question may be, how can we make the best of both worlds-technology and face-to-face, people-to-people connections? Just as fashions are redesigned and come back with a variation on a style from days-gone-by, I believe it is time for redesigning and revitalizing face-to-face (P2P) communication skills.

We need to get the balance right! People-to-people (P2P) communication skills remain one of the primary success factors in business, even in this age of technology. There are many situations-often those involving conflict, hurt feelings, high priority, or a large sum of money-that demand business people take the time and trouble to get in the same room to share information. Video-conferencing has become a good simulation and cost-effective method when individuals are in remote locations, but there is still no substitute for good, old-fashioned, face-to-face communication.

Don't take my word for it...Let's take a look at what some of the experts are saying.

Tom Peters, internationally known business guru, says without reservation that you should constantly attend to your face-to-face communication. Not to do so, will lead to career disaster. "We believe in high tech, high touch," Peters writes. "No question, technology is the Great Enabler. But, paradoxically, now the human bit is more, not less, important than ever before."

Sheila Hodge, author of Global Smarts: The Art of Communicating and Deal Making Anywhere in the World, says "The modern office is full of gadgets-computers and the Internet, uplinks and downlinks, videoconferencing, and online databases. Many people think they should let the fancy technology handle the messy task of interfacing with people."

Jo-Ellan Dimitrius, in her book Reading People, talks about how young, technically oriented employees tend to communicate mostly in computer chat rooms.

"If you want to become a better communicator, you must make a conscious effort to engage other people (in person)," she writes. "Even the most entrenched Internet junkie can learn the true meaning of 'chat' if the desire is there, but you have to get off the couch and make it happen."

Gary McClain and Deborah Romaine in their book, The Everything Managing People Book, put it this way..."Consistent, daily face-to-face communication promotes more than just good feelings; it also promotes effective and collaborative teamwork."

"One of the most critical areas of communication to get right in business is the one-on-one situations-especially offering advice, constructive feedback, and annual performance appraisals," says Chris Roebuck in Effective Communication.

One of my favorite quotes stated very simply by Margaret Wheatley, Turning to One Another: Simple Conversations to Restore Hope for the Future, says "I can believe we can change the world if we start talking to one another again."

Sounds like we're on to something here...So, what can you do? Start out by taking an honest look at your communication methods and your attitude about technology vs. (P2P) face-to-face interaction. Are you e-mailing more and meeting less for financial reasons? Are you avoiding human contact mostly because of a lack of interpersonal skills? If the latter is true, you need to take action before it's too late.

The next time you are tempted to send an e-mail, text message or make a phone call for other than routine purposes, stop! Get back to basics. Go out of your comfort zone and, instead, send the e-mail, text message or make the call to set up a face-to-face, in person meeting with the person behind the technology! Why? Because it works!

Make the people-to-people connections... You and your business will be glad you did!

A Positive Workplace Means Business! TM

Mary Jane (MJ) Paris, Founder and President of Positive Impact Consulting Services, LLC in Shelton, CT, brings a broad base of experience to her practice gained from more than 25 years in people management, sales, retail banking, training, recruiting, coaching, project management, event planning and community leadership.

14

Speech Synthesis

Speech synthesis is the artificial production of human speech. A computer system used for this purpose is called a speech synthesizer, and can be implemented in software or hardware. A text-to-speech (TTS) system converts normal language text into speech; other systems render symbolic linguistic representations like phonetic transcriptions into speech.

Synthesized speech can be created by concatenating pieces of recorded speech that are stored in a database. Systems differ in the size of the stored speech units; a system that stores phones or diphones provides the largest output range, but may lack clarity. For specific usage domains, the storage of entire words or sentences allows for high-quality output. Alternatively, a synthesizer can incorporate a model of the vocal tract and other human voice characteristics to create a completely "synthetic" voice output.

The quality of a speech synthesizer is judged by its similarity to the human voice and by its ability to be understood. An intelligible text-to-speech program allows people with visual impairments or reading disabilities to listen to written works on a home computer. Many computer operating systems have included speech synthesizers since the early 1980s.

Overview of Text Processing

A text-to-speech system (or "engine") is composed of two parts: a front-end and a back-end. The front-end has two major tasks. First, it converts raw text containing symbols like numbers and abbreviations into the equivalent of written-out words. This process is often called *text normalization, pre-processing,* or *tokenization*. The front-end then assigns phonetic transcriptions to each word, and divides and marks the text into prosodic units, like phrases, clauses, and sentences. The process of assigning phonetic transcriptions to words is called *text-to-phoneme* or *grapheme-to-phoneme* conversion. Phonetic transcriptions and prosody information together make up the symbolic linguistic representation that is output by the front-end. The back-end—often referred to as the *synthesizer*—then converts the symbolic linguistic representation into sound.

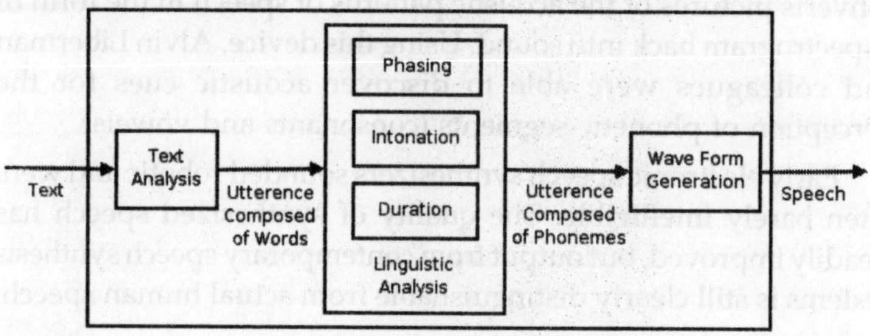

History

Long before electronic signal processing was invented, there were those who tried to build machines to create human speech. Some early legends of the existence of "speaking heads" involved Gerbert of Aurillac (d. 1003 AD), Albertus Magnus (1198–1280), and Roger Bacon (1214–1294).

In 1779, the Danish scientist Christian Kratzenstein, working at the Russian Academy of Sciences, built models of the human vocal tract that could produce the five long vowel sounds (in International Phonetic Alphabet notation, they are [aÐ], [eÐ], [iÐ], [oÐ] and [uÐ]). This was followed by the bellows-operated "acoustic-mechanical speech machine" by Wolfgang von Kempelen of Vienna, Austria, described in a 1791 paper. This machine added models of the tongue and lips, enabling it to produce consonants as well as vowels. In 1837, Charles Wheatstone produced a "speaking machine" based on von Kempelen's design, and in 1857, M. Faber built the "Euphonia". Wheatstone's design was resurrected in 1923 by Paget.

In the 1930s, Bell Labs developed the VOCODER, a keyboard-operated electronic speech analyzer and synthesizer that was said to be clearly intelligible. Homer Dudley refined this device into the VODER, which he exhibited at the 1939 New York World's Fair.

The Pattern playback was built by Dr. Franklin S. Cooper and his colleagues at Haskins Laboratories in the late 1940s and completed in 1950. There were several different versions of this hardware device but only one currently survives. The machine converts pictures of the acoustic patterns of speech in the form of a spectrogram back into sound. Using this device, Alvin Liberman and colleagues were able to discover acoustic cues for the perception of phonetic segments (consonants and vowels).

Early electronic speech synthesizers sounded robotic and were often barely intelligible. The quality of synthesized speech has steadily improved, but output from contemporary speech synthesis systems is still clearly distinguishable from actual human speech.

Electronic Devices

The first computer-based speech synthesis systems were created in the late 1950s, and the first complete text-to-speech system was completed in 1968. In 1961, physicist John Larry Kelly, Jr and colleague Louis Gerstman used an IBM 704 computer to synthesize speech, an event among the most prominent in the history of Bell Labs. Kelly's voice recorder synthesizer (vocoder) recreated the song "Daisy Bell", with musical accompaniment from Max Mathews. Coincidentally, Arthur C. Clarke was visiting his friend and colleague John Pierce at the Bell Labs Murray Hill facility. Clarke was so impressed by the demonstration that he used it in the climactic scene of his screenplay for his novel *2001: A Space Odyssey*, where the HAL 9000 computer sings the same song as it is being put to sleep by astronaut Dave Bowman. Despite the success of purely electronic speech synthesis, research is still being conducted into mechanical speech synthesizers.

Synthesizer Technologies

The most important qualities of a speech synthesis system are *naturalness* and *Intelligibility*. Naturalness describes how closely the output sounds like human speech, while intelligibility is the ease with which the output is understood. The ideal speech synthesizer is both natural and intelligible. Speech synthesis systems usually try to maximize both characteristics.

The two primary technologies for generating synthetic speech waveforms are *concatenative synthesis* and *formant synthesis*. Each technology has strengths and weaknesses, and the intended uses of a synthesis system will typically determine which approach is used.

Concatenative Synthesis

Concatenative synthesis is based on the concatenation (or stringing together) of segments of recorded speech. Generally, concatenative synthesis produces the most natural-sounding synthesized speech. However, differences between natural variations in speech and the nature of the automated techniques for segmenting the waveforms sometimes result in audible glitches in the output. There are three main sub-types of concatenative synthesis.

Unit Selection Synthesis

Unit selection synthesis uses large databases of recorded speech. During database creation, each recorded utterance is segmented into some or all of the following: individual phones, diphones, half-phones, syllables, morphemes, words, phrases, and sentences. Typically, the division into segments is done using a specially modified speech recognizer set to a "forced alignment" mode with some manual correction afterward, using visual representations such as the waveform and spectrogram. An index of the units in the speech database is then created based on the segmentation and acoustic parameters like the fundamental frequency (pitch), duration, position in the syllable, and neighboring phones. At runtime, the desired target utterance is created by determining the best chain of candidate units from the database (unit selection). This process is typically achieved using a specially weighted decision tree.

Unit selection provides the greatest naturalness, because it applies only a small amount of digital signal processing (DSP) to the recorded speech. DSP often makes recorded speech sound less natural, although some systems use a small amount of signal processing at the point of concatenation to smooth the waveform. The output from the best unit-selection systems is often indistinguishable from real human voices, especially in contexts for which the TTS system has been tuned. However, maximum naturalness typically require unit-selection speech databases to be very large, in some systems ranging into the gigabytes of recorded data, representing dozens of hours of speech. Also, unit selection algorithms have been known to select segments from a place that results in less than ideal synthesis (e.g. minor words become unclear) even when a better choice exists in the database.

Diphone Synthesis

Diphone synthesis uses a minimal speech database containing all the diphones (sound-to-sound transitions) occurring in a language. The number of diphones depends on the phonotactics of the language: for example, Spanish has about 800 diphones, and German about 2500. In diphone synthesis, only one example of each diphone is contained in the speech database. At runtime, the target prosody of a sentence is superimposed on these minimal units by means of digital signal processing techniques such as linear predictive coding, PSOLA or MBROLA. The quality of the resulting speech is generally worse than that of unit-selection systems, but more natural-sounding than the output of formant synthesizers. Diphone synthesis suffers from the sonic glitches of concatenative synthesis and the robotic-sounding nature of formant synthesis, and has few of the advantages of either approach other than small size. As such, its use in commercial applications is declining, although it continues to be used in research because there are a number of freely available software implementations.

Domain-specific Synthesis

Domain-specific synthesis concatenates prerecorded words and phrases to create complete utterances. It is used in applications where the variety of texts the system will output is limited to a particular domain, like transit schedule announcements or weather reports. The technology is very simple to implement, and has been in commercial use for a long time, in devices like talking clocks and calculators. The level of naturalness of these systems can be very high because the variety of sentence types is limited, and they closely match the prosody and intonation of the original recordings.

Because these systems are limited by the words and phrases in their databases, they are not general-purpose and can only synthesize the combinations of words and phrases with which they have been preprogrammed. The blending of words within naturally spoken language however can still cause problems unless the many variations are taken into account. For example, in non-rhotic dialects of English the *"r"* in words like *"clear"* /ÈkliĐY/ is usually only pronounced when the following word has a vowel as its first letter. Likewise in French, many final consonants become no longer silent if followed by a word that begins with a vowel, an effect called liaison. This alternation cannot be reproduced by a simple word-concatenation system, which would require additional complexity to be context-sensitive.

Formant Synthesis

Formant synthesis does not use human speech samples at runtime. Instead, the synthesized speech output is created using an acoustic model. Parameters such as fundamental frequency, voicing, and noise levels are varied over time to create a waveform of artificial speech. This method is sometimes called *rules-based synthesis;* however, many concatenative systems also have rules-based components.

Many systems based on formant synthesis technology generate artificial, robotic-sounding speech that would never be mistaken for human speech. However, maximum naturalness is not always the goal of a speech synthesis system, and formant synthesis systems have advantages over concatenative systems. Formant-synthesized speech can be reliably intelligible, even at very high speeds, avoiding the acoustic glitches that commonly plague concatenative systems. High-speed synthesized speech is used by the visually impaired to quickly navigate computers using a screen reader. Formant synthesizers are usually smaller programs than concatenative systems because they do not have a database of speech samples. They can therefore be used in embedded systems, where memory and microprocessor power are especially limited. Because formant-based systems have complete control of all aspects of the output speech, a wide variety of prosodies and intonations can be output, conveying not just questions and statements, but a variety of emotions and tones of voice.

Examples of non-real-time but highly accurate intonation control in formant synthesis include the work done in the late 1970s for the Texas Instruments toy Speak & Spell, and in the early 1980s Sega arcade machines. Creating proper intonation for these projects was painstaking, and the results have yet to be matched by real-time text-to-speech interfaces.

Articulatory Synthesis

Articulatory synthesis refers to computational techniques for synthesizing speech based on models of the human vocal tract and the articulation processes occurring there. The first articulatory synthesizer regularly used for laboratory experiments was developed at Haskins Laboratories in the mid-1970s by Philip Rubin, Tom Baer, and Paul Mermelstein. This synthesizer, known as ASY, was based on vocal tract models developed at Bell Laboratories in the 1960s and 1970s by Paul Mermelstein, Cecil Coker, and colleagues.

Until recently, articulatory synthesis models have not been incorporated into commercial speech synthesis systems. A notable exception is the NeXT-based system originally developed and marketed by Trillium Sound Research, a spin-off company of the University of Calgary, where much of the original research was conducted. Following the demise of the various incarnations of NeXT (started by Steve Jobs in the late 1980s and merged with Apple Computer in 1997), the Trillium software was published under the GNU General Public License, with work continuing as gnuspeech. The system, first marketed in 1994, provides full articulatory-based text-to-speech conversion using a waveguide or transmission-line analog of the human oral and nasal tracts controlled by Carré's "distinctive region model".

HMM-based Synthesis

HMM-based synthesis is a synthesis method based on hidden Markov models, also called Statistical Parametric Synthesis. In this system, the frequency spectrum (vocal tract), fundamental frequency (vocal source), and duration (prosody) of speech are modeled simultaneously by HMMs. Speech waveforms are generated from HMMs themselves based on the maximum likelihood criterion.

Sinewave Synthesis

Sinewave synthesis is a technique for synthesizing speech by replacing the formants (main bands of energy) with pure tone whistles.

Challenges

The process of normalizing text is rarely straightforward. Texts are full of heteronyms, numbers, and abbreviations that all require expansion into a phonetic representation. There are many spellings in English which are pronounced differently based on context. For example, "My latest project is to learn how to better project my voice" contains two pronunciations of "project".

Most text-to-speech (TTS) systems do not generate semantic representations of their input texts, as processes for doing so are not reliable, well understood, or computationally effective. As a result, various heuristic techniques are used to guess the proper way to disambiguate homographs, like examining neighboring words and using statistics about frequency of occurrence.

Recently TTS systems have begun to use HMMs (discussed above) to generate "parts of speech" to aid in disambiguating homographs. This technique is quite successful for many cases such as whether "read" should be pronounced as "red" implying past tense, or as "reed" implying present tense. Typical error rates when using HMMs in this fashion are usually below five percent. These techniques also work well for most European languages, although access to required training corpora is frequently difficult in these languages.

Deciding how to convert numbers is another problem that TTS systems have to address. It is a simple programming challenge to convert a number into words, like "1325" becoming "one thousand three hundred twenty-five." However, numbers occur in many different contexts; "1325" may also be read as "one three two five", "thirteen twenty-five" or "thirteen hundred and twenty five". A TTS system can often infer how to expand a number based on surrounding words, numbers, and punctuation, and sometimes the system provides a way to specify the context if it is ambiguous. Roman numerals can also be read differently depending on context.

Similarly, abbreviations can be ambiguous. For example, the abbreviation "in" for "inches" must be differentiated from the word "in", and the address "12 St John St." uses the same abbreviation for both "Saint" and "Street". TTS systems with intelligent front ends can make educated guesses about ambiguous abbreviations, while others provide the same result in all cases, resulting in nonsensical (and sometimes comical) outputs.

Text-to-phoneme Challenges

Speech synthesis systems use two basic approaches to determine the pronunciation of a word based on its spelling, a process which is often called text-to-phoneme or grapheme-to-phoneme conversion (phoneme is the term used by linguists to describe distinctive sounds in a language). The simplest approach to text-to-phoneme conversion is the dictionary-based approach, where a large dictionary containing all the words of a language and their correct pronunciations is stored by the program. Determining the correct pronunciation of each word is a matter of looking up each word in the dictionary and replacing the spelling with the pronunciation specified in the dictionary. The other approach is rule-based, in which pronunciation rules are applied to words to determine their pronunciations based on their spellings. This is similar to the "sounding out", or synthetic phonics, approach to learning reading.

Each approach has advantages and drawbacks. The dictionary-based approach is quick and accurate, but completely fails if it is given a word which is not in its dictionary. As dictionary size grows, so too does the memory space requirements of the synthesis system. On the other hand, the rule-based approach works on any input, but the complexity of the rules grows substantially as the system takes into account irregular spellings or pronunciations. (Consider that the word "of" is very common in English, yet is the only word in which the letter "f" is pronounced [v].) As a result, nearly all speech synthesis systems use a combination of these approaches.

Languages with a phonemic orthography have a very regular writing system, and the prediction of the pronunciation of words based on their spellings is quite successful. Speech synthesis systems for such languages often use the rule-based method extensively, resorting to dictionaries only for those few words, like foreign names and borrowings, whose pronunciations are not obvious from their spellings. On the other hand, speech synthesis systems for languages like English, which have extremely irregular spelling systems, are more likely to rely on dictionaries, and to use rule-based methods only for unusual words, or words that aren't in their dictionaries.

Evaluation Challenges

The consistent evaluation of speech synthesis systems may be difficult because of a lack of universally agreed objective evaluation criteria. Different organizations often use different speech data. The quality of speech synthesis systems also depends to a large degree on the quality of the production technique (which may involve analogue or digital recording) and on the facilities used to replay the speech. Evaluating speech synthesis systems has therefore often been compromised by differences between production techniques and replay facilities.

Recently, however, some researchers have started to evaluate speech synthesis systems using a common speech dataset..

Prosodics and Emotional Content

A recent study reported in the journal "Speech Communication" by Amy Drahota and colleagues at the University of Portsmouth, UK, reported that listeners to voice recordings could determine, at better than chance levels, whether or not the speaker was smiling. It was suggested that identification of the vocal features which signal emotional content may be used to help make synthesized speech sound more natural.

Dedicated Hardware

- Votrax
  - SC-01A (analog formant)
  - SC-02 / SSI-263 / "Arctic 263"
- General Instruments SP0256-AL2 (CTS256A-AL2, MEA8000)
- Magnevation SpeakJet (www.speechchips.com TTS256)
- Savage Innovations SoundGin
- National Semiconductor DT1050 Digitalker (Mozer)
- Silicon Systems SSI 263 (analog formant)
- Texas Instruments
  - TMS5110A (LPC) (obsolete?)
  - TMS5200 (obsolete?)
- Oki Semiconductor
  - MSM5205
  - MSM5218RS (ADPCM)
- Toshiba T6721A
- Philips PCF8200.

Outlets with Speech Synthesis

Apple

The first speech system integrated into an operating system was Apple Computer's MacInTalk in 1984. Since the 1980s Macintosh Computers offered text to speech capabilities through The MacinTalk software. In the early 1990s Apple expanded its capabilities offering system wide text-to-speech support. With the introduction of faster PowerPC-based computers they included higher quality voice sampling. Apple also introduced speech recognition into its systems which provided a fluid command set. More recently, Apple has added sample-based voices. Starting as a curiosity, the speech system of Apple Macintosh has evolved into a cutting edge fully-supported program, PlainTalk, for people with vision problems. VoiceOver was included in Mac OS X Tiger and more recently Mac OS X Leopard. The voice shipping with Mac OS X 10.5 ("Leopard") is called "Alex" and features the taking of realistic-sounding breaths between sentences, as well as improved clarity at high read rates. The operating system also includes say, a command-line based application that converts text to audible speech.

AmigaOS

The second operating system with advanced speech synthesis capabilities was AmigaOS, introduced in 1985. The voice synthesis was licensed by Commodore International from a third-party software house (Don't Ask Software, now Softvoice, Inc.) and it featured a complete system of voice emulation, with both male and female voices and "stress" indicator markers, made possible by advanced features of the Amiga hardware audio chipset. It was divided into a narrator device and a translator library. Amiga Speak Handler featured a text-to-speech translator. AmigaOS considered speech synthesis a virtual hardware device, so the user could even redirect console output to it. Some Amiga programs, such as word processors, made extensive use of the speech system.

Microsoft Windows

Modern Windows systems use SAPI4-and SAPI5-based speech systems that include a speech recognition engine (SRE). SAPI 4.0 was available on Microsoft-based operating systems as a third-party add-on for systems like Windows 95 and Windows 98. Windows 2000 added a speech synthesis program called Narrator, directly available to users. All Windows-compatible programs could make use of speech synthesis features, available through menus once installed on the system. Microsoft Speech Server is a complete package for voice synthesis and recognition, for commercial applications such as call centers.

Text-to-Speech (TTS) capabilities for a computer refers to the ability to play back text in a spoken voice. TTS is the ability of the operating system to play back printed text as spoken words.

An internal (installed with the operating system) driver (called a TTS engine): recognizes the text and using a synthesized voice (chosen from several pre-generated voices) speaks the written text. Additional engines (often use a certain jargon or vocabulary) are also available through third-party manufacturers

Internet

Currently, there are a number of applications, plugins and gadgets that can read messages directly from an e-mail client and web pages from a web browser. Some specialized software can narrate RSS-feeds. On one hand, online RSS-narrators simplify information delivery by allowing users to listen to their favourite news sources and to convert them to podcasts. On the other hand, on-line RSS-readers are available on almost any PC connected to the Internet. Users can download generated audio files to portable devices, e.g. with a help of podcast receiver, and listen to them while walking, jogging or commuting to work.

A growing field in internet based TTS is web-based assistive technology, e.g. 'Browsealoud' from a UK company. It can deliver TTS functionality to anyone (for reasons of accessibility, convenience, entertainment or information) with access to a web browser. Additionally SPEAK.TO.ME from Oxford Information Laboratories is capable of delivering text to speech through any browser without the need to download any special applications, and includes smart delivery technology to ensure only what is seen is spoken and the content is logically pathed.

Others

- Some models of Texas Instruments home computers produced in 1979 and 1981 (Texas Instruments TI-99/4 and TI-99/4A) were capable of text-to-phoneme synthesis or reciting complete words and phrases (text-to-dictionary), using a very popular Speech Synthesizer peripheral. TI used a proprietary codec to embed complete spoken phrases into applications, primarily video games.
- IBM's OS/2 Warp 4 included VoiceType, a precursor to IBM ViaVoice.

- Systems that operate on free and open source software systems including GNU/Linux are various, and include open-source programs such as the Festival Speech Synthesis System which uses diphone-based synthesis (and can use a limited number of MBROLA voices), and gnuspeech which uses articulatory synthesis from the Free Software Foundation. Other proprietary software also runs on GNU/Linux.
- Several commercial companies are also developing speech synthesis systems : ABC2MP3, Acapela Group, AT&T, Cepstral, CereProc, DECtalk, IBM ViaVoice, IVONA TTS, Loquendo TTS, NeoSpeech TTS, Nuance Communications, Orpheus, SVOX, YAKiToMe!, Voice on the Go, and Voxette.
- Companies which developed speech synthesis systems but which are no longer in this business include BeST Speech (bought by L&H), Eloquent Technology (bought by SpeechWorks), Lernout & Hauspie (bought by Nuance), SpeechWorks (bought by Nuance), Rhetorical Systems (bought by Nuance).

Speech Synthesis Markup Languages

A number of markup languages have been established for the rendition of text as speech in an XML-compliant format. The most recent is Speech Synthesis Markup Language (SSML), which became a W3C recommendation in 2004. Older speech synthesis markup languages include Java Speech Markup Language (JSML) and SABLE. Although each of these was proposed as a standard, none of them has been widely adopted.

Speech synthesis markup languages are distinguished from dialogue markup languages. VoiceXML, for example, includes tags related to speech recognition, dialogue management and touchtone dialing, in addition to text-to-speech markup.

Accessibility

Speech synthesis has long been a vital assistive technology tool and its application in this area is significant and widespread. It allows environmental barriers to be removed for people with a wide range of disabilities. The longest application has been in the use of screenreaders for people with visual impairment, but text-to-speech systems are now commonly used by people with dyslexia and other reading difficulties as well as by pre-literate youngsters. They are also frequently employed to aid those with severe speech impairment usually through a dedicated voice output communication aid.

News Service

Sites such as Ananova and YAKiToMe! have used speech synthesis to convert written news to audio content, which can be used for mobile applications.

Entertainment

Speech synthesis techniques are used as well in the entertainment productions such as games, anime and similar. In 2007, Animo Limited announced the development of a software application package based on its speech synthesis software FineSpeech, explicitly geared towards customers in the entertainment industries, able to generate narration and lines of dialogue according to user specifications. The application reached maturity in 2008, when NEC Biglobe announced a web service that allows users to create phrases from the voices of Code Geass: Lelouch of the Rebellion R2 characters.

TTS applications such as YAKiToMe! and Speakonia are often used to add synthetic voices to YouTube videos for comedic effect, as in Barney Bunch videos. YAKiToMe! is also used to convert entire books for personal podcasting purposes, RSS feeds and web pages for news stories, and educational texts for enhanced learning.

Software such as Vocaloid can generate singing voices via lyrics and melody. This is also the aim of the Singing Computer project (which uses the GPL software Lilypond and Festival) to help blind people check their lyric input.

Document eBook Speaker

Android application MultiReader speaks several document formats using TTS.

Speech Recognition

Speech recognition (also known as automatic speech recognition or computer speech recognition) converts spoken words to text. The term "voice recognition" is sometimes used to refer to speech recognition where the recognition system is trained to a particular speaker-as is the case for most desktop recognition software, hence there is an element of speaker recognition, which attempts to identify the person speaking, to better recognize what is being said. Speech recognition is a broad term which means it can recognize almost anybody's speech-such as a call-centre system designed to recognize many voices. Voice recognition is a system trained to a particular user, where it recognizes their speech based on their unique vocal sound.

Speech recognition applications include voice dialing (e.g., "Call home"), call routing (e.g., "I would like to make a collect call"), domotic appliance control and content-based spoken audio search (e.g., find a podcast where particular words were spoken), simple data entry (e.g., entering a credit card number), preparation of structured documents (e.g., a radiology report), speech-to-text processing (e.g., word processors or emails), and in aircraft cockpits (usually termed Direct Voice Input).

History

The first speech recognizer appeared in 1952 and consisted of a device for the recognition of single spoken digits Another early device was the IBM Shoebox, exhibited at the 1964 New York World's Fair.

One of the most notable domains for the commercial application of speech recognition in the United States has been health care and in particular the work of the medical transcriptionist (MT).

According to industry experts, at its inception, speech recognition (SR) was sold as a way to completely eliminate transcription rather than make the transcription process more efficient, hence it was not accepted.

It was also the case that SR at that time was often technically deficient. Additionally, to be used effectively, it required changes to the ways physicians worked and documented clinical encounters, which many if not all were reluctant to do.

The biggest limitation to speech recognition automating transcription, however, is seen as the software. The nature of narrative dictation is highly interpretive and often requires judgment that may be provided by a real human but not yet by an automated system. Another limitation has been the extensive amount of time required by the user and/or system provider to train the software.

A distinction in ASR is often made between "artificial syntax systems" which are usually domain-specific and "natural language processing" which is usually language-specific. Each of these types of application presents its own particular goals and challenges.

Applications

Health Care

In the health care domain, even in the wake of improving speech recognition technologies, medical transcriptionists (MTs) have not yet become obsolete. Many experts in the field anticipate that with increased use of speech recognition technology, the services provided may be redistributed rather than replaced. Speech recognition is used to enable deaf people to understand the spoken word via speech to text conversion, which is very helpful. Speech recognition can be implemented in front-end or back-end of the medical documentation process.

Front-End SR is where the provider dictates into a speech-recognition engine, the recognized words are displayed right after they are spoken, and the dictator is responsible for editing and signing off on the document. It never goes through an MT/editor.

Back-End SR or Deferred SR is where the provider dictates into a digital dictation system, and the voice is routed through a speech-recognition machine and the recognized draft document is routed along with the original voice file to the MT/editor, who edits the draft and finalizes the report. Deferred SR is being widely used in the industry currently.

Many Electronic Medical Records (EMR) applications can be more effective and may be performed more easily when deployed in conjunction with a speech-recognition engine. Searches, queries, and form filling may all be faster to perform by voice than by using a keyboard.

High-performance Fighter Aircraft

Substantial efforts have been devoted in the last decade to the test and evaluation of speech recognition in fighter aircraft. Of particular note are the U.S. program in speech recognition for the Advanced Fighter Technology Integration (AFTI)/F-16 aircraft (F-16 VISTA), the program in France on installing speech recognition systems on Mirage aircraft, and programs in the UK dealing with a variety of aircraft platforms. In these programs, speech recognizers have been operated successfully in fighter aircraft with applications including: setting radio frequencies, commanding an autopilot system, setting steer-point coordinates and weapons release parameters, and controlling flight displays. Generally, only very limited, constrained vocabularies have been used successfully, and a major effort has been devoted to integration of the speech recognizer with the avionics system.

Some important conclusions from the work were as follows:

1. Speech recognition has definite potential for reducing pilot workload, but this potential was not realized consistently.
2. Achievement of very high recognition accuracy (95% or more) was the most critical factor for making the speech recognition system useful — with lower recognition rates, pilots would not use the system.
3. More natural vocabulary and grammar, and shorter training times would be useful, but only if very high recognition rates could be maintained.

Laboratory research in robust speech recognition for military environments has produced promising results which, if extendable to the cockpit, should improve the utility of speech recognition in high-performance aircraft.

Working with Swedish pilots flying in the JAS-39 Gripen cockpit, Englund (2004) found recognition deteriorated with increasing G-loads. It was also concluded that adaptation greatly improved the results in all cases and introducing models for breathing was shown to improve recognition scores significantly. Contrary to what might be expected, no effects of the broken English of the speakers were found. It was evident that spontaneous speech caused problems for the recognizer, as could be expected. A restricted vocabulary, and above all, a proper syntax, could thus be expected to improve recognition accuracy substantially.

The Eurofighter Typhoon currently in service with the UK RAF employs a speaker-dependent system, i.e. it requires each pilot to create a template. The system is not used for any safety critical or weapon critical tasks, such as weapon release or lowering of the undercarriage, but is used for a wide range of other cockpit functions. Voice commands are confirmed by visual and/or aural feedback. The system is seen as a major design feature in the reduction of pilot workload, and even allows the pilot to assign targets to himself with two simple voice commands or to any of his wingmen with only five commands.

Helicopters

The problems of achieving high recognition accuracy under stress and noise pertain strongly to the helicopter environment as well as to the fighter environment. The acoustic noise problem is actually more severe in the helicopter environment, not only because of the high noise levels but also because the helicopter pilot generally does not wear a facemask, which would reduce acoustic noise in the microphone. Substantial test and evaluation programs have been carried out in the past decade in speech recognition systems applications in helicopters, notably by the U.S. Army Avionics Research and Development Activity (AVRADA) and by the Royal Aerospace Establishment (RAE) in the UK. Work in France has included speech recognition in the Puma helicopter. There has also been much useful work in Canada. Results have been encouraging, and voice applications have included: control of communication radios; setting of navigation systems; and control of an automated target handover system.

As in fighter applications, the overriding issue for voice in helicopters is the impact on pilot effectiveness. Encouraging results are reported for the AVRADA tests, although these represent only a feasibility demonstration in a test environment. Much remains to be done both in speech recognition and in overall speech recognition technology, in order to consistently achieve performance improvements in operational settings.

Bibliography

Barnett, Marya A. (1983). *Replacing teacher talk with gestures: Nonverbal communication in the foreign language classroom.* Foreign Language Annals.

Damen, Louise (1987). *Culture Learning: The Fifth Dimension in the Language Classroom.* Addison-Wesley: USA.

Feldman, Robert S. (1992). *Applications of Nonverbal Behavioral Theories and Research.* Lawrence Erlbaum Associates, Inc.: New Jersey.

Hartley, Peter (1993). *Interpersonal Communication.* Author: New York.

Koch, Robert (1971). *The teacher and Nonverbal Communication. Theory Into Practice* , pp: 231-242.

Pennycook, Alastair (1985). *Actions speak louder than words: Paralanguage, Communication, and Education.* TESOL Quarterly.

Philippot, Pierre, Robert S. Feldman, Erik J. Coats. (1999).*The Social Context of Nonverbal Behavior.* Maison des Sciences de l# Homme and Cambridge University Press : Cambridge.

Soudek, Miluse and Lev I. Soudek. *Non-verbal Channels in Language Teaching.*

Wackman, Daniel (1987). *Handbook of Communication Science,* Newbury Park, CA: Sage.

Wolfgang, Aaron (1984) *Nonverbal Behavior: Perspectives, Application, Intercultural Insights.* C. J. Hofrege, Inc. Lewinston, NY.

Index

❑❑❑